THE POWER OF THREE

OTHER BOOKS BY JACQUELINE AULD

MASSEY AND SPARKS

1. The Children of Gaia

2. An Old Evil

THE
POWER OF THREE

A Massey & Sparks crime thriller

BOOK 3

JACQUELINE AULD

SHUFFLE

THE POWER OF THREE

ISBN: 978-1-7385390-4-8

Published worldwide by Jacqueline Auld
under her Shuffle Books brand

Copyright © Jacqueline Auld 2024

The right of Jacqueline Auld to be identified as the author of this work has been asserted in accordance with the Copyright, Designs and Patents Act 1988.

All rights reserved. No part of this book may be reproduced or distributed in any form without prior written permission from the author, with the exception of non-commercial uses permitted by copyright law.

This book is a work of fiction. Names, characters, organisations, places, events and incidents are either the products of the author's imagination or used in a fictitious manner. Any resemblance to actual persons, living or dead, or actual events is purely coincidental.

SHUFFLE

For all the wonderful people who have brought
Cresswell Pele Tower back from the brink and
created such a fascinating community
resource in the process.

CHAPTER 1

Saturday, 12 October 2024

Three women clattered through the door of the rugby club in a rush of swirling autumn leaves, cackling loudly as the gust of wind at their backs stood their hair on end and flapped the skirts of their sparkling black party dresses.

Where the hell had they come from? If DCI James Massey – second row lock forward and star player of today's charity match – hadn't stepped sidewards, he'd have been knocked flat despite his size. He'd only just walked through the door himself. Surely, he couldn't have failed to hear three noisy women so close behind him.

His look of surprise set the trio cackling even louder. With an appraising look the oldest, maybe forty-five to fifty, moved closer, impelling him to step backwards towards the wall. 'Tell you what girls,' she said, twirling a lock of chestnut hair around one index finger. 'He's a bit of alright, isn't he?'

He leant back, registering a barely-there inflection in her otherwise Northumbrian accent. Something musical. Scandinavian perhaps? She took another step towards him. He detected a fruity wine on her breath.

'Needs a few tips, I think though,' she said.

The youngest of the three; tall, with long dark hair disturbingly like his wife's, raked smoky eyes down the length of him and cocked a provocative hip. 'Yeah, like don't stand in the way of the door.'

The comment set all three off on a fresh paroxysm of shrill laughter, until the first woman reached up to stroke a feather-soft finger across his cheek, and they all fell silent, holding their collective breath, eager to see his reaction.

Massey held his own breath, feeling distinctly uncomfortable, a heady combination of the three women's perfumes invading his nostrils and cloying at the back of his throat.

The woman patted his cheek with her open palm, and he pulled his head back as far as it would go, feeling his still damp hair brush the wall.

'I mean about what the future holds for him. You'd like that, wouldn't you, sweetie?' She gave him a moment to respond, but he didn't take her up on it. 'So here is my prophesy for you…'

The other two women fluttered their fingers, jangling wrists full of bracelets.

'… Before the clock strikes twelve tonight, I foresee that you will be forced to revisit a time from your past that you would far rather forget.'

Her friends crowded in further and chortled a chorus of theatrical 'oohs'.

Massey breathed out and rolled his eyes. Of course he would. He'd played a good game this afternoon and the Northumbria Police team had smashed the locals, but in the original charity match eleven years ago he'd fumbled the ball with disastrous consequences for his team and he knew he'd end up being reminded of that by the Ellington & Cresswell lads before the night was out, if only to offset their own team's poor performance today. Yes, he might prefer to forget it, but he could cope with a bit of piss-taking. It was all part of the game.

He wasn't so keen on the game being played out around him now though, but his tormentors showed no signs yet of becoming bored with him.

The youngest – the one with hair like Helen's – took up the challenge and slunk in closer.

He took another step back. His heel hit the skirting board.

With her face inches from his, her smouldering eyes staring up at him from beneath thick black false lashes, the woman straightened the button-down collar of his Oxford cotton shirt and trailed pointed red fingernails down his chest. 'I foresee a fabulous revelation.' She flashed a dimpled grin and glanced at each of her friends in turn. 'But beware, it will have tricky conditions attached.'

Another chorus of theatrical 'oohs', chortling hoots, and rattling jewellery. Way too close for comfort.

'My turn.' The third woman elbowed the other two out of the way until she stood as close as she could get to him. The most buxom of the three. Plump olive skin, striking hazel eyes and purple-glossed lips. He felt her black lace-clad breasts pressing against his upper abdomen. She cocked her head and morphed her face into a mask of tragedy, raising herself up onto the tips of her toes and leaning into him.

'I foresee…' She lifted an index finger towards each of her companions and beamed a wicked smile. '… that you will face *death* before next the moon wanes, and only you can decide if you want to live or die.'

The cackling chorus this time, inches from Massey's ear drums, deafened him.

With a clatter of high heels and a rattle of jewellery, the trio turned as one and pushed their way through double doors into the bar, leaving him standing in the entrance hall with his mouth open.

Putting a hand to his racing heart, he breathed an embarrassed sigh of relief and caught the eye of a chuckling doorman, mobile phone raised, videoing the whole thing.

Bastard.

***

The function room in the Ellington & Cresswell RFC clubhouse was full to bursting. He'd been right about the piss-take, but not for fumbling the ball at the previous match. On the way to the bar, he ran a gauntlet of locals already watching the video.

Eventually, complementary pint in hand, he made his way from the crowded bar to the half dozen large Formica-topped tables claimed by the Northumbria Police contingent and took the chair Detective Sergeant Christine Sparks had saved for him between herself and Detective Constable Andrew Donaldson. He knew he'd be in for a lot more good natured ribbing before the night was out once this lot got wind of the video too. He'd have a word with that doorman later, when his racing heart had calmed down and his legs didn't feel quite so shaky.

'What's up?' Sparks demanded.

'Nothing.' He shook his head and tried to smile. 'Just something stupid.'

Sparks looked at him from under her brows. 'Not nothing then.'

'Nothing worth fussing about, Christine. Jesus, you're worse than my mother.' She'd been treating him like an invalid who'd just undergone major surgery lately, rather than as someone who'd been deserted by his wife. She meant well, he knew that, but he was pig sick of sitting at home brooding; he needed to get back out and start enjoying himself again.

He turned his attention to the others at the table. His immediate boss, Detective Superintendent Lou Portas sat next to Detective Inspector Guy Keegan. He'd become good friends with Keegan over the past year or so, although their relationship could easily have gone the other way after everything that had happened.

Keegan and Portas were more than just friends, although nothing romantic, as far as he could tell. Portas might be single but, despite his characteristic bluster, Keegan was a devoted family man with two teenage daughters. Looked like his wife wasn't here tonight though. Sarah, was that her name?

Dawn Alder, Andrew Donaldson's girlfriend – soon to become fiancée, by the look of it – was engrossed in a lively discussion with Forensic Pathologist Lorraine French.

One of his team mates today sat in the eighth place at the table. Darren Albright, known as Dazzle, most often shortened to Dazz, which his first name would undoubtedly have been anyway, whatever his surname was. Dazz's marriage, like his own, had recently come to grief, although he'd heard on the grapevine that Dazz and his ex managed to maintain a cordial relationship, unlike his own with Helen. But then they had two children together, whom they were both equally determined to protect, whereas his own marriage to Helen had ended up being childless, which in itself had been a major aspect of their problems.

Dazz raised his glass. 'The place hasn't changed a bit, has it? Takes me back.'

It took Massey back too. More than eleven years back. Another charity event in the summer of 2013, of which today was a replay, although in aid of a different cause this time.

A night he usually remembered for all the wrong reasons.

Although he and Dazz hadn't exactly been the youngest players on the police fifteen back then, today they'd definitely been the oldest. He still recognised a few faces around the room; blokes who'd been around the same age he and Dazz were now, and the oldest on the Ellington and Cresswell first team back then. Their playing years were firmly behind them now though. Most had thickened out into middle age. That's what time does to men; turns muscle into flab, makes it harder to maintain strength. And worse, it could cause hair to disappear.

Perhaps that was all Massey had to look forward to now, becoming fat and weak and bald.

He ran his hand over his own slightly greying but still thick dark hair. Wasn't a tendency to baldness supposed to be a genetic thing? He had a vague memory, aged only four, of his biological father – only in his mid-twenties at the time – already sporting a mega high forehead when he'd walked out of their lives. Massey had celebrated his own fortieth just a few days ago, which made him feel old, but he'd yet to find hanks of hair on his pillow in the morning, so maybe it wasn't Massey senior he took after, fingers crossed. Didn't mean it wouldn't happen eventually though.

Actually, in the only photo still in existence of both his biological parents together, the abusive bastard looked to be of only average height. Unlike himself. Come to think of it, the men on his mother's side of the family weren't that tall either.

His mind drifted back to his three female tormentors. If there was any truth in that third prophesy, then maybe he didn't have long to worry about his hair falling out anyway.

Not that he believed in prophesies.

He gave a brief laugh that earned him another sharp look from Sparks.

So far, thankfully, he'd seen no sign of one particular face and, listening to the chatter around him, he began to relax. Not that there'd been any reason to suppose she'd have been here tonight anyway. She'd been a visitor to Cresswell eleven years ago. A tourist, staying at one of the local caravan parks, on her second week of a fortnight's holiday from her life somewhere further south. She'd probably told him where, but he couldn't remember now. Or maybe she hadn't. So brief and so intense had been their encounter, there'd been no time and no need to explore anything beyond their overwhelming physical attraction to each other.

She could have had no idea of the devastating consequences their carnal encounter had wrought on his life. She'd have simply enjoyed the rest of her holiday, returned home afterwards, and probably never even thought about him again.

If only he'd been able to do the same.

***

The drinks flowed. Massey's table managed to score second place in a fund-raising general knowledge quiz, and he avoided becoming a last minute lot in the charity auction by sneaking to the gents at an opportune moment. Of course, the speeches cast a veil of sadness over the proceedings for a while, referring as they did often to the murder of the rugby club's former president, retired Northumbria Police Chief Superintendent Duncan Kingsley, more than a year ago. But once the last speaker stood down at around half nine and the music restarted, the party atmosphere resumed immediately, just as Kingsley would have wished.

It was Kingsley who'd been the driving force behind the original charity match back then. And behind today's charity match too, although his murder last summer had been the reason the event – initially scheduled to take place on the tenth anniversary – had been postponed for more than a year. And, having had a foot still in both camps, Kingsley wouldn't have minded Ellington & Cresswell getting trounced today by the Northumbria Police squad in a stark flip of the match score back then.

He found himself on the dance floor a couple of times. Once with Lou Portas, and immediately afterwards with Lorraine French. He noticed Sparks refusing the efforts of Dazz to get her up to dance, but at least she looked to be letting the bloke down gently. This time last year she'd have bitten his head off for even being brave enough to ask.

He also noticed her eyes wandering towards a neighbouring table once or twice, the occupants of which he didn't know but he'd gathered they had something to do with the community development work currently going on at Cresswell's ancient pele tower, for which today's charity match and tonight's event were raising much needed funds.

A couple of times, back at the table, Massey felt an itch on the back of his neck and turned to find himself under scrutiny from the far side of the room by his three tormentors. Each time he turned, they raised their glasses to him and burst into cackling laughter. He couldn't actually hear them above the music, but his subconscious filled in the blanks and sent shivers up his spine.

He still felt weirdly discomfited by his gut reaction to their attention at the door, and just as discomfited by the fact he felt that way.

Was this how women felt when hassled by a group of rowdy males?

He tried to dismiss the thought. Three males onto a lone female must be a far more terrifying experience than the one *he'd* suffered under the attentions of three brazen women, none of whom, without the heels, would even have come up to his chin.

He was a big strapping bloke for heaven's sake. So why did he feel he'd been assaulted? And those prophesies. It was as well he wasn't overly superstitious, or he'd be fretting for the next few weeks about that last one. He took a long draught of his beer, determined to brush off the unease the women had caused. The glass rattled against his teeth as a hand patted him on the shoulder.

'I hear you had the pleasure of meeting my wife and her mates earlier.'

Massey looked up into the face of the Ellington & Cresswell Head Coach Ben Quinn, one of the older blokes he'd played against in the original match. 'Your wife?'

'One of the three you met at the door, so I'm told. My apologies.'

On the other side of the table, Detective Inspector Guy Keegan rose to his feet and grabbed Quinn's hand in a hearty shake.

'Good to see you again, mate. What's this you say? James and *three* women?'

Quinn laughed. 'I'm told Ursula and her little coven over there had a bit of fun with him at the door earlier. Surprised you haven't seen the video yet. All of our lads have. Anyway, once again, my apologies. Ursula and her friends are playing three witches in an amateur production of Macbeth at the pele tower at Halloween. They're getting in some early practice by harassing the visitors. They did the same thing last year. All in jest though, eh James?'

Massey looked across the dance floor towards the three women, the sparkles of their black dresses catching the flashing disco lights as they bent to speak to someone sitting at a table against the back wall. 'If you say so, Ben. Which one is your wife?'

'The one on the left. That's Ursula.'

Chestnut hair, the instigator of the whole prophesy malarkey; the one who'd told him that by midnight he'd be forced to revisit a time from his past that he'd rather forget. Well, she'd missed the mark so far. All in all, he was enjoying himself more than he'd thought he would, given that this was his first social outing since Helen had walked away from their marriage.

It was nowhere near midnight yet though.

'Technically,' Quinn continued, 'Ursula might still be my wife., we are still married, but we're separated. It's hard to break a thirty year habit though, and we do still get on alright, which is just as well since we still live together.'

A young woman joined them. 'Are you talking about Mam? I hear she and her mates have been up to their tricks again?'

Quinn put his arm around her and kissed her cheek. 'What's wrong? Have the two of you been rowing again?'

'Nothing to do with Mam. It's that bloody Finn Barron, as usual.'

Quinn gave her shoulders a bracing squeeze. 'Gentlemen, meet my daughter, Fleur. Ardent promoter of women's rugby at a grassroots level at the club here and around our local communities. Fleur, this is Guy Keegan and James Massey.'

Pretty in a snub-nosed, fresh-faced way, Ben's daughter looked like a feminine version of him. She bore no resemblance at all to Ursula, she of the chestnut hair. She nodded to both of them and raised her glass towards Massey. 'That was a good game you played today. We didn't stand a chance.'

He smiled. 'Thanks. I didn't know you had a women's team here.'

Fleur jutted her chin. 'Not for much longer, if Finn Barron has his way. He's a Neanderthal. He doesn't approve of women "ruining the game", as he calls it. And he's already making it clear that when he officially becomes president, he'll be fighting against it. All because of the rubbish my mother and her mates spun last year. He'd never —'

'Let's not get into all that now,' her father said, patting her arm. 'Our guests don't need to know all that.'

'Who are the other two women?' Keegan asked. 'Ursula's mates. Because if I wasn't married...'

Massey gave him a disparaging look, which Keegan returned with a shrug. 'What? I can dream,' he said.

'The one with the dark curly hair next to Ursula,' Quinn said. That's Betsy. Betsy Halliwell. She's a psychotherapist or some such thing. Runs a clinic out of her own home on Beach Road in Cresswell. And the tall girl, the youngest, that's Scarlett. Can't remember her surname, but she's actually one of Fleur's mates. Isn't that right, Fleur?'

'Donkeys ago, Dad. When we were still at school.'

Quinn gave her shoulder another squeeze. 'Not that long ago then. Scarlett works at The Plough along the road. Does a couple of shifts behind the bar at the club here too every now and then, when we're desperate. And...'

Massey only half heard the rest because the three women, realising they'd become the subject of discussion, turned to face them with knowing smiles. Between them, a fourth woman stared straight at him and the blood drained from his face. Everything around him: his friends and colleagues, the music and flashing lights; everything receded until nothing existed but the stare between the two of them.

Jesus wept, Trinny.

***

'James, are you okay?' He could feel Sparks' hawk eyes on him. 'You've gone white.'

Standing beside him, Keegan nudged his elbow. 'Seen a ghost, Flash?'

He slumped back down into his chair and reached for his drink. He couldn't speak, but he nodded his head to signal that yes, he was okay. And when he looked across the dance floor again, all four women had disappeared.

In vain, his eyes searched for them between the shifting shapes of dancers, for Trinny in particular: the woman with whom he'd committed his one and only act of infidelity. Who, over eleven years ago, had lit the slow-burning fuse that eventually blew his marriage apart.

But no, that wasn't fair. Whatever damage had been done that night all those years ago to his relationship with Helen, he'd done himself. He should have been stronger. He could have resisted. He'd been the married one, after all, not Trinny.

And not only had he been married, but Helen had been pregnant too, and the stress of finding out about his one night stand the following day, their third wedding anniversary no less, had caused her to miscarry their baby. And, however much they'd tried since, she'd never conceived again. So he was doubly, triply responsible for the fallout from a couple of rampant, illicit, lust-filled hours.

But good grief, he'd never experienced anything like the attraction he'd felt for Trinny. Not before, nor since. He'd felt drunk with lust. Brass bands, fireworks, the lot. Even now, just the thought of how thoroughly they'd possessed each other that night made his knees turn weak. In fact, several times over the years he'd wondered if she'd somehow managed to slip some sort of magical aphrodisiac potion into his drink, which was rubbish.

No such thing as magic.

He could... he *should* have said no. It was no good trying to blame Trinny. In fact, now he thought about it, he couldn't remember if he *had* even told her he was married before falling into bed with her?

He pulled his chair further in towards the table to hide an unwanted erection and forced his mind towards the most ignominious aspects of his behaviour that night in order to damp it down; to the shame he still felt at how he'd slunk away from Trinny's caravan in the night while she slept, already full of guilt and remorse for what he'd done, hoping against hope that she would disappear back to wherever she came from at the end of her holiday and never, ever try to contact him.

And she hadn't. He'd never seen nor heard from her since. *So what the hell is she doing back here now?*

All these years later he still had no idea exactly how Helen had found out about what he'd done. But somehow she had, and she'd lost their baby as a result. A terrible tragic and painful loss at twenty-one weeks gestation, less than a week after a scan, at which they'd been told that everything was progressing well, and the baby was growing normally.

He'd wondered at the time if Trinny herself had told Helen. But even if she'd wanted to, he couldn't see how she could have known Helen's name or how to find her. He'd even thought it could have been one of his own team mates. Someone who'd spotted them sneaking away from the party, who felt aggrieved about the error he'd made on the pitch that had lost them the match. But, while they might not all have been bosom buddies, he couldn't see any of them wanting to do him that sort of harm. A gossipy word in the wrong ear though maybe? Although that would have taken far longer than just the following day to percolate down to Helen's ears. So perhaps his own guilty conscience had simply made him behave differently, and Helen had picked up on it and drawn her own conclusions.

He gave himself a mental shake. No point trying to work it out now, after all these years. However it happened, the fact was it had. And it was purely his own actions that had killed his child and blighted his marriage. When it came right down to it, if he'd kept his dick in his pants, he and Helen would likely have had a happy marriage and he'd be father to a ten year old daughter now.

CHAPTER 2

Ten minutes later, Dazz Albright tried to claim Sparks' attention again. Clearly not a man to give up easily. Lou Portas had moved down two tables to talk to Chief Superintendent Crowder, and Andrew Donaldson was giving it large on the dance floor with Dawn, displaying a fluent exuberance that amazed Massey, given the lad usually came over as being gangly and awkward.

Over his left shoulder, the Ellington & Cresswell Club Captain, Michael Duffy had joined Guy Keegan and Ben Quinn in conversation. It would be rude to continue sitting all alone at the table with his back to the three men now that the shock of spotting Trinny had worn off and he was no longer likely to embarrass himself.

Back on his feet, he gave the room a furtive scan. No sign of her or the three women. He began to doubt that the face he'd spotted had even been hers?

'... not convinced it was them,' Michael Duffy was saying. 'I mean, what did they have to gain?'

Massey had missed the beginning, but it wasn't difficult, given the context, to gather that the men were discussing the murder of retired Chief Superintendent Duncan Kingsley, in July last year, for which three men were about to be charged. According to the press.

'The case must be pretty strong against them,' Keegan replied. 'Or else the press have got it wrong.'

'Strong in what way?'

'Sorry. Even if we knew, we couldn't discuss it. But we're out of the loop anyway. It's Durham Constabulary carrying out the investigation, not us.'

'Why is that?' Ben Quinn asked. 'I've never understood why they should be investigating a case in Northumberland.'

Keegan looked uncomfortable. He took a long draught of his beer and shifted his weight from one foot to the other.

Massey took pity on him. 'It's because it happened just as we were undergoing an internal investigation ourselves following that Children of Gaia business last summer.'

An investigation that had resulted in Superintendent Lou Portas' predecessor, Oliver Hitchins being charged with murder, some junior officers being drummed out of the force, and Keegan himself being demoted from DCI down to DI when all the favours he'd done Hitchins came to light. Although at least Keegan had kept his job.

Keegan nodded his thanks for the intervention. 'Duncan might have been retired for a couple of years by then,' he said, 'but no-one wanted to risk getting it wrong. There was enough of the brown stuff flying around already.'

Quinn accepted the explanation without further question. After all, the scandal had been splashed all over the news and across every daily newspaper for weeks at the time.

'I agree with Michael though. I don't think those three men did it. I mean, Duncan knew them pretty well, didn't he? They'd done all that work for him in his garden, and he'd even given them a contract to keep it maintained. He wouldn't have done that if he hadn't rated them and their work. But anyway, somehow Finn got their number—'

'From the side of their van.' Duffy said, rolling his eyes.

Quinn laughed. 'Probably. Anyway, Finn decided he wanted something more extravagant, and he arranged for them to come round to give him a quote on the exact same day he'd already invited everyone round for a barbecue—'

Duffy gave a disparaging harrumph. 'You can't tell me that wasn't deliberate.'

Quinn pressed his lips together and lifted his chin in sage agreement. 'So Duncan was there with Elena, and we were there too, weren't we Michael? And we all had to listen to Finn bragging about what he wanted done.'

'Typical of the bloke. Whatever Duncan had, that bastard had to have too, only better.'

'Haven't spoken to Finn for years,' Keegan said, 'Probably not since the first match. But he seemed to be a decent bloke.'

'And so he was – back then. But he's changed over recent years. He's—'

'And that wife of his is just as bad,' Quinn butted in. 'If not worse. Ideas of grandeur has Verity. She's the one pushing him all the time.'

Duffy rolled his eyes again. 'Or at least that's what Finn tells everyone.'

Massey remembered the old Finn Barron. Big and brash, captain of the Ellington & Cresswell first team back then; a hard player, but a good laugh at the party after the game. He remembered Verity too, although nothing like the woman Quinn described, and he couldn't imagine Barron being pushed around by her. The person he'd met had been overcome with gratitude and emotion by the huge sum of money the match had raised in aid of their disabled son. Funds to send him to America for life-saving treatment.

'How's the son now?' he asked. 'Luke, is that his name?'

'He died a couple of years after she brought him back from the US,' Duffy said. 'The treatment didn't work.'

'Oh God, I'm sorry. I didn't know. They must have been devastated.'

'Verity was, certainly. Don't think she ever properly got over it. But it would have been a relief to Finn. He'd never come to terms with the lad's disabilities. And he *was* just the boy's stepdad when all comes to all, not his biological father. So, well…'

Massey hadn't known that either. 'Do they have other kids?' he asked, when Duffy's voice trailed off.

'None. So Finn always had to go one better in everything else; to compensate. Duncan had two strapping sons you see. Good lads. Decent rugby players too, Milo is particularly good. They're both here somewhere tonight. Have you met them?'

'I'm not sure.' Massey took the opportunity to scan the room again for a sign of Trinny, but didn't spot her. 'Did either of them play today?'

'No. Finn wasn't happy about them playing on the first team now they've moved out of the area. But come on, it was a charity match for heaven's sake, that *their* dad had organised. If anyone should have been on the team, it was his boys. And that's just one example of Finn taking his duties as temporary club president way too enthusiastically. He's alienating a lot of people, you know. Splitting the club down the middle. If he gets in—'

Quinn gave Duffy a nudge. 'Come on Michael, our guests don't need to know about all our petty squabbles. This is supposed to be a fun night.'

'I'm surprised that's all still up in the air?' Keegan said. 'It's more than a year now. I thought the election for club president would have been all over bar the shouting.'

'I reckon Finn's deliberately drawing out the process, in the hope all the competition will die away. But Ben here is still standing.' Duffy clapped Quinn on the shoulder. 'Isn't that right, Ben.'

'Not just me. Len Stafford's still in the running too.'

'Len hasn't the heart for a battle over it though,' Duffy said.

Quinn snorted. 'Me neither, but someone else needed to stand. I'm doing it for Fleur. She's right. Finn doesn't like there being a women's team at the club. If you ask me, Milo should have stood. A bit unconventional, but a young club president could be a good thing. And it would have really put the wind up Finn. Especially after Duncan had been telling everyone how he hoped the lad would follow in his footsteps at the club.'

Duffy looked surprised there was so little beer left in his glass. 'Your Ursula didn't exactly help though, did she? Her and her mate, telling Finn's fortune; saying the presidency would be his just as soon as Duncan stood down. And then what did you do but wind him up even more by saying the club could have a woman president one day? He knew perfectly well who you—'

'Talking about me, gents?'

All four turned abruptly to find Finn Barron himself standing behind them, that Edinburgh burr of his still broad after so many years living in the North East of England. Had he heard their entire conversation above the noise of the party? Barron made a show of shaking hands and congratulating Massey on his game. 'Can I get anyone a drink?' he asked. 'Oh, and can I introduce—'

A woman slid out from behind Barron's bulk. Petite and graceful, dressed in low-cut floating layers of midnight blue, her heart-shaped face and cascading copper hair a stunning foil for huge chocolate brown eyes.

Eleven years had hardly changed her.

In shock, Massey's eyes sought out the dark mole he remembered right above her heart that emphasised the rise and fall of her breasts.

She directed a demure, dimpled smile towards each of the men in turn, leaving Massey until last, giving him a moment to raise his eyes to a more decent level before looking innocently up into his face. 'Trinity Moon. How do you do? 'I believe we may have met before. A long time ago.'

Understatement of the year. Of the decade.

CHAPTER 3

'Howay, Christine, just one dance.'

'Bloody hell Dazz, *piss off*.'

Dazz Albright ramped up a beseeching puppy dog expression that Sparks imagined had served him well throughout his life. But for all she couldn't help but like the bloke – no-one could ever not like Dazz – she was immune to such ploys. And besides, she needed to know who the red setter bitch was. The woman who'd commandeered Massey's attention behind her, who'd caused his brain to turn so suddenly to mush earlier. But with Dazz prattling in her ear, she couldn't hear what they were saying, and her patience was wearing thin.

When Massey had that funny turn earlier, when his jaw had just about hit the floor, she'd followed the direction of his rabbit-in-the-headlights gawp and spotted the woman staring back at him from the cover of her friends. At first she'd thought, typical bloke, eyes on stalks as soon as he spots tits hanging out on any woman passable in the looks department. But then she'd noticed the woman's covetous expression. Like a lioness spotting its prey from the undergrowth. If she'd smacked her lips the woman couldn't have made her intentions towards Massey any plainer. And he could do without that sort of complication right now.

So she'd kept track of the woman. She'd watched her melt into the background and gradually slink her way around the room. A few words here and there to people she must know. All men. Using them for concealment whenever Massey's eyes swept the room searching for her. Stealthily keeping out of his sight until she was ready to pounce.

She and Massey must know each other. And not just as passing acquaintances. Massey and the red setter had history. Something had happened between them, and it didn't take a genius to figure out what. But had it happened before Helen, or during his marriage?

Much as she'd disapprove of the latter, it hardly mattered anymore. He was a free agent now, although in no fit state emotionally for any hanky-panky tonight. Especially not with a woman who looked as if she'd like to eat him alive.

Even an old flame can burn.

And anyway, he'd had way too much to drink tonight to be thinking rationally, as evidenced by his reaction when he'd first spotted Red.

'Come on, Christine. One dance, that's all.'

'For the last time, Dazz. *Bugger off*. I am *not* getting up to dance. With you or anyone else.'

Dazz pointed a drunken finger towards her face and moved it in circles. 'You… are no fun. Do you know that? You're a… a joy killer. Nope, scrub that. Wha' do I mean? Help me out. Killjoy, that's the one. That's what you are, Christine. You're a freaking killjoy.'

She rolled her eyes. 'Go pester Lorraine instead. She'll dance with you.'

He wheeled around and looked doubtfully at the pathologist. 'She will? You think?'

'Absolutely. Now go on. Bugger off.'

He drained his glass, rolled his shoulders a couple of times, and held his arms out towards her. 'Last chance, Christine. One dance.'

'Bloody hell Dazz, just go away, will you.' She got to her feet and turned her back on him to emphasise the message, glancing at the time on her Fitbit as she did so. If she could keep Massey distracted and out of Red's clutches for just another half an hour, then their minibuses would be here to take them all home.

She'd be saving him from himself.

Someone had to.

CHAPTER 4

The hire company had sent an executive coach for them, rather than the three minibuses they'd expected – arranged just that afternoon, it emerged during the journey, by a proud Chief Superintendent Crowder as a special treat for the winning team. Plush reclining seats with armrests, rather than the cheap vinyl bench seats of the minibuses they'd arrived in, and toilet facilities included.

Dazz Albright had closeted himself inside just as soon as the coach had taken the first bend, and could be heard above the sound of raucous singing noisily purging his stomach. Those two shots of vodka he'd downed after failing to persuade anyone to get up and dance with him must have caused all the beer and buffet food he'd consumed.to curdle.

Sparks directed a raised eyebrow look at Massey, beside her. 'Are you going to tell me who she is?'

'Who?'

'You know perfectly well who. That dangerous looking red setter with her tits hanging out. The one who beat a hasty retreat as soon as I joined your little group.'

'Finn had only just introduced her. I didn't exactly have time to talk to her.'

'But you already knew her, didn't you?'

Massey sighed and rolled his eyes. 'Okay. If you must know, I met her once eleven years ago.'

'Hmm, methinks you did more than just meet her.'

He sighed and shook his head. The sort of psychic connection that he and Sparks had developed in their working partnership could be invaluable. It meant they could pretty much read each other's thoughts. But sometimes it ended up being a real pain in the arse.

Like now.

He looked around for salvation from a conversation he absolutely did not want to have with his sergeant right now.

'The woman stalked you. All around the room. Just waiting for her chance to isolate you from the group and take you down.'

He gave an uncomfortable laugh. 'Take me down?'

'Go in for the kill. Drag you away to her lair and rip off your knickers.'

He snorted a laugh. 'Knickers? No way do I wear knickers.'

'Okay then, kecks, shreddies, dogs. Whatever the hell you men like to call them, she definitely wanted to remove them.'

'Would that have been so bad?' He was a single bloke now. If he wanted to get intimate with a woman, he damn well would. He wasn't about to let his sergeant get away with trying to dictate his love life now that Helen had left him. *Although, Trinny for heaven's sake.*

'The way she was acting; yes it would. Too sneaky by half that one. You're not up to that sort of nonsense. Not in your state. For one thing, how the hell would you have got home afterwards?'

'Um, taxi? And what do you mean, in my state? I'm not dying. My wife left—'

'That's if she even let you go to tell the tale. Just saying. What's that song about some nightmare hotel, by that American band; The Eagles was it? Something about checking in but never being able to leave. That could be you with—'

'Hotel California. Are you on something, Christine?' He laughed again, real amusement in it this time. 'Where did you dredge that one up from?'

'It's true. And it's just as well I dragged you out of there. She could have a dungeon full of poor deluded sods back at her place, one for each day of the week. So, you never know, I could have saved your life tonight. You'll be grateful tomorrow.'

He could have kissed Keegan, purely for the distraction he brought, when he leant over from the opposite seat and held out his iPhone, a video already playing on the screen. Until he saw what it was. Three raucous women, and himself backed against a wall, looking for all the world like a giant frightened rabbit caught in headlights.

'Let me see,' Sparks demanded.

He rolled his eyes. Jesus. This would be all around the force by tomorrow. It probably already was.

***

Sliding the key in the front door, Massey waited for the emptiness to claim him. The strangeness. The brooding shadows. The house telling him he should somehow have been able to prevent this jagged rip in the fabric of their existence. His, Helen's, and their little home, all tied to each other, belonging together. Until that day almost five weeks ago when he'd come home late from work to find The Note. Written in Helen's uptight spikiness, each phrase razor sharp; all the unspoken words she'd left poised over his head for so many years finally falling. Like a sword of Damocles. And still he had no idea why. Or why now, at least.

Stepping into the hall, locking the door behind him and moving into the kitchen, his every movement in the house seemed to reverberate as if the rooms had been empty for years, as if all the furniture, the carpets, the curtains refused to absorb the echoes, in protest. Helen had left him with almost everything except for the couple of suitcases of clothes and toiletries she'd walked out with. At first, that fact had made her departure feel temporary, as if she'd simply gone off somewhere to clear her head and would be back in a week or so. It had given him hope that things might turn out okay in the end.

For a while, at least.

Until the third day, when in the midst of his emotional turmoil he finally noticed the yawning gap on the alcove shelves in the lounge and realised that she'd taken their vinyl record collection, that only he ever listened to. Why the hell had she taken them? More than half were by artists she didn't even like. And a good few meant a lot more to him than just the music they contained. Those he'd held onto out of sentiment. Ones that predated his life with Helen. The soundtrack to his life before she'd come into it. His childhood and early teens. His first romance. Music he'd hunted down on vinyl especially. There was even one there that had belonged to his biological father. Oddly enough, it was an original edition of the Eagles' *Hotel California* album, the title song of which Sparks had referenced earlier.

After the non-comprehension had come the anger, because the only reason Helen could possibly have had for taking the vinyl was to hurt him, and she'd succeeded. It hurt like a bitch every time he thought of it. As if she'd deliberately rammed a thumbnail hard into his tender unguarded flank and twisted it. And for a long time he couldn't help *but* think of it, because she could have had no other motive for taking them. If she'd kneed him in the balls it couldn't have hurt as much, because at least that would have been an impulsive reaction, not a premeditated act designed to specifically cause him anguish.

Listening to his collection had always been his go-to decompression method following a hard and harrowing case. His music had helped him through the long months of his adored stepfather's terminal illness and death last year too. He'd have wallowed in his music now, if Helen hadn't taken them. Which, of course, was exactly why she had. To knock away his crutch. To make sure that getting over her departure would be as hard and unforgiving a journey as possible.

She knew him so well. Yet he can't have known her at all. When had she become so spiteful and vindictive? Had his own actions made her that way?

Unshed tears pricked his eyes again. Just as they'd done every day since she'd gone.

He sniffed as he reached a tumbler down from a cupboard. The sound of glasses clinking together on the shelf sounded unnaturally loud in the darkness, and the noise when he turned on the tap to let the water run sounded thunderous as it hit the stainless steel. He didn't feel drunk, although he'd put away a lot more beer than he was accustomed to tonight. But to be on the safe side, he drank two glasses of water then filled the tumbler again to take upstairs to bed with him. No reason to sit up moping. Every reason to pull the duvet over his head and pray for sleep to grant him a few dead hours towards some obscure total he'd found himself working towards.

Time heals, apparently, although no-one ever mentions how long it takes. And since he no longer had his vinyl to listen to, he reckoned the more hours he could spend asleep, with his conscious mind disengaged, the better. Let his subconscious mind get on uninterrupted with processing his grief for as long as possible.

If only it were that simple.

Fifty minutes later, he still lay wide awake in the spare bed with his conscious mind refusing to switch off. *His* bed now, not the spare, because, ever since the day she'd left, he hadn't wanted to sleep in the one he'd shared with Helen.

But it wasn't Helen who occupied his thoughts in these small hours. It was Trinny. The sight of her tonight, hardly changed after so long. That remembered dark mole, so perfectly circular it could have been glued on, causing a twist in his gut as soon as he spotted it again.

Trinny's demeanour though, when they came face to face, had betrayed no quickening of the heart for being so close to him, while his own had flapped around in his ribcage. The exact same animal response to her closeness he'd experienced the moment he'd first set eyes on her. And yet, she'd looked as if she barely cared.

And, when it came down to it, why should she? They didn't exactly know each other. They'd shared a few stolen hours together more than a decade ago, during which they'd explored every inch of each other's body, yes, and they must have had some sort of conversation, however basic, although he had zero recollection of anything they'd talked about. But he'd abandoned her as soon as she'd fallen asleep, slinking away from her caravan in the night, ashamed already of his own behaviour, drowning in guilt over the damage he could potentially have caused to his marriage, to his pregnant wife and unborn child.

The damage he *had* done, once Helen found out.

But Trinny couldn't have known anything of that. And even if she had, she had every right to feel he deserved it, after the way he'd left her.

He closed his eyes, allowing the images to crowd in. He and Trinny entwined, writhing in passion, hot damp flesh melting together.

Eleven years on, her power to entrance him hadn't waned. But the fact she'd seemed completely unaffected by her closeness to him tonight had dented his pride. *Had it not.*

He punched the pillow, flipped it over onto the cold side and slammed his head back down.

She *had* teased him tonight though. He hadn't imagined that. And if Sparks could be believed, she'd made it her business to get close to him, which must mean something.

He should have caught her later, away from the others, arranged a date. After all, Helen had left him. He was free to do what he liked with whomever he liked.

They could have…

She might have…

Jesus Christ! Even inside his own head he sounded pathetic.

Perhaps all she'd wanted was to face the man who'd treated her so badly back then. Show him that she really didn't give a toss about him.

He groaned, pulled the duvet up around his shoulders and screwed his eyes shut, trying to conjure up some sheep to count. Anything to count. He couldn't care if they were polka-dot pixies so long as they sent him to sleep.

After another ten minutes, he gave up and went downstairs to make himself a hot chocolate, like his mother used to make for him when he was poorly. Then, just as he was finally drifting off to sleep in the armchair, his phone rang.

Unknown number. He accepted the call. 'Hello?'

The caller hung up.

CHAPTER 5

Sunday, 13 October 2024

Sparks rolled onto her back and treated herself to a big feline, full-body stretch, feeling a couple of vertebrae crack as she arched her back and yawned. Sunday morning. Not yet light outside. No work today. She felt bored already.

When her mother had first moved into a care home eight months ago, Sparks had lived alone for a while in the house she'd grown up in; the first time in her entire life she'd lived on her own. She'd found it difficult to cope with at first.

For one thing, her relationship with her mother hadn't exactly been a happy one, so she'd felt no nostalgia for the house. For another, she'd always known that she'd have to move eventually. The house would need to be sold to pay for her mother's care package once the nest egg her father had left ran out. And not being one to sit around at the best of times when there were things to be done, she'd been keen to get the process underway. Her mother, stricken as she was by the rampaging beast of dementia, would never be coming back home. She already had all the belongings she was likely to need in what remained of her life at the care home with her. Everything else had to go.

For the first couple of months, she'd spent most of her free time clearing out all the crap that had built up over the years, the detritus of a family unit that no longer existed, at least not in the form it once held.

Her brother Ian had helped now and then, particularly when it came to going through all the personal stuff: old photos, sloppy love letters between their parents, comical school reports from their own childhoods, a collection of holiday postcards from long dead relatives. They'd each retained a few mementos and had worked together to digitise the best of the rest. In fact the process had even helped them to rebuild their fractured relationship. To a point. But mostly, she'd found herself enjoying the task on her own, and gaining a better understanding of her parents as people in the process.

For weeks she'd haunted a selection of local charity shops, donating sacks full of freshly laundered old-fashioned clothes and soft furnishings that she couldn't imagine anyone ever wanting to buy, boxes of books, china and ornaments. She'd lost count of the times she'd visited the tip to dump mountains of old newspapers and magazines and anything too broken or obsolete to be of any use to anyone in its current form. And once all of that was done, she'd tackled a bit of painting and decorating. Not too much. Just enough to freshen the place up a bit and make it more inviting to prospective buyers.

The house had sold quickly and Sparks, having already put down a deposit on a two bedroomed flat in Whitley Bay, was able to complete in double quick time and move into her new home before the spring had properly given way to summer. If she squinted, she even had a sea view – from one window at least.

With property prices just on the turn, they'd got a good deal both ways. Her childhood home had sold for above its estimated value, which was excellent news for the coffers of her mother's self-funded care, while her own new home had been reduced in price for a quick sale only the day before she'd first spotted it online. It had been on the market for some time, despite the sea view. The drawback to buyers, Sparks reckoned, being the lack of a dedicated parking space. But that didn't worry her, she'd found a garage to rent only a few streets away, and she didn't mind the walk. In fact she mostly ran the distance to and from her front door anyway.

She swung out of bed now, drank a glass of water, ate a banana and a handful of raisins, then dressed in running gear. She'd need to do double the distance this morning to make up for all the greasy buffet food she'd eaten last night at the charity match bash.

***

Wearing a small backpack, Sparks jogged down to the south end of Whitley Bay beach and turned north. Running on dry sand for added resistance, she covered the full length of the beach before climbing to The Links footpath and taking a left fork just before St Mary's Lighthouse, where she bounded along the cliff path to Seaton Sluice. She passed no-one on the path in the semi-darkness, not even a dogwalker.

Over the bridge, she ran down onto another beach, making for the waterline, dodging a dog that dashed in and out of the sea with half a tree in its mouth, its owner nowhere to be seen. A mongrel of some sort, although it could easily be one of those extortionately priced designer crossbreeds with a stupid name and she wouldn't know it. She wasn't a dog person, and the subject irked her; mongrel puppies that would previously have been unwanted and of little monetary value, had become expensive sought-after designer accessories as soon as they'd been seen on social media with some celebrity bimbo and given a stupid made-up name. Like Cockadoodle or Yorkipoo or Boxweiler. The dogs that is, not the bimbos. Although most of *them* had ridiculous names these days too. But whatever label they carried, and however nice an animal, the dogs were still mongrels to her.

She swerved to avoid the dog, which had abandoned the tree in favour of trying to trip her up. It really was an ugly thing. Maybe this one *was* just a plain mongrel from an unplanned union, or surely it would be on a lead. The owner wouldn't have wanted to let it out of their sight. Not for the money they'd have had to pay for it.

And talking about dogs. Something else that narked her was how do all the local supermarkets could justify the price they charge for bones with barely a picking of meat left on them. Bones that would previously have ended up on the butcher's floor and sold for pennies to dog owners were now selling for as much as prime steak, simply because they'd been labelled 'barbecue spare ribs'. Not quite the same as designer mongrels, but it got on her wick, nonetheless. Misrepresentation in both cases. Same principle, different subject. Blatantly obvious marketing rubbish, yet people fell for it every sodding time.

Sticking to the wet sand now, dodging more dogs – and their owners this time – and leaping three old wooden groynes, she didn't slow her pace until she'd passed the remains of the World War One and Two artillery battery, freshly painted earlier in the year for the D-Day commemorations, and the twin side-by-side rows of beach huts at Blyth's South Beach.

Climbing the ramp up to the promenade by the lifeguard station, she allowed herself a few moments bent forward, hands on knees until her breathing regulated, disappointed in herself for not having completed the full length of the beach. But she knew her body well, and she needed enough energy to run back home. By the time she got back, she'd have done around three times her normal morning run.

Taking off her backpack, she reached inside for the water bottle she always carried, and groped around for the energy bar she'd brought with her. She finished the bar in two bites and stowed the wrapper in a litter bin near where she stood.

The Mermaid Car Park wasn't exactly full, but there were a good few more people here than she'd encountered elsewhere on her run, and not just dog owners. A group of middle aged women of all shapes and sizes performed warm-up stretches under the guidance of a shrill-voiced harridan, while two young men in wet suits carried boogie boards into the surf. A couple sitting on a memorial bench stared at the horizon, their legs encased in sleeping bags, as if they'd spent the night there. The two big rucksacks and three overstuffed plastic bags at their feet could easily contain all their worldly possessions, so maybe they had nowhere else to go.

Sparks jumped as a bicycle zipped past her from behind, catching under its wheels the strap of the backpack she'd laid on the ground by her feet. She yelled and the rider threw a lame apology over his shoulder.

Prick.

Stowing her water bottle away, keeping her eyes on the group of women, Sparks did a few stretches of her own to keep her muscles flexing while she allowed her mind to linger on the subject she'd pushed away so far this morning. Her boss. DCI James Massey. Her best friend. Possibly her only real friend, if she didn't count colleagues or Ellie Morgan, Massey's mother. She should call him. Check he was okay after last night.

She glanced at the time on her Fitbit. Not yet eight. Was that too early for a social call on a Sunday morning? Would he hang up on her? He hadn't been exactly grateful she'd saved him from that red-haired man-eater last night.

Definitely something dodgy about that one.

And not just her.

When Sparks had seen that video on Keegan's phone last night, she'd recognised the three women who'd accosted Massey at the rugby club door as the same three who'd been hanging onto Red's every word on the other side of the dance floor. She didn't believe for a moment *that* was a coincidence. They'd deliberately targeted him. And all that mumbo jumbo they'd spouted. Making predictions. Beyond weird.

They reminded her of a play she'd been in at school once. A Shakespeare tragedy. Macbeth. The weird sisters.

How apt is that?

She needed to find out who Red was. Who all of them were in fact. Although Red must have been behind what the other three had done. She was the one Massey had history with.

She'd need to do it surreptitiously of course. He wouldn't thank her for interfering. At least that's what he'd call it, although she'd prefer to think of it more as looking after his interests. Watching his back.

All the way home, she occupied her mind with how she might discover the identities of the women, without Massey finding out, and failed to come up with even one, short of doing a bit of undercover investigating up in Ellington and Cresswell one day and quizzing the locals. And that was out. She'd stick out like a sore thumb on her own.

It wasn't until she put the key in her front door that she thought of asking Dazz to go with her. In his drunken stupor, having just returned from chucking his guts up in the coach's on-board facilities, he'd hung over the back of her seat breathing puke fumes over her, and scribbled his number on the back of a receipt he'd found in his pocket.

She'd told herself at the time that she'd make him regret doing that.

No time like the present.

CHAPTER 6

Dazz looked like shit when Sparks arrived to pick him up. No chance of him dazzling anyone or anything in this state. It had taken a bit of effort to persuade him to stop feeling sorry for himself and get himself up and out, and she knew she'd end up having to listen to tales of woe about his marriage breakup before the day was done. Looking at him now, waiting for her at the kerb, squinting against the unseasonably hot autumn sun, as if he'd lived underground for the last decade, she seriously doubted her own sanity.

Did all men fall apart when they ended up on their own?

But if this was the price of having a semi-willing co-pilot on this scouting mission, then so be it.

She could *look* interested when she needed to. She didn't have to actually listen.

'Jesus, Dazz. Don't you own a comb?'

He had the sort of thick dirty blond cow-licked locks that didn't take well to being groomed at the best of times, but this morning he looked like he'd stuck his fingers into an electrical socket.

He raked those same fingers through his hair, making it look ten times worse before patting it down and stroking it into some semblance of style.

'It's fine. See.'

'Or an iron?'

The hooped rugby shirt he wore had clearly been trampled by a herd of rampaging rhinos before he'd picked it up off the floor and put it on.

'Body heat will sort that before we get to where we're going. Wherever the hell that is. Remind me why it's me you've rumbled out of bed and not James.'

She indicated to pull away from the kerb. 'Because it's *about* James. That woman, last night.'

'What woman?'

'The redhead who hunted him down.'

Dazz burst out laughing. 'Hunted him down? In Ellington and Cresswell RFC? Lucky man.'

She glanced sideways at him. 'Her and her mates. They were all messing with him, and I want to know why.'

He laughed again. 'Are you jealous? Is that what this is? Because—'

'What? No, I'm not bloody jealous. I'm concerned. Can't I be concerned about my boss?'

'But why? So a woman came onto him last night. So what. Good for him. He did better than me if that's the case.' Eyebrows raised, clearly remembering the umpteen times she'd rebuffed his advances at the party, he gave her a long look that she chose to ignore.

'Have you watched the video?' she demanded.

'What video?'

'Of James being attacked by a band of women at the door of the club.'

He screwed up his face. 'Oh yeah, I think I did, lucky bastard. Can't remember much of it though. I was a bit distracted.'

'I'm not surprised, the state you were in. It'll be on your phone. I think Keegan put it on that WhatsApp group the team has going.'

She took the A189 north off the Moor Farm roundabout at Annitsford while he scrolled through his messages.

'Got it.' He watched for a few moments and emitted a loud bark. 'Who the hell shot this?'

'Must have been the bloke on the door.'

Dazz continued to watch, punctuating his viewing with the occasional sharp burst of laughter.

'Christ. Look at his face… priceless.'

'It's not funny, Dazz. They assaulted him.'

'Bollocks. It's hilarious. But none of these three women are redheads.'

'No. She was with them in the club later though. Hiding behind them. Biding her time.'

'For what?'

'Before she pounced. I managed to get a photo of her. I'll show it to you, once we get parked up.'

'You still haven't told me what we're supposed to be doing, and why you've dragged me out of my pit to help you.'

'We're going to find out who she is. It'll be easier if there are two of us.'

'Why don't you just ask James who she is?'

'I did. He wouldn't tell me.'

'Maybe because it's none of your business. Are you sure this isn't just jealousy, Christine? Because that's what it's coming across as to me. And if you think I'm going around knocking on doors on my day off, you can turn this car around now.'

'I am not jealous. And we are not going to be knocking on doors.'

'So what are we doing?'

'I only want to find out her name. All of their names in fact, but hers in particular. It would have looked odd, just me asking on my own.'

'It's still going to look odd with both of us.'

***

Sparks parked up in the pitted car park of The Drift Café at the far end of Cresswell, taking the last spot between two huge SUVs, glad her car was only small.

'Why here?' Dazz asked.

'It's still too early to go anywhere else, and I thought you might like a coffee to perk you up a bit. A full English breakfast too if you like. Then we can have an amble through the village, ask a couple of locals. And if we still have no joy, we can call in at the Plough at Ellington.'

He patted his well-muscled stomach. 'Not sure I'm up to anything massive to eat yet after drinking so much alcohol last night.'

'You threw most of that back up on the way home. Your belly must be empty. My treat.'

'Hmm.'

He raised his eyebrows and breathed in through gritted teeth, considering his options.

'Still don't fancy the full English. I need something sweet. Do they do cakes?'

'Whatever.' She scrolled through her phone's gallery and clicked on the sneaky image of Red she'd taken last night. 'Look, this is the woman we're looking for. Keep an eye open for her.'

'Woah,' Dazz took the phone from her to get a better look. 'She's a bit of alright, isn't she?'

'I don't know Dazz, is she? Something to do with the tits hanging out, perhaps?'

Amused, he gave her a sidelong look. 'It's everything about her, actually. You certainly can't accuse her of being plain. She's beautiful, and sexy as hell. I wouldn't kick her out of bed, that's for sure.'

Sparks snatched her phone back and flung open the car door. 'Ready?'

At the counter, he ordered a large latte with an extra shot, a huge slice of carrot cake with thick cream cheese frosting, and then wavered over something to go with it, stuck between a slice of Malteser tiffin or a raspberry and poppy seed muffin with orange drizzle. Eventually – after an elbow in the ribs from Sparks, who nodded towards the lengthening queue of people behind them – he opted for the tiffin.

Sparks sent him to find a table with instructions to text her the number, while she ordered a pot of tea and a cheese scone for herself and tried to engage the young female cashier in conversation. But the pressure of the queue won out.

'Sorry,' the cashier said. 'We're too busy just now for me to stop and natter. But if I get a few minutes later, I'll come and find you.'

The woman looked sincere enough. Sparks mumbled begrudged thanks and went to find Dazz, knowing those minutes were unlikely to arrive given how busy the place had become since they'd come in. He'd bagged the smallest table, tucked away in a corner of the room, and sat sideways on his chair, examining a flyer that had been left on the windowsill beside him. 'Look at that,' he said.

Sparks leant over him and grabbed the flyer. 'Cresswell Macbeth. Saturday 26th October at Cresswell Pele Tower.' How strange. She'd only just been thinking this morning about her own part in a school production of Macbeth a long time ago. 'So?'

'So, look at the picture.'

'What about it?'

Below the headline, the flyer bore a spooky image of Macbeth's three witches around a cauldron. An actual photo, rather than a graphic cartoon image.

'The three women you're looking for,' he said. 'The ones who… "assaulted" James. That could be them.'

'Could be anyone.' Sparks examined the image closer. The print quality wasn't the best, and the women were wearing wigs and stage make-up, so there was no way to tell if these were the same three women, although it would make sense of the mumbo jumbo they were spouting during their assault on Massey. The predictions they made; telling him he was going to face *death*, for God's sake, before the moon wanes.

Which was when?

She pulled out her phone and tried to search for the Cresswell Pele Tower website but had no service.

Dazz checked his phone. Only one bar.

A waitress, who looked hardly a day over twelve but had to be at least sixteen, arrived with their order, and Dazz dug in straight away, licking his lips and moaning in pleasure as he swallowed a huge bite of carrot cake.

Sparks brought up the photo of Red. 'Do you know her?' she asked the waitress.

'No, sorry.' The girl's eyes flicked towards the busy counter, and she hurried away.

'That'll send your blood sugar through the roof,' Sparks said, when he finished. 'That lot must have had twice the calories of a full English.

He smacked his lips and gave her one of his trademark twinkling grins. 'I know.'

'You'd better not spew it all back up in my car.'

'Mmm-mm. Not a chance.'

She had to admit it, the sugar rush seemed to have perked him up no end.

***

The village was packed with parked cars now, their owners presumably down on the beach. Sparks thought she'd scored lucky in the small, packed car park adjoining the ice cream shop in the village when she spotted another car just pulling out of a space, until she realised by the size of the queue that the staff here wouldn't have time to answer her questions either, without having to wait at least half an hour. And Dazz would end up ordering some humongous multi-flavoured, multi-scoop sugar cone monstrosity and would want to eat it in the car – her car – and that wasn't happening.

Where the hell did he put it all? There wasn't a picking of fat on the bloke.

She drove further along the coast road, past the village hall and an ornate swinging sign for a Blue Moon Bakery, which she couldn't actually see and so dismissed. A bakery, off the street front, was hardly likely to be open on a Sunday.

She drove as far as the gateway to a place called Golden Sands Holiday Park, filled with static caravans. Nothing else in sight along the road beyond that but caravans on the right, the North Sea on the left and another small car park she probably also wouldn't be able to find a space in.

Despondent, she turned the car around in the gateway and headed back the way they'd come. She hadn't banked on the village being so full of happy campers and day trippers in October, all keen on making the most of the unseasonably hot weather.

How the hell could they spot any locals amongst this lot; they'd probably be staying well out of the way.

Maybe this mission hadn't been such a good idea after all, at least not on a red hot Sunday.

'Where to next, oh wise one?' Dazz said.

Sparks took the left turn sharper than she'd intended onto the Ellington road. 'Are you taking the piss?'

He held up both hands. 'No, not me. I'm just along for the ride, and looking forward to a hair of the dog and a three course Sunday lunch at the Plough.'

'You can't possibly be hungry again already. You must— *Shit!*'

She braked hard, only just missing a woman who'd decided to dash across the road in front of them. Skinny jeans, turquoise and white striped beach cover-up with the hood raised to frame a pale face, half hidden by huge sunglasses. 'Stupid cow!' she shouted out of her open window.

Dazz laughed. 'Back to the subject. Those cakes were emergency sustenance. Thank you, by the way. But the sugar rush isn't going to last long. Soon, my blood sugar will crash again, and I'll turn into a morose dick, crying on your shoulder, bending your ear about how hard done by I am since my wife left me. Do you really want to have to deal with that?'

Sparks couldn't help herself. The corners of her mouth began to twitch, then she burst out laughing. That was exactly what she'd thought she'd be subjected to when she saw the state of him earlier.

The car in front, already crawling, slowed further to allow the one ahead of it to pull up onto the grass verge between two traffic cones. A gate set in a high stone wall stood open, a waist-high A-board next to it. A man in a hi-vis vest bent to talk to the driver. On an impulse, Sparks clicked on her indicator and pulled onto the grass too.

'What are you doing?' Dazz cried. 'You said we were going to the Plough. Is it too late to say lunch is on me?'

'The Plough won't be open for another quarter of an hour. And it'll be hectic for a while after that. We'd probably need to book a table anyway if you want to eat. How about you check if they've got any tables left in an hour or so, while I...' She leant across him towards the passenger window. '... have a word with this man.'

The thought of having dinner with Dazz, even just Sunday lunch, had become a strangely attractive one, and she couldn't keep a smile from her face as hi-vis man approached.

'Is that the way into the Pele Tower?' she asked.

'It is, miss. We have a free guided tour starting in...' He pushed up a shirt sleeve and consulted his watch. '... exactly fifteen minutes. You're okay to park next to that gentleman. The guide will be waiting at the top of the path.'

She pointed towards the A-board. 'Is that a poster for Cresswell Macbeth?'

'Yes it is. Saturday the 26th. Two performances: afternoon and evening. You can buy tickets from the guide if you're interested.'

Dazz finished a call he'd been making. 'Thought I'd better call them. Didn't want to risk their online booking system this late in the day. We have a table for two booked at half two. Only slot they had left.'

Table for two. The expression conjured something far more intimate than what it would be in reality, but she liked the sound of it. The fact that Dazz seemed happy to prolong the time he spent in her company gave her a warm feeling too.

'Good,' she said. 'Plenty of time to explore this place.'

A wide path through wooded grounds led them up a gentle slope towards the tower, its ancient stone projection scarred diagonally by what looked like the remnants of a roof line. Something must have been attached to it at some point.

Noticing the direction of her gaze, a man at the top of the path stepped forward. 'That's where the old mansion house was attached,' he said.

Surprised, Sparks gave him a second look. and recognised him from last night. Average height, dark hair, neatly trimmed beard. As good looking as she remembered.

'Are you here for the tour,' he asked, addressing both of them.

'Um yes, why not. We stopped on a bit of an impulse really.'

'Impulse is good.' His eyes crinkled in the corners as he looked directly into hers. Perhaps he recognised her from last night too. 'We can work with that.'

'Actually, mate…' Dazz sidled in closer, in a move clearly designed to infer they were a couple, although he steered clear of actually touching her. '… it's the Cresswell Macbeth thing you've got coming up that interests us.'

The man nodded. 'Really? That too is good. We have tickets on sale now. Twelve quid each. Includes a Halloween buffet and a spooky lantern display. All in aid of the tower's community fund, like the match and the party last night.'

Dazz looked stunned for a moment.

'You were there? I didn't see you.'

The man gave a short laugh. 'I'm not surprised. *Mate*. I think you'd already had a skinful by the time we got there. I'm Tom Kirk, by the way'

'Good man,' Dazz said, and shook Kirk's hand.

Having clearly bonded in a way she didn't get, Sparks shook her head, knowing the opportunity to ask about the three witches on the poster had been wrested from her. But if Kirk wanted to sell them tickets for the play, the opportunity would arise again; she just needed to bide her time. She glanced at her Fitbit. Exactly twelve o'clock. 'Are we the only ones here for the tour?'

'There's another couple who came in just before you; they're having a wander around the outside. We'll wait for them before we go in. And there's a big group of women who went straight over to the garden. They might join us later, they said, but gardening's more their bag.'

An older couple emerged slowly from the path to the left of the tower, taking their time, stepping up onto a long stone mounting block and pointing out to sea, considering no-one's time but their own. Retired, no doubt. Sparks had to stop herself from yelling at them to get a move on.

Eventually, with a family of four joining behind them at the last minute, Tom Kirk led the way through a heavy wooden door into a cool cavernous space.

CHAPTER 7

Exhausted, Massey slumped down into a sun lounger, taking his first breather of a long day. To fill the empty hours, he'd spent the time since waking beating the back garden into submission. He'd scalped the lawn, savaged some shrubs and hacked back perennials, wondering if he'd ever get to see them all bloom again next year. The house would probably need to be sold if he and Helen couldn't find their way back together, if their break-up actually ended up in – dirty word – divorce.

Who was he kidding. There was no 'probably' about it. Helen still refused to speak to him, or to engage with him in any way at all during five whole weeks. But then he remembered her Catholicism. Did her church even recognise divorce? Did she intend to just leave him in limbo?

He couldn't cope with that. The whole business with his vinyl collection had caused something to shift in his heart. If she could do that to him, knowing how important the albums were to him, was she even the person he'd fallen in love with anymore? Could he ever love the person she'd become?

To be fair, he'd done his best to see it from her point of view. Eleven years back, Helen must have been asking herself whether she could still love the person *he'd* proven himself to be through his infidelity. And he was well aware that, as hard as it had been for him to bear, the loss of their child had been a complete devastation for her; a wound she'd never recovered from. And one that he had caused. Back then, she'd decided to save their marriage, and he'd felt so pathetically grateful. But had she ever really, truly forgiven him?

Probably not. In fact, scrub that. Definitely not. Deep inside, he'd always known that. It had just taken eleven years for her to realise she never ever could. A question formed at the edge of his mind. The first time it had occurred to him in all the time she'd been gone. He pushed it away, trying to banish it, but it persisted.

Has she found someone else?

Determined not to dwell on the thought, he stared at the back fence, becoming mesmerised by the greyness of the painted wood. Urban Slate, if his memory served; the colour they'd chosen for it, together.

As he stared, the upright planks began to warp and writhe in his vision, and it took a few moments to realise how dizzy he felt, and then a few more to click that he'd been out in the sun all day with nothing to eat or drink. He hadn't eaten yesterday either, after the smoothie and banana he'd consumed before the match. He'd fancied none of the buffet food his colleagues had piled high on their plates at the party. In fact he hadn't been able to stomach many meals recently, and only the necessity of having to eat enough of the correct nutrition during training and prior to the game had prevented him from starving himself.

His mother had rung earlier to ask him over for lunch and he'd told her he'd think about it, with no real intention of going, but maybe he should.

He looked at the time on his mobile. Almost half four. He'd left it way too late. She'd have eaten lunch and done the dishes hours ago.

A takeaway then. He could order in. But was there anywhere open at this time on a Sunday? And could he be arsed to eat it anyway, by the time it arrived?

He gave a big sigh, running dirt encrusted hands over his face, feeling the sun-burnt flush in his cheeks. He should have worn sun screen.

As he got to his feet, to go and clean himself up, he paused as his phone vibrated on the wooden table next to him. The same unknown number as last night. It had rung a couple of other times through the day too, still with no-one speaking when he answered. Helen probably, having bought herself a new phone. Trying to mess with his head even more than she had already. He accepted the call but said nothing, remaining silent until the caller eventually hung up. Two could play silly buggers.

In the end, after stowing away his gardening tools and having a quick shower, he pulled a couple of bags of microwaveable rice with vegetables from the back of a cupboard. When the machine pinged, he transferred the rice to an oven-proof dish and mixed in his last tin of tuna, then topped the lot with slices from the dried up end of some extra mature cheddar and stuck it under the grill.

He'd grown tired of feeling pathetic. He was a single bloke now, responsible for his own health and wellbeing, and more than capable of feeding himself properly and getting on with life. First stop tomorrow after work, the supermarket to stock up on some decent food.

Before settling down to watch an old movie on Sky, he remembered to give his mother a call and apologised for not having turned up for lunch, knowing the best way to reassure her he was fine was by allowing her to hear how much brighter and more positive he sounded now than when she'd called him this morning. Which, to be fair, was exactly how he did feel. A hard day of physical graft in the unseasonably hot sun had been good for him. Perhaps he wouldn't need to count polka-dot pixies tonight to get to sleep.

But when his phone rang just before seven and he saw Sparks' name on the screen, he had a premonition she wasn't calling for just a chat. He may end up getting no sleep after all tonight.

CHAPTER 8

As soon as Sparks hung up, Massey had called Keegan. After all, Keegan knew the old guard from Ellington and Cresswell RUFC far better than he did.

'Shit. I can't drive,' he'd said. 'I've been drinking.'

'If you want to go up there, I'll drive you.'

'Thanks Flash. If you're okay with that, I'd be grateful.'

Massey spotted him now in his headlights, waiting by his gate.

'You took your time,' Keegan said, as soon as he climbed in. 'And how the hell did Sparks find out about this first?'

'She was up there already.'

'Why?'

Massey shrugged. 'No idea. You can ask her when we get there.'

Keegan ran both hands through his thick thatch of dark hair, unable to sit still.

'Anyone inside?

'They think Ben's inside. Not sure about Ursula and Fleur. Sparks said the blaze was already well out of hand by the time the Fire Service arrived. I'm not sure how she even knows it's Ben Quinn's house. Why would she?'

They drove in silence for a while, until Keegan – fidgeting constantly in the passenger seat as if his piles were playing up – could stand it no longer. 'Ben called me this morning, worried about all that stuff he and Michael Duffy were saying last night. About Duncan Kingsley's murderer still being out there. What if they were right?'

Massey indicated right onto Cresswell Road in Ellington. Already, they could smell burning. 'Kingsley didn't die in a fire. Durham know who killed him—'

'Do they though? Both Ben and Michael told us last night they think Durham have cocked up.'

'— and we don't know that anyone has died tonight yet.'

Above the tree line, a hazy orange glow became more defined as they moved further towards their destination. Eventually, as the sea view opened up before them, they saw the burning house almost at the bottom of Cresswell Road on the left, two or three up from the junction. Flames still licked the sky, but the soaring inferno Sparks described had been subdued. Two fire appliances had driven up onto the wide grass verge to allow closer access to the fire. An ambulance stood at the kerb with its doors open, a shape on a stretcher inside. Still alive, if the frenetic activity of the paramedics was anything to go by.

'That's too small to be Ben,' Keegan said. 'It must be Ursula or Fleur.'

They saw Sparks talking to a uniformed police officer, who'd used his squad car to block the road and kept a close eye on members of the public on both sides.

She spotted them and pointed to her own car over to their right, on a wide grass verge, nose in to a stone wall. Massey pulled in behind it. In his mirror, he spotted someone else he knew standing right next to Sparks. Dazz Albright. What the hell was he doing up here today? Were he and Sparks together?

A stocky figure detached itself from the crowd of rubberneckers as they climbed out. Michael Duffy clasped Keegan's hand in both of his. 'You came. Thank you.'

'Michael, What do you know?' Keegan asked.

'They're telling us nothing, but I can see that's Fleur they've brought out. She doesn't look good...' A single tear escaped his eye.

'They'll look after her. She'll be taken off to hospital in no time. What about Ben?'

'They haven't found him yet.' Duffy's face twisted. 'Oh God...'

Massey knew the two men had known each other since childhood. 'What about Ursula? Is she in there too?'

'No, I've spoken to her. She's on her way.'

'Anyone else missing?' His brain had focussed immediately on Trinny, simply because she'd been on his mind all day, although why she would possibly be inside Ben Quinn's house, he had no idea. But the first person his eyes landed on was Finn Barron, seemingly entranced by the licking flames, his wife Verity clinging to his arm. He scanned the rest of the crowd, the flashing lights of emergency vehicles casting a flickering glow across their faces. No Trinny.

Sparks rolled her eyes and nodded her head in the direction of the ice cream shop on Beach Road, beyond another patrol car roadblock on the far side of the action. 'Over there.'

Even with the voluminous dark coat she wore billowing in the wind, Trinny looked tiny from this distance. But with all that long burnished red hair streaming loose, it could be no-one else. Massey felt the impact at the exact moment their eyes met, even from so far away, like an electrical current, or the flash of steel blades clashing together. But then she turned and walked out of his view, and even when he craned his neck he couldn't spot her.

When he turned back towards his colleagues, he caught a raised eyebrow enquiry from Dazz towards Sparks', and a confirming nod in return. He could guess what that was all about, but he still had no idea why the pair of them should be here today. Together. On the day a huge blaze destroyed the house of a man they were all talking to last night.

And then he heard a shout from the direction of the flames. Someone else found inside.

It had to be Ben. Dead or alive, they couldn't yet tell.

CHAPTER 9

When Massey arrived with Keegan in tow, Sparks had noticed his quizzical look when he spotted Dazz. He'd have said something to her about it, if that Duffy bloke hadn't collared them first, but she knew he'd get round to it eventually.

She couldn't decide whether it had been luck that she and Dazz had still been in the Plough when the news came through, or fate. They'd noticed the ripple of alarm that had passed through the staff, including the youngest of the three women she was looking for, who looked much different in her staff uniform from the glamorous vamp of last night. Then a wave of concern murmured through the people at the bar, then through the diners. And then they heard the news too. A huge house fire. In Cresswell.

'Don't like the sound of that,' Dazz had said.

'Me neither.'

Dazz had already paid, so they'd left immediately. She'd enjoyed Dazz's company far more than she could ever have considered possible.

At first, they'd talked about the reason for their outing in the first place. Tom Kirk had confirmed the three witches in the Cresswell Macbeth poster were the same three who'd hassled Massey at the door of the club. He'd even told them their names. He'd claimed not to have known Red though, or seen her at the party, and Sparks couldn't decide whether or not she believed him, until eventually he'd admitted that he *may* have seen her around at other times, but it was a grudging admission, which had raised Sparks' bullshit antennae, and his attractiveness had waned considerably.

Perhaps he was another poor sod Red had ensnared.

After a while, their conversation had drifted to other subjects, and she'd found it hard to believe how much they had in common. They'd both grown up locally and their birthdays were only a day apart. Different years though, Dazz being closer to Massey's age. Like her, Dazz had only one sibling, and a parent with dementia, although his father was still in the early stages and being cared for at home by his mother, while her own father was dead, and her mother had been resident in a specialist care home for the past eight months. They discovered they were both fitness freaks too, although her preference was for running, while Dazz's was for team sports. And, weirdly, they both also had double-jointed elbows. But how that subject had come up, she couldn't now recall.

Then, when they'd run out of things they had in common to talk about, they started exploring their differences, and she couldn't help but feel flattered by how interested Dazz had seemed in everything she'd said. The whole day with him had been a completely new experience for her. People usually found her difficult, mostly because she had no problem in telling them what she truly thought. But with Dazz it was different. He found her directness funny, and that had made her laugh at herself, something she couldn't ever remember being able to do before.

He *had* mentioned his family and marriage break-up eventually, but as a matter of fact. As a part of who he was, rather than in a woe-is-me way. And then immediately, determined to leave it at that, he'd steered the conversation back around to Red and the three witches. She respected, and was thankful for his determination not to talk about it, because she had no wish to delve any further into the subject of his marriage.

It was in the middle of telling him about how she'd once been in a production of Macbeth herself at school, as a fourth witch called Hecate, that they'd heard the news about the house fire.

'I thought there were only three witches in Macbeth,' Dazz had said, on their way out to the car.

Sparks had shrugged. 'Apparently, in some versions there are four.'

'You should have told what's-his-name at the tower, Tom Kirk. He might have been a little more forthcoming, if you had.'

***

When they'd arrived at the scene, firefighters were still in the process of assessing the situation and deploying hoses. No men had yet been sent inside.

Sparks knew they could read the smoke of a fire as they approached the location to help get a line on the exact position and size of the blaze within a building. They could tell by the colour and intensity of the smoke the type of materials likely to be burning inside and the precautions they'd need to take. Before they'd even arrived, the crews would have been weighing up these factors, hoping no-one was inside. No cars on the drive, but that meant nothing. If the occupants couldn't be found elsewhere, the crews had to assume they could be inside. Staring up at the voracious towering flames when she and Dazz had got there, Sparks hadn't envied the firefighters who'd have to go in there looking for anyone trapped.

Only one patrol car had arrived before them, so they'd made themselves known to the officers and helped to establish wide cordons on either side of the house to keep the public at bay, But soon, as more troops arrived, their services had become redundant, and Sparks found a moment to call Massey.

A shout went up. They were bringing someone out. Small, so not the bloke she'd met last night. By the time they knew it was the daughter Fleur, Sparks saw Massey arriving with Keegan, and noticed his puzzlement when he spotted Dazz there too, no doubt wondering why they were together. No way did she want to have to enlighten him, but she didn't need to. Not once that Duffy bloke collared him and Keegan, and it wasn't long anyway before he started craning his neck looking for Red, who she'd spotted earlier on the far side of the road blocks. A speck in the distance, but unmistakably her.

'Over there,' she told him, nodding her head in the direction of the ice cream shop.

And then another shout went up. Someone else confirmed still inside. But no sooner had a team of firefighters got themselves lined up to re-enter, than a loud crack sounded, followed by a groan. Then a huge flare and a belch of smoke vomited from the front of the building.

CHAPTER 10

Shaking from head to foot, Verity Barron clung to her husband's sleeve, transfixed in horrified fascination by the burning house, still ablaze after so long, although the huge flames that had earlier leapt into the sky had retreated into a black smoking maw; a void that spat amber sparks into the star-speckled night sky every time something shifted inside, and throbbed with an aura that made her feel dizzy. She'd thought it visible only to her, but beside her Finn stared at the remains of his friend's house with an intensity that frightened her. Perhaps he could see the aura too.

She had no idea how many hours ago Ben's body had been taken away. Everything felt so... distant. Someone in the crowd earlier had said young Fleur would die too, and even if she survived she'd be maimed, scarred for life. Oh God, of course she would. Inside as well as out. What sort of life could she live, with... with scars like that?

Verity clutched the cloth of Finn's sleeve, in an effort to stop an agitated tremor. She saw her knuckles were bleeding again, but resisted the impulse to pull the sleeves of her own white quilted coat over them. She didn't want blood on that. White for purity and cleanliness. And honesty. Although she couldn't describe her mind as pure or honest anymore, and her hands hadn't felt clean since...

Oh God, this was all her fault. Her thoughts had led to this. To... to Ben's death. And Fleur... poor, poor Fleur. But she hadn't intended *this*. Oh God no. Not at all. She'd just thought... If Ben could just, stand down. Allow Finn to...

She felt one knee give way and tried to shift her weight onto the other foot.

Finn had worked so hard at the club since Duncan died. The position should be his, not Ben's or anyone else's. They'd both worked hard for it really, because without her pushing him, he'd have been happy to continue living in Duncan's shadow, when she knew he'd be far better at the job than Duncan could ever have been.

But… She shook her head, trying to clarify her thoughts. But that was then. Before… oh God… before Duncan's murder. She'd wished Duncan gone. And then he was. And now, while Finn kept putting off the election because he said he couldn't be sure of winning, she'd wished Ben gone too. Finn's greatest rival. And now he *was* gone… and it was her fault… oh God…

She wrapped both arms tighter around Finn's, clutching hard to keep herself from falling, turning her face into his shoulder to hide from the throbbing aura. Her legs buckled, and at last Finn dragged his attention back from the burning house. His eyes wide like saucers, he grabbed her by the shoulders and shook her, his grip the only thing holding her up.

'Did you see… in the flames? Did you see him?'

'We should go, Finn. Take me home. We shouldn't be here.'

After one long last look towards the burning house, he thrust his arm across her back, his big right hand gripping her ribs below her armpit, preventing her from falling. He glanced around them constantly, concerned more, she couldn't help noticing, with how her behaviour would look to others than about her wellbeing. But most of the villagers had already gone, drifting away gradually, like the tide from the shore.

***

Massey watched Finn and Verity Barron squeeze through the gap beside the gate onto the field below the tower's boundary wall in order to circumnavigate the road blocks, their dark silhouette against the moonlit sky incongruous as they cut across the grass together. Like a pantomime horse walking sideways as Finn held his wife pinned to his side, since her legs appeared unable to hold her upright.

Shock, he supposed.

Whatever issues there'd been between the men more recently, Finn had known Ben well since their young teenage years when he'd moved down from Scotland. Verity surely couldn't have failed to get to know Ben and his family too. She may not have grown up around here – he seemed to recall she spoke in a soft Irish lilt – but she'd probably lived here with Finn for at least as long as she hadn't. Longer than twenty years anyway. More than enough time to get to know Ben well too.

But then he remembered what Ben had said about Verity at the party on Saturday. Something about her having ideas of grandeur. That it was her who pushed Finn towards bigger and better things.

At the time, his mind had conjured up a vision of Verity as a Hyacinth Bucket type, which was way different to the Verity Barron he remembered from the first charity match party. But then he'd noticed her here tonight with Finn and seen how painfully thin and wraith-like she looked, and the contrast jarred in his mind.

She'd suffered other tragedies too, of course. As well as her son, she'd lost her first husband, although not by fire as far as he knew, so perhaps seeing such horrific evidence tonight of Ben's death – and possibly Fleur's too since she may yet die as a result of the burns and smoke inhalation she's suffered – had simply brought those emotions of loss flooding back.

He watched their receding figures now, moving diagonally across the field. Finn doing the walking and dragging Verity along beside him. Heading for the Lynemouth road on a trajectory that would take them beyond all the buildings he could see, towards the holiday park he knew lay along there somewhere.

CHAPTER 11

Monday, 14 October 2024

Massey arrived at work early and made straight for the office of his immediate boss, DSU Lou Portas. He'd called her last night and brought her up to speed with what had happened in Cresswell and the fact that some of her officers had ended up there unofficially. She had coffee already brewing in her vintage French percolator.

'You haven't told me how Christine Sparks and Darren Albright managed to be up in Cresswell together when the fire broke out.' Her tone held an accusatory edge.

'That's because I have no idea. Things were a bit manic last night. I never had the chance to ask either of them.'

She sighed and moved over to the filing cabinet to pour the coffee. 'I know, I appreciate that. Sorry. I need a gallon of coffee to make me feel human today.'

She did seem a bit out of sorts this morning. Not her usual cool, calm self at all.

She noticed him looking. 'Don't mind me. Things are a bit manic at home. I have family staying for a few days. Not used to having kids around the place.'

This was the most she'd ever shared of her private life with him. When he'd first met her, he'd imagined that the crude pottery pen holder on her desk might have been made by a son or a daughter at school. He'd heard since that she was unmarried, but that didn't necessarily mean she was childless.

'I was as surprised as anyone that Christine had gone back up there so soon after the charity match,' he said.

'Is there something going on between her and Darren?'

'What, Christine? No, I can't see it.'

In all the time he'd known Sparks, he couldn't remember her ever having had a boyfriend. Or a girlfriend come to that. Not one that she'd told him about anyway and, while they were close, it was really none of his business. Anyway, for the last two or three years she'd had a lot to deal with: the death of her father, whom she'd adored; finding herself, in the midst of her grief, having to take over from him as the main carer for her mother, who in her worsening dementia didn't even recognise her own daughter.

Even though they worked on the same team, he hadn't really got to know Sparks himself until he'd been asked to mentor her when the stress of everything happening at home had impacted on her job, to a point it could have cost her the career she loved so much. From that moment on they'd become fast friends, as well as colleagues, but that didn't mean they shared the really personal stuff with each other.

'You saw them at the party too,' he said. 'Dazz was arseholed. Pestering her for a dance every five minutes. And she wanted nothing to do with him.'

'Yet now they're going off for days out together. She isn't the reason that Darren and his wife split up, is she?'

'What? No. Absolutely not.'

'Then there has to be a reason they were there.'

'I'll ask her.'

Having already given it some thought, he suspected he knew exactly why Sparks had gone there, although he didn't hold out much hope of her admitting it.

But why Dazz had got involved was a mystery.

Portas placed a coffee down in front of him and sank back into her squashy leather executive chair. 'God, I need this.'

'Any news from the hospital on Fleur?' he asked.

'Not yet. Guy's going to let me know if he hears anything, but I'm not holding out much hope of her surviving.' She slammed her hands on the desk. 'It's a bugger not being in the loop, isn't it? We have no authority here, not until we know whether that fire was anything more than an accident.'

'And possibly not even then if Durham snaffle it. I told you what Ben Quinn and Michael Duffy said about Durham going after the wrong men on Duncan Kingsley's murder. If the fire turns out to have been a malicious firing – and I'm going to stick my neck out and say it was, which would make it arson and Ben's death murder – then what's to say it isn't connected to Duncan's death?'

'What's to say it is? Supposition; that's all. Sounds from what you and Guy have told me, that's all they had; no hard proof that anyone else was involved. Durham will have done a good job on the Kingsley inquiry. They wouldn't be set to charge those men without a solid case against them – if indeed they *are* planning to charge them.'

Massey blew out his cheeks. He knew that. But the fact Ben Quinn had died not even twenty-four hours after he and Duffy had claimed that Kingsley's murderer was still out there stank. And he knew Keegan felt the same.

'I'll talk to the Chief Super,' Portas said. 'But there's nothing else we can do until the postmortem is finished and we have the fire investigation report.'

***

Sparks knew she'd be in for an inquisition from Massey when she got to work, and she figured the sooner the better; get it over with. He'd arrived before her, and she parked her car next to his. She didn't find him in the MIT room though, or in his little cubbyhole office. Most likely, he'd be with Portas.

She made herself a coffee and logged onto the system. A couple of emails awaited her on open cases, but she couldn't concentrate on responding to them just yet while she was still trying to work out what she could say to Massey. He'd want to know why she and Dazz had been up in Ellington and Cresswell together.

So, rock or hard place? Admit she'd persuaded Dazz to go with her to find out who Red and the other three women were, or claim it was a date, which it definitely was not.

They *had* got on well together though. Extremely well. Unexpectedly well. Way better than she got on with almost anyone other than Massey.

But they weren't an item. God no.

For a start, she wasn't in the market, and he came with way too much baggage.

She glanced at her mobile and saw an unread text from Dazz. She had no intention of even reading it, let alone responding. Not for a while at least.

'Morning, Christine. Come into my office for a moment, will you?'

Massey's voice made her jump. She hadn't heard him come in.

She closed the door behind her and took the seat he nodded to.

'Superintendent Portas asked me why you were up in Cresswell already yesterday,' he said. 'With Dazz Albright of all people. Something you want to tell me?'

'Nope.'

'It doesn't matter. I have a pretty good idea anyway why you were there, although not why you had Dazz in tow. You were sticking your nose into things that don't concern you.'

Sparks looked down at the floor.

'Look Christine, I know you have my best interests at heart but really, it's none of your business.'

She couldn't help herself. 'What isn't, sir?'

Massey rolled his eyes and held up his hands. 'Not going there. Just tell me how the hell Dazz Albright ended up there, with you of all people.'

What did he mean, of all people? 'I asked him. He said yes. That's it.'

'You were doing everything you could to shake him off on Saturday night. What changed?'

'Yeah well, I felt a bit guilty about that.'

Massey's laugh came out as a snort. 'Just be prepared for Portas to quiz you. Both of you. Better get your stories straight. She wants to know why you went back up there. She thinks there's something going on between the two of you.'

'Well there's not. And even if there was, it's none of her business.'

Massey shook his head and laughed again. 'Pot and kettle, Christine.'

Time to change the subject. 'Have we heard anything yet, about the fire?'

'Not yet. Looks dodgy to me though.'

'Way too intense for it just to have been an accidental blaze. Has to have been an accelerant used. What about the daughter, is she in any fit state to be questioned?'

'It's not our case. Not yet. And it might never be, not if it links somehow to Duncan Kingsley's murder.'

That hadn't even occurred to her. 'Do you think it will?'

'We'll find out eventually, but it could take a while.'

***

As it happened, Massey found out later that day, when he was called to a meeting in Chief Superintendent Crowder's office. Portas was already there, along with Nicola Pendleton, the force's Media and Comms Manager; Nathan Buffet, Northumberland Fire and Rescue Service's Chief Fire Officer; and another man, introduced by Buffet as Greg Ferguson, a specialist Fire Investigation Technical Officer.

'Take a seat, Massey. Coffee is on its way.'

Massey had passed Crowder's usually ultra-efficient secretary on his way in, looking more tense than usual. This meeting must have been sprung on her too at the last minute if she hadn't already had the refreshments sorted.

'Alright then,' Crowder said, once they were all settled. 'I called this emergency meeting because some issues have arisen concerning a house fire in Cresswell last night that we need to get out in front of as soon as possible. You'll have gathered by your presence here Massey that it's your team I want on this. That would have been the case anyway, even before I heard about the um...' He gave a sidelong look at Portas and then peered at Massey over the top of his glasses. '... purely coincidental and unofficial attendance at the incident by members of your team.'

'The fire *was* deliberately set then?' Portas asked.

'So I'm informed. At the very least we have a case of murder, grievous bodily harm and arson with the intent to endanger life. Mr Ferguson, perhaps you could explain.'

Ferguson cleared his throat and adjusted the collar of his shirt. Massey wondered whether he was unused to being thrust into the limelight, or uncomfortable about being called to make a report on an investigation that could barely have started yet. He got his answer as soon as the man spoke.

'You need to understand that we are still in the preliminary stages of our investigations, and so there's not much I can tell you. So I may not, um…'

'What he's trying to say,' Nathan Buffet butted in, never a man to leave a pause unfilled, 'is that we have identified the seat of the fire in the cellar of the house, close to an electrical outlet, with what looks to be a small appliance – probably a craft tool of some sort – plugged in and switched on. That on its own would not necessarily indicate intent, but the fact that a significant amount of flammable materials had been piled close to the outlet does point us in that direction.

'As my colleague was no doubt about to explain, it could take weeks, or even months for us to meticulously examine every iota of damage and systematically process and interpret the scene fully. But that is not the only evidence we have.'

He nodded towards Crowder.

'As you know, we have been working closely with your Community Policing team and other partners throughout the night. In the early hours of this morning, we heard from the hospital caring for the daughter of the deceased that, as well as smoke inhalation injuries and extensive, potentially life-changing burns, she has an injury to her head consistent with having been hit hard from behind with a blunt object. We're still waiting on initial postmortem findings on the deceased to find out if he too had been similarly incapacitated.'

'Couldn't the injury have been caused by falling debris?' Portas asked.

'Highly unlikely, according to the girl's consultant.'

'So, attempted murder then, by an as yet unknown third party.' Nicola Pendleton said.

Ferguson sniffed and butted in before the fire chief could get a word in. 'The deceased could have attacked his daughter and set the fire himself before being overcome by fumes. But that would depend on the volatility and toxicity of the materials that fuelled the fire, and any accelerant used. It would still constitute arson with intent, of course. However, if we find that the deceased also suffered blunt force injuries, then yes, unknown third party.'

Pendleton unconsciously mirrored his sniff, but said nothing.

It took another full half hour of discussion for the gathering to gain a good understanding of where each element of the Fire Service investigation was at, and for Crowder to thank Buffet and Ferguson and send them on their way.

***

As the door closed behind the two fire officers, Pendleton shrugged her shoulders and straightened the neck of her blouse. 'You'll forgive me, Chief Superintendent, but I'm not sure why you needed me here for this meeting.'

'Because whatever this is, it's possible it could have links to the death of my predecessor, retired Chief Superintendent Duncan Kingsley, which is currently being investigated by Durham Constabulary. If you can believe anything the press says, it seems they're about to charge three men with his murder. However, Duncan Kingsley and Ben Quinn – the deceased in this house fire – were good friends, and they were both involved in Ellington & Cresswell RFC. In fact Kingsley was the driving force behind the charity match played between Ellington & Cresswell and our own police fifteen on Saturday, the day before the fire. And at the party afterwards, Quinn expressed his opinion to two of our officers that Durham have got the wrong men.'

'I see,' Pendleton said, although Massey wasn't so sure she did.

'So,' Crowder continued, moving across to the window and staring unseeingly out, 'if this house fire turns out to be arson to cover the murder of Ben Quinn and the attempted murder of his daughter, or connected in any other way to that of Duncan Kingsley, then there are a dozen ways this could all go tits up for the Northumbria force, and I for one would prefer to get out in front of it.

'Even if these current events turn out not to be connected in any investigative way to Kingsley's murder, you know as well as I do Nicola, that the press are sure to come up with all sorts of conspiracy stories relating to last summer's shitstorm that led to our force having to hand over the inquiry into the murder of one of our own retired officers to another force. And I do not want any of us to have to relive any of that.'

'Point taken, Sir.' Pendleton said, sniffing again.

'What about Durham?' Massey asked.

'We have to inform them officially, but I'll do everything in my power to hold onto this one. It looks like they believe they know the killers of Duncan Kingsley now. They'll not want to muddy the waters unless and until they're forced to.'

CHAPTER 12

6 pm on a Monday, the Snowy Owl was quiet despite the good weather, which had stayed sunny, although not quite as hot as it had been the day before. The lack of fellow customers suited them fine.

Keegan had arrived first and got the drinks in. Still working on Operation Casper cold cases, his working week was strictly nine to five, Monday to Friday, which Massey suspected, after the demands of his previous role, bored the shit out of him. His own working week depended entirely on what they had going on, although as DCI it was his job to adhere to budgetary requirements as much as possible, which included his team sticking to a thirty-seven hour week unless overtime had been expressly permitted. However, a lack of overtime pay never prevented him, nor any members of his team from regularly exceeding their allotted work hours.

With the sun dipping further below the horizon, they sat outside in the beer garden. As soon as they got settled, Keegan stroked his beard and gave Massey a worried look. 'Well?'

'Looks like arson, and there's evidence Fleur was knocked unconscious by a heavy blow that was not consistent with falling debris.'

'I knew it. Tell me your team is investigating.'

Massey nodded, still uncomfortable more than a year later with the fact that the MIT he now led used to be Keegan's team, until his demotion from DCI to DI. 'For now we will be,' he said. 'But you know as well as I do that we may not be able to hold onto it.'

'Give over looking at me like that,' Keegan said. 'What happened to me was my own doing, not yours. I'm happy with where I'm at now. It's your team. You've earned it.' He laid a hand on his chest. 'I'm thankful I'm still in the job instead of having to ponce around the Metrocentre or Eldon Square as a security guard.'

Massey laughed out loud at the thought of coming across Keegan working security while out on a shopping trip. Then he remembered; it was always Helen who'd dragged him out to such retail netherworlds. He'd never choose to go shopping in those places on his own.

Shit, food shopping. He hadn't had the time, and there was nothing at all left in the house. 'You fancy something to eat?' he asked.

Keegan patted his beer belly and thought about it for a moment. 'I could manage one of their burgers, if you insist.'

Massey went back inside to order. When he returned, Keegan was waiting with more questions. 'What about Ben's injuries?'

'The PM hasn't been completed yet.'

'Crowder's not really going to hand it over to Durham though, is he?'

'He thinks they'll not want anything mucking up the case they're building against the three workmen.'

'And yet, it's connected. I can feel it in my water.'

Massey agreed. But all he could do was to ensure the fire, Ben's death and Fleur's injuries were investigated to the fullest ability of his team and their partners.

'Sparks tell you what she and Albright were doing back up at Cresswell yesterday?'

'She told me something, but it wasn't the truth.'

'She's not what split up Dazzle's marriage though, is she? Can't imagine her as a homewrecker, but you know what the force is like for gossip. That's what'll go around anyway. Plenty of people saw them up there together.'

Keegan was the second person to voice that thought today. 'Nah. I'd lay money on it.'

'Would you even know if they did have something going? You've been a bit wrapped up in your own problems lately.'

'I'd know.'

'And what is happening between you and the lovely Helen then? Any chance of a reunion?'

'You tell me. I still have no idea why she left, and she won't respond to my calls or texts.'

Keegan ducked his head, a gesture that caught Massey's attention, as if Keegan knew something about why Helen left. But how could he?

CHAPTER 13

Tuesday, 15 October 2024

By first thing Tuesday morning the MIT incident room bustled with activity, with the inquiry into the house fire, the death of Ben Quinn and the injuries to his daughter now in full swing. As usual, DC Ana Horvat had everything in hand. She'd updated the big screen with all the headline information they had so far and had handouts ready for the briefing, which was due to start in – Massey looked at his watch – less than ten minutes.

His usual team complement had been joined this morning by the Fire Investigator, Greg Ferguson – on his own today – and by Police Inspector Brian Truman, who'd been leading the Neighbourhood Policing Team efforts so far in Cresswell.

Massey had asked Sparks to get an update from the hospital on Fleur's condition and she'd moved into the corridor, away from the noise, to make the call. They'd need to interview Fleur, if she was up to it, as soon as possible.

Sparks must have encountered Portas on her way back in, because they entered the room together. He heard Portas asking her if she'd had a good weekend and saw Sparks' features tighten. She gave him a little shake of her head as she passed him, from which he gathered they weren't going to be able to interview Fleur any time soon. Although perhaps the nod had been an appeal for rescue from Portas' questioning.

If so, tough. He wasn't ready yet to forgive her for sticking her nose where it wasn't wanted.

***

Massey called the briefing to order and made a quick round of introductions for the benefit of the newcomers.

Detective Inspector Madge Brown, who'd been made up permanently in rank from Detective Sergeant after acting in the role early in the year had brought in a tin of chocolate biscuits from M&S and offered them round. 'Still left over from Christmas,' she said. 'You're saving me from myself.'

With Christmas being almost ten months past, several people paused before taking a bite.

'Don't be daft; they're still in date. Only just, mind. So they need eating.'

Madge had transferred up from West Yorkshire not yet two years ago, and late in her career. It was no secret she intended to retire as soon as she'd completed her thirty years next January, and Massey would miss her steadying influence on the team.

'Alright then,' he said. 'Now we all know who's who, let's get down to business. As you know, we are investigating a house fire that broke out in Cresswell at the home of Mr Benjamin Quinn in the early evening of Sunday 13th of October, which resulted in the death of Mr Quinn and catastrophic injuries to his daughter Fleur, who I've just been informed has been put into an induced coma, so we are unlikely to be able to find out what she knows anytime soon.

'Initial investigations carried out by Fire and Rescue point to the fire having been set deliberately, and we also have a report from the consultant in charge of Fleur Quinn's care that she suffered a skull fracture consistent with her having been attacked with a heavy blunt object. We do not yet know whether her father suffered similar injuries; we're still waiting on the initial postmortem report on that. Now Gary, could you tell us where you're up to on this?'

Ferguson ran a hand over a scalp of sandy stubble and stood up. He nodded to Ana, who brought up a presentation on the big screen with a large image of the Northumberland Fire and Rescue Service badge on the front page, the red and yellow stripes of its county shield and banners appearing almost fluorescent.

'Morning all,' he said, as he dusted biscuit crumbs from his shirt and flicked to the next slide of his presentation. 'As I'm sure you'll all recognise, this is a satellite image street map of Cresswell, and that there…' He wiggled the cursor over a grey oblong towards the bottom of the main road into Cresswell from Ellington, a little up from the junction onto Beach Road. '… is the property in question; a three-storey, stone-built, detached house made up of first floor, ground floor and a half cellar or, if you happen to be a Yank, second floor, first floor and a half basement.'

He flicked to the next slide. 'This here is a three-dimensional representation of the layout of the whole property, and these images below are floor plans for each storey. You'll notice that the cellar has only half the floorspace of the house above it. It can be accessed from inside the house and also through this door here, down a couple of steps from a small courtyard at the rear of the property. So maybe that makes it a basement in the UK too, rather than a cellar. No idea, but I'm told that family and friends refer to it as the cellar.'

He paused for a moment to give his audience time to peer at the screen and rustle the papers before them to find the same images in the printout of his presentation.

'We believe the seat of the fire to have been in the cellar, which the homeowner clearly used not only as storage, but also as a base for his hobbies. That red cross there indicates where Mr Quinn's body was discovered in the cellar, close to the stairs to the kitchen. Miss Quinn was discovered unconscious in the kitchen. There she is, that cross there.'

He clicked the controls again and the slides flipped to an image of a triangle. 'Now, I don't expect any of you to know everything about what the job of a fire investigator entails, just as I don't know all the ins and outs of your jobs. So I'm going to assume that the majority of you don't know a great deal about the principles of fire, its chemistry and how it spreads, and I think it will help if I explain a little about how a fire develops first before we get into what we can see already from the fire scene at Cresswell. You'll have to forgive me if you do already know this.'

He turned back to the screen. 'This here is the fire triangle. It represents the three factors necessary for a fire to start and to continue to burn. As you can see, a fire needs an ignition source. That could be a spark or a naked flame, or an electrical appliance, or a hot surface, that sort of thing. It also needs oxygen, which is always present in the air, but can also be got from any oxidised substances. And lastly a fire needs fuel, which could be solids, liquids or gases; anything combustible. Take away any one of those three things and either the fire will not start, or it will be immediately extinguished.

'But once it *has* started, the molecules in the fuel will break down and release a vapour, or gas: a process known as thermal decomposition, or pyrolysis. Being hot, the gas rises and displaces the colder air above it, which further feeds the fire with oxygen, while the hot gases above ignite, causing the fire to spread upwards. And so you have the process of fire, from induction, which involves these three factors here…' He wiggled the cursor over the triangle. '… to the growth of the fire, which will continue to burn violently until it reaches flashover, i.e. when it can't develop any further because it is already consuming all the combustible material available to it.'

Massey glanced around at the faces of his team, all rapt with attention, and wondered how many of them had latent pyromaniac tendencies. He liked a good fire himself but put that down to his boyhood scouting forays, where he learned to build a campfire. Dyb, dyb, dyb, and all that.

'Okay then.' Ferguson clicked the control to bring up a photo of the blackened cellar room. 'Back to Cresswell, although you're not going to be able to see much detail in this image, and what you can see, you probably won't recognise without me telling you what it is, but here goes. See that black lump in the middle of the shot there?' He wiggled the cursor. 'That's what's left of a table that Mr Quinn evidently used as a desk and a workspace. It would have sat at right angles to the wall at the bottom of the stairs that lead up to the kitchen. You might not be able to make it out, but on the wall above it – the stairs are on the other side, see – is a double electrical socket. Here it is in close-up.'

He clicked the remote again to the next slide and wiggled the cursor.

'You see that. Something's been left plugged in, and the switch is down, so we can see that an appliance of some sort has been left with power running to it, and we think we can tell what that something is – or was. We think it's a pyrography pen. That was one of his hobbies apparently, according to his wife. He used to make things like wooden boxes and garden plaques and burn decorative designs on the surface with the heated metallic point on the end of a pyrography pen. He even had a little online business going to sell them.'

He clicked again.

'Now look at this next one. That black mound against the remains of the table, and that lump of material on top. See that? And this one here showing the other side of the room. Right next to the remains of a big chest freezer are all those empty metal shelves that, according to Mr Quinn's wife, should be filled with all sorts of stuff. Paint tins and thinners, rolls of wallpaper, Christmas decorations, jigsaws, photo albums and what have you. All highly flammable, and none of it is where it should be. No trace of any of it on the shelves. While all of this material over by the table…' Another click and a wiggle. '… should not be there at all.

'Now, it is going to take us quite some time before we'll be able to say without a doubt that these deposits here by the table are the remains of the same types of materials that should have been on those shelves, and I doubt we'll ever be able to state categorically that they are precisely the same items that were last seen on the shelves. But the theory we have developed is this: that someone – and we can't say who, that's your job – carried all that flammable material across the room and stacked it on and next to the table, close to an electrical implement intended to burn wood, that was plugged into an electricity socket that was left switched on.

'So remember that fire triangle? Here, you have your ignition – the hot pyrography pen, you have a room full of oxygen and an open door to the kitchen to pull more in, and you have an immediate fuel source of highly flammable material piled up there.' He finished with a last emphatic wiggle of the cursor.

'Arson then,' DC Andrew Donaldson said. 'With intent.'

'Or reckless arson,' Massey said. 'The perpetrator may not have intended to kill, but has recklessly endangered life in the process of arson.'

'Fine line,' Portas said.

'They may have thought the house was empty when they set the fire, so maybe only malicious firing. Perhaps it was empty, but then Ben and Fleur returned while they were still in the house.'

'In which case they attacked both of them and left them there, imagining that the fire would consume any evidence.'

***

It took a while for the murmuring to die down. When it did, Massey thanked Greg Ferguson and asked Brian Truman to bring the team up to date with how far the Neighbourhood Policing Team had got.

Truman, a tall sparely built man with prematurely greying hair, coughed and swigged down the remains of his coffee before speaking in a nasal Mackem accent. 'Okay then, as you know, our role initially was one of assisting the emergency response at the time of the blaze and in the immediate aftermath. Since then, we've been intelligence gathering. Carrying out house to house enquiries, starting with those properties close to Stoneyriggs. That's the name of the Quinn house, by the way.' He gave a sidelong look at Greg Ferguson. 'We've covered most of the village now, including the two holiday parks, and we're in the process of getting it all recorded. But I have to warn you that we've found nothing of note. No-one in the village saw anyone. No sightings of Mr Quinn or his daughter, or anyone else going into or coming out of Stoneyriggs during the time frame in question, other than the one early report of Mr Quinn arriving home at around half eleven in the morning.'

'Or they're not saying so, if they did see anything,' Madge Brown said.

'Indeed. But you need to understand that few of the locals would have been out and about. They like to keep their heads down when there are a lot of visitors about. It was an unusually hot day for the time of year, which always brings in a load of day-trippers on top of all the holiday makers in the two holiday parks, even in October.'

Day-trippers like Sparks and Albright, Massey thought. He glanced at Sparks and found her glaring back at him. 'Point taken,' he said. 'But now it's escalated to arson with intent, grievous bodily harm and possible homicide, we'll need to revisit some, if not all of those interviews. And we need to put out an appeal for information from any non-residents who were in Cresswell that day. Is there anywhere in the village we might be able to use as a temporary base?'

'There's the village hall, or Cresswell Pele Tower. They're both within spitting distance of Stoneyriggs. Or there's St Bartholemew's Church further up Cresswell Road. The hall is probably your best bet, and it has a conservatory at the back that looks directly out onto the sea.'

'We won't be there for the scenery.' Massey said, nodding to DC Donaldson. 'Andrew, see what you can organise please?'

'Will do.' Donaldson woke the screen of his laptop and made a couple of clicks. 'Sir, the preliminary postmortem report just arrived.'

Massey brought the document up on his phone and quickly scanned the main points, zeroing in on one particular paragraph. Blunt force trauma to the back of the head. Likely inflicted by a blow from behind.

'We have a homicide,' he said.

CHAPTER 14

'This really isn't on.' Fist clenched and chin jutted, Margaret Charlton wrapped her arms tighter across her bosom and shook her head. 'Bookings will have to be cancelled. Folks won't be happy. And what sort of a mess are you going to be making of the place? Because I won't be cleaning up after you all.'

'That's absolutely fine, Mrs Charlton,' Donaldson said, a red flush creeping up his neck towards the ginger of his hairline. 'We wouldn't want to put you—'

'It's Miss Charlton, young man, not Mrs. I'm from a long line of Charltons, part of Cresswell's history for hundreds of years. And it's all very well you saying you wouldn't want to put me out, when you're doing just that by being here at all. We're decent people. That fire was a tragic accident; nothing more. We don't need a load of policemen breathing down our necks all hours of the day and night.'

'I'm sorry, Miss Charlton, but this has all been agreed by the chair of your committee, Mr Len Stafford. I spoke to him myself just this morning and—'

'Well, he's said nothing to me. Len had no right to make such an arrangement when it's me who has to deal with things. Ringing around, disappointing people, putting the place to rights when you've finished wrecking it. He might at least have had the decency to talk to me himself before making a decision.'

'That's between you and Mr Stafford, Mrs – I mean Miss Charlton. He said it would be fine to collect the keys from you.'

Donaldson glanced along Beach Road to his left, beyond the village hall, where he could see DC Phil Jackson staring longingly at the menu in the ice cream shop window, probably deliberately looking away. No help forthcoming from that quarter.

'Well, I'll be having words with him about that. Why can't he give you his own keys? I'm going to need my set for going in to do the cleaning.'

'That won't be necessary, Miss Charlton. We'll look after the place for the duration of our stay. You won't need to bother yourself about anything.'

'Hmph! Well, I am not happy about this, not at all. I want that on record.'

'Understood, Miss Charlton.'

'Now I'm going to have to get my shoes on and come along there with you to show you what's what? And I warn you, you can't be having the heating blasting all day, every day mind you. Energy's far too expensive for that.'

'You don't need to come along. We can sort ourselves out.'

The last thing he wanted was to spend any longer in the woman's presence than absolutely necessary. But he might as well talk to himself.

'That's non-negotiable, young man. How would you know about the alarm unless I come along and show you?'

Miss Charlton slammed the door in his face.

He was on his third astonished blink by the time she opened it again, while fastening the zip of a jade green knee-length coat, her black-stockinged feet now shod in a pair of tan leather brogues.

'Come along then,' she said. 'I don't have all day.'

***

Miss Charlton led him through a set of white double-glazed doors into a spacious entrance lobby and through into a main hall that Donaldson had seen already in 360 degree images on the website: a long room with a polished wood floor, pale walls and grey-green paintwork.

After the heat of the sun outside, he shivered.

'We've had the heating on for the toddler's group this morning, so you'll find the place quite comfortable.'

Miss Charlton opened a door on the left and allowed him to step inside a small room.

'Fully fitted kitchen. Everything you should need, although I'll thank you to leave the supplies in the cupboards alone; they belong to our regular users.' She swept him back out into the main hall. 'Also along this wall: ladies and gents toilets, and a disabled one too, of course. And you'll find plenty of tables and chairs in this cupboard here.'

Distracted by a series of framed panels arranged around the walls of the main hall, Donaldson zoned her out. One panel in particular: 'Cresswell Lifeboat Station 1875-1944', captured his attention. 'That's this building, isn't it?'

'What? Oh, yes. This was the old lifeboat station originally. Many of my ancestors helped man the lifeboat. My grandfather served on the Martha. Not my father though. Killed at Dunkirk, he was, when I was just a baby. Slaughtered on the beach, like so many others, before he could get to one of the boats. The day before his twenty-first birthday, it was. Bloody Luftwaffe.'

Donaldson had estimated her age to be somewhere around seventy-five, but if she was a baby in 1940 when the Dunkirk evacuation took place, she must be in her mid-eighties by now. 'I am so sorry,' he said.

'Nothing for you to feel sorry for, is there young man? Your grandad probably wasn't even a twinkle in your great grandad's eye back then. Now look, through here, this is the conservatory.'

An oval table large enough to seat eight, or ten at a pinch, occupied most of the space in what was more a sunroom than a conservatory. Vertical blinds had been drawn back from the half-height windows as far as they would go to make the most of the view directly out to sea. Donaldson stood transfixed, trying to decide whether the tide was coming in or going out. But then a thought snapped him back to the moment. 'Apart from yourself and Mr Stafford, who else has a set of keys for the building?'

'There are four sets altogether. Mine and Len's, and then there's Anne's set. She runs the toddler sessions we do here every weekday during term-time. And, of course, Finn Barron. He has a set.'

'We'll need to keep all of them while we're here. Do you have contact details for those people please?'

Miss Charlton huffed a huge impatient sigh. 'You'll have to come back along the road with me, if you want that information now.'

***

By the time Donaldson returned to the Village Hall, he found DC Jackson waiting for him. 'Thanks for the help, Phil,' he said.

'You were doing fine on your own. Me and battle-axes don't get on. What's happening then?'

'I've got one set of keys for the place, but there are three more. One of us is going to have to go and collect them.'

Jackson pulled a coin from his pocket. 'Heads or tails.'

Driving past the blackened shell of Stoneyriggs on his way to collect the first set of keys, Donaldson wished he'd insisted on using a coin from his own pocket.

You could never be one hundred percent sure with Phil.

***

It had turned six thirty by the time he returned to the village hall, to find the tiny car park full and a marked van directly outside the front door.

'Glad you're back, Andrew,' Massey said, as soon as he walked in the door. 'We're going to need your help to get this lot set up.'

A uniformed officer dumped a printer and a tangle of cables next to a pile of other equipment on a table set up in Donaldson's absence. 'That's the last lot, gov,' he said.

'Thanks Dave. Much appreciated.' Massey turned back to Donaldson. 'Phil said you were off picking up keys. Everything okay?'

Donaldson placed two sets on the table closest to him, where Phil Jackson was busy tying himself into a knot while trying to untangle cables. 'I only managed to pick up these two. The woman who runs the toddler sessions wasn't at home. I spoke to her though, and she said she'll get her husband to drop them off here as soon as he gets in from work. No problem with Len Stafford; he handed his set over without a fuss. But a Mr Finn Barron wasn't happy about parting with his. Something to do with rehearsals for a play at the tower. He refused point blank. Insisted on calling Stafford, who of course told him to hand the keys over. But he still took some persuading, at least until he'd managed to speak to someone else, whose name I didn't catch, to rearrange the rehearsals. And even then he made me sign a receipt for them.'

Massey laughed. 'Here, you keep one lot, and I'll take a set. Alright then Andrew, as soon as you've given Phil a hand with this lot, you can show me how to work the alarm and then you're both done for the day. We have a full day of interviews booked in for tomorrow. We can use the conservatory for that, although I need to find some screens from somewhere to put in front of all that glass to give the room a bit of privacy. I'm sure we have some presentation stands back at HQ somewhere; they would do. I'll make a call. See if we can get them brought straight over.'

CHAPTER 15

Two things Massey still had to do before clocking off. He'd checked again with the hospital. No change in Fleur's condition, just as he expected. But that was most likely where he'd find Ursula, who he needed to speak to. He also had to go to a supermarket. He had nothing decent in the house left to eat. He'd volunteered to buy in some provisions for their stay at the village hall so that he'd have no excuse not to do his own shopping at the same time. Otherwise he'd probably have said bugger it and lived off takeaways every night for the foreseeable. But he was determined not to fall into that trap.

He was a perfectly capable adult, responsible for his own health and wellbeing. He'd been telling himself the same thing over and over since Sunday and it was beginning to feel like a mantra.

He'd asked Sparks to meet him at the Northumbria Specialist Emergency Care Hospital at Cramlington, but then wondered if having her with him was the wisest move, given she'd made it her business to find out not only about Trinny, but about the three women who'd accosted him at the rugby club on Saturday, and Ursula had been their ringleader.

Sparks waited for him in the lobby, and they made their way through the labyrinthian corridors to intensive care, the circular construction of the main building making him feel like a tiny silver ball in one of those maze puzzles he'd had as a child.

***

If he didn't already know who she was, he could never have associated this broken woman in the corridor with the provocative man-eater he'd encountered on Saturday. Wearing a shapeless, pale green tunic over black leggings, chestnut hair scraped into a dull messy bun and her face devoid of make-up, she looked ghostly pale, her eyes swollen from all the tears she'd shed.

She recognised him and had the grace to look embarrassed. 'You have come to arrest me for assaulting a police officer?' The foreign musical inflection in her voice sounded more pronounced today. 'I am sorry about that. We had a good bit to drink already, I think, before we got to the club. Just a bit of fun, that is all.'

'That's not why we're here.'

'Of course not. I understand. My husband… Benjamin. My poor Ben. He…' She shook her head, struggling to maintain her composure. 'And my daughter, she is not well.'

Through the glass of double doors, inside some sort of near but not quite horizontal glass tube, they saw the shape of someone he couldn't possibly have recognised as the brightly passionate young woman he'd met at the charity party.

'It is hyperbaric oxygen therapy, they give her. For the smoke inhalation; the carbon monoxide, and the heat. They cannot fix her burns until they first fix her throat and her lungs. She is in the induced coma now so she can start to heal herself. Perhaps for six weeks or so. Or longer, they say. Perhaps. And then, when they wake her up, they say she can be transferred to Newcastle, to the Royal Victoria Infirmary for reconstructive sur—' She raised her hand to catch a sudden sob. '—surgery. I am sorry. I cry too much. It is not good for my Fleur. I need to be strong for her.'

Six weeks or more in an induced coma? It couldn't be worse news for the investigation. Fleur could have seen the person who attacked her and her father. She could be the only person who did, and now they wouldn't know for weeks, if at all.

If she even survived that long.

'If this is too much for you right now Ursula, we can talk another time.'

She took hold of his hand in both of hers. 'We can talk now. You are a good man. I am sorry for the other night, for… you know.'

They sat on a line of chairs in the hushed corridor a few metres from the door of Fleur's room, one at either side of Ursula, keeping their voices low. They'd agreed he should do the majority of the questioning.

Apart from anything else, he didn't trust Sparks to stick to only what they needed to know for the purposes of the investigation.

'When did you last see Ben or Fleur before the fire?' he asked.

'That is easy. It was at the party at the rugby club on Saturday.'

So she mustn't have gone home after the party. 'When were you last in Stoneyriggs?'

'That too is easy. Benjamin and me, we had separated, but we still loved each other, in our way. I still live…' She sucked in a breath. '… lived there. I have seen the damage, on the photographs they showed me, and I know I cannot live there anymore. I don't know… I have no idea where I can go to live now. But that is a problem for another day, I think. Now you need to ask your questions, when I have already told other officers. I was home on Saturday until… let me see… around four. We had no interest in watching the match, you see, my friends and me, so we met at Scarlett's place, because she lives closest to the rugby club. We got ready for the party there and we… we had a lot to drink. I am sorry.'

Massey noticed Sparks roll her eyes. 'You don't need to keep apologising, Ursula. Really, it's fine. So you're saying you didn't go back to Stoneyriggs after the party? Why not, if you still lived there?'

'I have said this before. To the other officers. I stayed at Betsy's. We had plans for Sunday morning, you see. We were going out for the day, to the Metrocentre. Just Betsy and me. Not Scarlett. She had to work.'

'What time did you and Betsy go out, and what time did you get back?'

Ursula flung her hands in the air. 'I don't understand why you are asking me all these questions again. Is it because you think I might have set my own home on fire, killed my husband and made that…' She gestured back along the corridor, her lips twisting in horror. '… that terrible thing happen… to my own daughter?'

'No, no Ursula. Not at all.' He moved to catch hold of her flailing arms, then thought better of it. 'These are just routine questions that we have to ask, so we can get a clear idea of where people were at certain times and what they may have seen. Sometimes, especially when they're under extreme stress – as you are now – people can forget things, so we ask the same questions more than once in case they've remembered anything more. Now, what time did you and Betsy go out on Sunday and what time did you get back?'

'Aagh!' Ursula lifted her chin and tried to control its tremble. 'I believe you. I do. I am sorry, but it is so… difficult. But I tell you the same thing I told the others. We got the bus on Sunday morning in Cresswell at nine thirty, but we did not get to the Metrocentre until after twelve. We had to change buses, you see, in Ashington, and again in Newcastle. When we got there, we had lunch first and did some shopping, and then we caught a bus back to Newcastle and we had a drink in a pub. I cannot tell you what time it was when I got a call from Michael to tell me what had happened. He had tried to call more than once but my phone was at the bottom of my handbag, and I didn't hear it. I called a taxi straight away and we both came back. All this, you can check. My phone is in the room. I will get it for you.'

'No, don't worry about that just yet. We can have a quick look before we go.'

Everything she'd told them could be checked in numerous ways: a quick word with Duffy, CCTV on the buses and at the Metrocentre, confirmation from the taxi firm, as well as by talking to this Betsy woman. He tried to recall what Ben had said at the party about his wife's friends. Betsy's surname began with an 'H', he was pretty sure about that. Three syllables. And didn't Ben say she was some sort of shrink? Psychiatrist, psychologist, psychotherapist. He had no idea what the difference was.

'Now, I'd like to talk to you about Ben. I understand you told the Fire Investigator you believe things had been moved around in the cellar. We now think this was done by the person who set the fire, to help it spread quickly, but we don't yet know if Ben was attacked first and then the fire was set to cover it up, or if he surprised the perpetrator in the process of starting the fire and was killed in their effort to escape…'

Ursula's face crumpled, but she fought to get it under control. 'And what about Fleur?'

'We believe Fleur to have been attacked after Ben, but it's possible it happened the other way round. We need to find out about both of them as people. Their habits. Any plans they had that day. It could help us to understand the order of things, which may in turn help us figure why this happened and who is responsible.' He paused while Ursula blew her nose. 'Fleur was found in the kitchen, so the person who hit her could have been on their way back upstairs to escape from the house…'

'No! It cannot have happened like that.'

'What do you mean?'

'They did not need to go up to the kitchen to escape after they hurt Ben in the cellar. They could have gone out from the cellar into the garden and walked round. And if it was Fleur they wanted to hurt, why would they then go down into the cellar where Ben was when they did not need to?'

***

'She had a point,' Sparks said once they were eventually back outside. 'Could they have specifically gone looking for Fleur after killing Ben? Risky, if they'd already set the fire. Or did they attack Fleur first and then deliberately go looking for Ben in the cellar. And what motive could anyone have for targeting them both?'

She stopped in her tracks.

'What if they were there for Fleur, but she shouted for her dad, so they had to go and sort him out too?'

'One problem with that. Fleur was hit from behind, which suggests a surprise attack, so she was hardly going to be able to shout for Ben. We need more precise details of where they fell and the position they were likely in before the fire took hold.' He shook his head to clear it, tiredness dragging at his thoughts. They started walking again. 'Look, I don't want to narrow our investigation, but so far there are only a couple of scenarios that make sense of what we know. Either Ben was the target, and the fire was set to cover his murder, in which case the killer must have encountered Fleur on their way in or out via the kitchen; or the overriding motive was to recklessly set the fire, and they found themselves having to deal with both Ben and Fleur in order to achieve that. Either way, they may not have known the door in the cellar led out into the garden. I should have asked Ursula if it was solid or glazed.'

They'd reached Sparks' car. Massey glanced at his watch. It was getting late, and he still needed to go shopping.

CHAPTER 16

Wednesday, 16 October 2024

Massey bought a local paper on his way to Cresswell on Wednesday morning. News on the arson was out. It wouldn't take long for speculation to mount into a possible connection to Duncan Kingsley's murder. Cresswell was a small village. And the press had long memories.

A squad car stood outside the village hall when he pulled up, its crew engaged in conversation with a fit looking man – built more on the lines of a marathon runner than a body-builder – who Massey half recognised.

He took his time parking up in the hall's small car park and unloading the bags of supplies while he flicked through his memory banks. Then he remembered. The man had been at the party on Saturday, with the people from Cresswell Pele Tower. The one Sparks had kept her eye on.

One of the squad car crew hurried over to help him with the bags, leaving him a hand free to unlock the door and sort out the beeping alarm. He asked Pele Tower Man to take a seat in the entrance lobby, while he got things sorted inside.

The officer dumped the bags down on the first table he came to. 'I understand you were after some screens, sir,'

'That's right,' He pointed to the glazed wall and doors into the conservatory at the far end of the main hall. 'To cover all that glass over there to make it more private, but I take it from your transport you haven't brought the ones I wanted.'

'Sorry sir, all the big display screens are needed elsewhere, so we've brought you all the pull-up banner stands we could lay our hands on. Did you know there's a cupboard at Area Command that's chocker-block full of them? Well, it was. It's not now, because they're all here.'

As he spoke, his colleague pushed his way through the double doors with half a dozen long narrow cases strapped across his shoulders, and another three cradled in his arms. 'Where shall I put these? We've got more in the car.'

Massey could cheerfully have told him where to put them but, thankfully, he spotted Donaldson in the doorway. 'Andrew, could you sort out this lot please, while I have a word with the guy in the lobby?'

***

'There's no problem,' Tom Kirk said. 'Not about having the rehearsals at the tower. We'd have been in there by next week anyway. The shows are only ten days away. We need to rehearse in the space the performances will actually take place. I'm only here now to arrange the best time to pick up all the props. They're in the big cupboards through there.'

Massey reached into his pocket for the bunch of keys. 'I assume there's one in this lot for the cupboard door then. You can take the props now, if you like.'

'No thanks. I'm on foot at the moment and that bloody cauldron is too big to carry. I'll come back with one of the volunteers later on, if that's okay.'

'It's Macbeth you're doing, isn't it? I met your three weird sisters on Saturday night.'

Kirk guffawed. 'So you did. I saw the video. But we have a problem; we're one witch down now that Ursula Kyteler... Well, you know.'

Kyteler, not Quinn? Interesting. Had Ursula gone back to her maiden name since the split, or did she keep her own surname when they married?

'Of course, it's tragic,' Kirk continued. 'We wondered whether we should cancel, out of respect. But we've sold so many tickets. Both performances are pretty much full now. And it's for a good cause. For the good of the village really. Halloween-themed too, so it's not like we could just postpone for a month or so. You wouldn't believe the calls and emails that have been flying around since we heard. But in the end, Ursula is okay with it, so the committee have decided to go ahead. There's a special meeting about it tomorrow evening at seven. We'd probably have held it here, but well... the rugby club are going to let us use one of their rooms instead.' They both stood. Kirk held out his hand and Massey shook it. 'Don't suppose you know anyone who could play the part of a witch, do you?'

Through the window, over Kirk's shoulder, Massey saw Sparks approaching the building and nearly said something he shouldn't.

'Tom!' she said, as she walked in the door.

'Christine. Good to see you're here to help sort us all out. You should drop in at the tower sometime. You know, if you'd like…'

'Thanks, but I think we'll have our hands full here.'

After agreeing a time to call back later, Kirk walked away in the direction of the tower, with Massey struggling to keep a serious look on his face. 'Stringing two blokes along now, are we? Should I give poor Dazz a call to put him in the picture?'

Sparks punched his arm. 'Hope you've brought coffee with you. And it had better be the good stuff.'

***

Massey took on board Donaldson's suggestion and agreed to the stands being used to partition off the main hall instead of just the conservatory, so that only the front end would be openly on view from the lobby while a more private workspace would be created behind.

Four of the team would be working from Cresswell for the duration: himself, Sparks, Donaldson and Jackson, while DI Madge Brown, and DCs Horvat and Laidler remained at Middle Engine Lane. The team had lost one member a couple of months ago, who had yet to be replaced. After having held the post of temporary DS since the New Year, Paul Scott had secured a permanent promotion on one of the new CID investigative teams, set up since the revised operational structure had come into being in March. Scott had acted as the teams receiver and exhibits officer on a number of high profile cases, a role now being covered by Rob Laidler, with Donaldson poised in Cresswell to feed anything relevant at this end to him.

They'd be losing Madge Brown soon too; yesterday, she'd officially named her retirement date, so Massey needed to talk to Lou Portas about recruitment. Madge was currently his only DI, when he could really do with two. With all the right training already behind her, Sparks should have had the opportunity to move up by now. But personal issues had stalled her progress for a couple of years. It was time she had her chance. Although if Sparks did go for promotion, he'd likely lose her from his team, and then he'd be three down.

All these thoughts still occupied his mind when the front door opened and the person first on their list for interview today walked in; Michael Duffy, looking a good ten years older than he had on Saturday night.

CHAPTER 17

Massey escorted Duffy to the conservatory through the newly created walkway and offered refreshments. Donaldson and Jackson had done a good job, placing the banners strategically to create both a screened off workspace on one side of the hall, with access to the kitchen and toilet facilities via this walkway on the other, and privacy from the public on all sides.

In the conservatory, one banner at right angles screened the view from the outside door without blocking its use as the fire exit. With the vertical blinds drawn across the windows and slanted, it was nigh on impossible now for anyone to see inside from the car park. Similar blinds on the seaward side had been drawn but left fully open. It was unlikely anyone would try to get a look inside from that direction.

This would be an informal witness interview. As far as they knew so far, Duffy had no motive to harm Ben Quinn or his daughter, although that could change at any point, so Massey wanted a second pair of eyes and ears in the room to ensure they missed nothing.

Sparks brought in three coffees on a tray, with a packet of custard cream biscuits.

'You met DS Sparks on Saturday, didn't you Michael?' Massey asked.

'Briefly. It's Christine, isn't it?'

'That's right. Two sugars, you said?' Sparks handed round the mugs then offered biscuits.

'Thanks for coming in Michael. You'll have seen the news this morning, that we're treating the fire at Ben's house as arson.'

'I did, but it's no surprise. The place went up way too quickly for anything else. I've just driven past there. First time since it happened. We're all still in shock. Anything I can do to help, of course, let me know. But if you're asking me who could have done it, then I'm sorry, I have no idea. No-one I know could possibly have done that; I don't know anyone capable of such a thing.'

'But the fact remains that someone did do this. We're asking everyone if they've seen or heard anything suspicious. Not only on the day of the fire but in the days and weeks leading up to it, as well as in the time since. We're also asking everyone where they were on Sunday in the hours before the fire was reported, so I'd like to get that bit out of the way first, if we can.'

Duffy frowned and gave them both a long look, but decided to co-operate without question. 'That's easy. The mother-in-law comes over every Sunday and the missus does a roast. I got up late, drank a couple of pints of water to combat the hangover – I sank a lot more on Saturday than I usually do these days – and then all of us sat down to roast pork and crackling. I was asleep in my chair in front of the telly when we heard the fire engines.'

'Thank you, Michael,' Massey said. 'Now, I know the two of you were good friends, so there's something else you could help us with. We're interested in hearing about anything Ben might have said, either directly to you or in your hearing, that might be relevant to his death.'

Michael shook his head and gave a small mirthless laugh. 'Absolutely nothing. We were the best of friends. We grew up together, went to school together. It's hard, knowing I'll never see him again.'

Massey gave a sympathetic nod. He'd lost someone close himself recently. His stepfather: the best friend he'd ever had. 'When was the last time you saw or spoke to Ben?'

'At the rugby club, after the party. We both stayed back a bit and helped with the clear up. But we talked about nothing really. Just the usual day to day chunter.'

'And what about at other times? Did he say anything that, with hindsight, you now think could be significant?' He waited for a few moments, allowing Duffy time to blink away the tears trembling in the corners of his eyes and re-examine the most recent conversations he'd had with his friend, but the man shook his head again and said nothing.

Time for a prompt.

'Perhaps Ben told you about something that might have been worrying him,' Massey prompted. 'Arguments he might have had, issues with neighbours, money he owed, or was owed to him. That sort of thing. It could be something that didn't seem important at the time. Something he might even have laughed off. Or perhaps he told you about something of value he had in the house, that might have been worth stealing and setting a fire to cover up. Something someone could have overheard about.'

Duffy tapped his fingers on his knees as he gave it some thought. 'No, There's nothing. Only what we told you on Saturday night about the election for club president.'

'Remind me about that please. I'm not sure Christine heard any of it.'

Duffy blew out a big sigh. 'That won't have anything to do with this though, surely. No-one's going to commit arson over who's top dog of a minor league rugby club.'

'I'd still like to hear about it,' Sparks said. 'I missed that part of the conversation on Saturday.'

The man sighed again and took a noisy sip of his coffee. 'Not much to tell. The club is still in the process of electing a new president after the murder of Duncan Kingsley last... year...' Duffy blinked in surprise at the sudden juxtaposition in his mind of the two deaths; that of his old friend Ben, who'd been standing in the election to replace Kingsley, whose murder a year ago had necessitated the vote. 'Good God, they can't be connected, can they?'

'Why do you think they might be?' Massey asked.

'I didn't. It's never occurred to me. Until now. But now I think about it, I can't see how it could be any other. Two murders... Because that is what you're saying here about Ben, isn't it? You think his death in that fire was murder.'

Massey said nothing.

Duffy sat forward in his chair; his hands formed into fists on the table in front of him. He shook his head and breathed hard through his nose like an outraged bull. 'You do, don't you? That is what you're saying here. Both men associated with the rugby club; one president, the other standing to replace him. And now there are only two candidates left: Len Stafford and Finn bloody Barron. One of them could be next on the list, and the other one did it. And I know where I'd put my money.'

***

At the end of the day, Massey checked all the doors were locked and set the alarm.

'Duffy really doesn't like Finn Barron, does he?' Sparks said. 'But could Barron really commit murder and arson to win the presidency of a poxy rugby club?'

'Less of the insults; it's a good club. But it's a fair question.' How could the presidency of a small Regional League rugby club generate a strong enough motive for one murder, let alone two?

'If he's right, Len Stafford might actually be in danger.'

'But, like you said, could the presidency of a small rugby club ever be enough motive for arson and murder?'

'I said *poxy* rugby club.'

'And I'm not going to.'

'Both Duffy and Quinn believed Durham are after the wrong men for Kingsley's murder?'

'Shame they didn't tell us who actually did do it, then. Let's hope Kingsley's family can shed some light.'

They'd called Elena Kingsley as soon as Duffy had left the hall. She'd agreed to talk to them that evening and to arrange for her sons, Milo and Dominic to be there too. They'd spent the time since then interviewing a string of locals in the conservatory, while Donaldson and Jackson chased down some of the people the neighbourhood team hadn't yet been able to contact. And now they were on their way to Forest Hall in two cars, so they could each go home afterwards without needing to trail all the way back up the coast to Cresswell.

Massey came off the A19 at Holystone and drove along the Great Lime Road to Feetham Avenue, checking in his mirror that Sparks was still behind him. He eventually found Park Drive after a couple of wrong turns, and the narrow potholed offshoot of it, where the Kingsleys had moved to, purely by chance.

CHAPTER 18

The wrought iron gate squealed as they pushed it open. Overhung by mature willow trees and crowded by evergreen shrubs, the winding garden path felt spooky in the gathering dusk. Elena Kingsley must have been listening out for them, and was already at the door before they reached it. Perhaps the gate had deliberately been left unoiled as a warning siren. After her husband had been so brutally murdered, he couldn't blame her for that.

They stepped into a hallway of polished black and white floor tiles and caramel painted walls hung with stark black ink figure drawings in ornate gold frames. 'Thank you for agreeing to see us, Mrs Kingsley,' he said.

'It's Elena. Go through. The boys are in the lounge.'

The black and white tiles gave way to a sumptuous oak flooring, although the caramel walls continued through on every wall but the chimney breast, which was painted a dark peacock blue.

Facially at least, the Kingsley boys looked alike – both dark haired and pale complexioned, but neither resembled their father. They were hardly boys anymore; Milo nineteen and Dominic eighteen, he understood. Both strong and fit, although given their difference in build they'd play different positions on the pitch.

The tallest stepped forward and held out his hand. 'Hi. I'm Milo. This is Dom – Dominic.'

'Good to meet you. I'm DCI James Massey, and this is DS Christine Sparks.'

'Please,' Elena said, 'take a seat. Can I get you anything?'

'No thanks,' he said. 'We won't disturb your evening any longer than necessary.'

They sat side by side on an unyielding black leather Chesterfield that faced an ornate white fireplace, above which hung a big gold-framed image of a monstrous monotone abstract shape, like one of those psychological perception test inkblots. He saw a gigantic moth. He wondered what Sparks saw.

'I don't know how we can help you. We've heard what's happened, of course. Such a tragedy. I knew Ben and Ursula quite well when we lived up there, before Duncan's...'

She paused for so long, Massey was about to jump in with a question, but eventually she gave her head an inpatient shake and carried on.

'... before Duncan's death. And of course the boys know Fleur. They were all at the same school. How is she?'

'Not good. She—'

'Why are you really here?' Dominic had taken a challenging step forward while their attention was on Elena, and may have moved further towards them, had Milo not put a warning hand on his arm.

Massey maintained a relaxed position, but Sparks shifted her weight in the heavy sofa. Just in case.

Elena wrung her hands. 'Dom, please—'

'Why come here? We haven't been up to Ellington or Cresswell since we moved here, apart from on Saturday, so how could we know anything about what goes on there now? But that's not why you're here at all, is it? This is about Dad.

'Dom, don't... please.'

'We appreciate how hard this must be for you all.' Massey kept his voice placatory.

'Oh yeah, really? You know exactly what we're going through, do you?'

'Dominic. Stop.'

Massey waited a couple of beats before speaking again. 'We're treating the fire at Ben's house as arson, We know both Ben and Fleur were attacked and left for dead in that house. So the fact that Ben and your father were not only friends, but also both involved with the presidency of Ellington & Cresswell RFC may be significant. That's why we need to ask—'

'The men who killed Dad have been identified.' Milo said. 'They're about to be charged with his murder. What happened at the weekend has nothing to do with that?'

'We can't know that yet. Were you aware that Ben was standing in the election for president?'

Both boys looked at each other. It was Milo who spoke. 'Finn Barron is president now. That's what he told us.'

Dominic clenched his fists until his knuckles turned white. 'The bastard wouldn't let us play on the team on Saturday. Did you know that?'

Sparks inched further forward.

'We heard,' Massey said. 'I'm sorry. But Finn Barron is only acting as temporary president at the moment, until the election. Ben was also a candidate.'

Dominic's laugh was bitter. 'He used to vote against Dad in every decision, you know, just for the hell of it. Anything to divide the members, trying to push Dad into standing down, yet always acting so nicey-nicey to him away from the club, as if he hadn't just shot him down in flames in the boardroom.'

'Let me get this straight,' Elena said. 'You're suggesting that Finn Barron killed Ben Quinn in that house fire just so he could be president of the rugby club, and that he killed my husband for the same reason? But surely, that's ridiculous.'

'No, that's not what we're saying. We don't yet know what happened. But we can't rule anything out.'

'Does DCI Flint know about this?' Milo demanded. 'Durham Constabulary have been investigating, not Northumbria Police. That's who's been dealing with Dad's case.'

DCI Flint was Massey's contemporary on one of the Murder Investigation Teams over on the Durham force. Massey had heard the name before, but had never met or spoken to the man.

'Durham are aware of this new development. We're keeping them updated—'

Dominic sneered. 'So that's all Ben's death is to you, is it? A "new development". Jesus. Unbelievable.' He stomped from the room, and would have slammed the door behind him, had Milo not caught it and followed him out.'

'Boys!' Elena's voice sounded weary, as if she knew full well they'd ignore her. 'I'm so sorry. They—'

'It's alright, Elena,' Massey said. 'Let them go. We can talk to them another time if necessary. Right now we're simply asking people where they were on Sunday and to think again about any conversations they may have had with Ben, or with Fleur, or about anything they may have heard that could give us a lead on who could have done this.'

'As for your first question, I can tell you exactly where we all were on Sunday. All three of us. We went to the cemetery in the morning to talk to Duncan – the boys told him all about the match and the party. He would have been proud, you know, even though they weren't allowed on the team. And then we all went for a meal at The Holystone and got home around six. Is that enough, or do you need to know what we did after that too?'

'No, that's fine. Thank you. We're asking everyone the same questions. Now, I realise you may not have been up to Ellington or Cresswell for some time, but perhaps you've kept in touch with some of your friends up there? Maybe not face to face; but telephone conversations, social media, WhatsApp, anything at all?'

'I haven't kept in touch with anyone.' Elena closed her eyes and laid her head back in her armchair, which looked a lot more comfortable than the hard leather of the Chesterfield sofa. She sighed. 'I'll give it some serious thought, I promise, but really there's nothing springs to mind.'

***

Massey felt his mobile phone vibrate again as they walked back down the garden path. Twice, while they were inside he'd felt it go. He swiped the screen. A text this time, and two calls he'd missed earlier. All from Helen.

Finally, she'd decided to return his calls.

Well, she'd have to wait until he got home. No way was he going to have what could be an uncomfortable conversation with his wife while Sparks earwigged, and they needed a quick chat about the Kingsleys before they went their separate ways.

They sat in his car, and he started the engine to get the heated seats going. The temperature had plummeted in the time they'd been inside.

'What did you think about that?' he asked.

'Both sons are still angry, which is to be expected. They really don't like Barron, do they?'

'We need to make speaking to Barron our first priority tomorrow morning.'

'With the wife – can't remember her name – or on his own?'

'Verity. Did you see them on Sunday outside Stoneyriggs? Finn almost had to carry her home.'

'She looked like a ghost in that white coat, hanging onto his arm. I thought she was going to collapse.'

'It might be worth seeing how they are together initially. They made excuses not to come to the village hall yesterday. I've a feeling they'll try the same tomorrow. So if the mountain won't come to Mohammed… First thing in the morning, we'll go and knock on their door.'

CHAPTER 19

Sparks waited until she saw Massey drive away and then took her time starting her own car, not wanting him to see which way she turned at the main road. It would take twenty minutes or so to drive back to Cresswell, but the rehearsal should still be in progress at the tower by the time she got there.

Hopefully.

Tom Kirk had extended the invitation when he and another man had collected the props that afternoon, and she'd dithered until now on whether or not to accept.

But why not, as long as she kept things professional? It could help her gain an insight into the local community. But that wasn't her main motivation. In fact it was last on the list. For a start, the other two witches might be there: which was a good reason not to tell Massey about going. Well, that and the fact he'd take the piss about her and Tom Kirk again, when there was nothing to take the piss about, and there never would be. Especially now she suspected him of lying about Red. And, if she was lucky, *she* might be there too.

And she had another reason for going, which she hadn't fully analysed yet. The whole idea of a performance of Macbeth – her favourite of all the plays she'd performed in herself at school – had wormed its way into her brain, and she wanted to see how it would look in such an ancient and atmospheric setting. She and Dazz had tickets for the evening performance. Or at least *he* had two tickets because he'd insisted on paying for them on Sunday, and she hadn't argued because she hadn't wanted to spoil the day, despite him trying to convince Kirk that they were an item. They weren't then, and they still weren't, although they *had* fallen into having long phone conversations every evening since their impromptu day out on Sunday had ended so traumatically.

***

The gate in the stone wall stood open.

Sparks followed the path up to the tower, where the sturdy wooden door also stood open. As she grew closer, she could hear lines from Macbeth being spoken aloud.

A woman's voice.

'Pronounce it for me, sir, to all our friends, for my heart speaks they are welcome.'

Reaching the doorstep, with the speaker still out of view, she tried to recall the scene being rehearsed, but a male voice spoke the next lines before she got there.

'See, they encounter thee with their hearts' thanks. Both sides are even — here I'll sit i' the midst. Be large in mirth; anon we'll drink a measure the table round.'

A momentary pause, before the male voice continued in a similar tone.

'There's blood on thy face.'

A loud crack sounded from inside, followed by a strident male voice. 'No, no, no!'

Peeking inside, Sparks spotted a short tubby man, with hair sticking out at all angles, waving a rolled-up sheaf of paper in one hand. In the other, he held a hardback book, which he slammed on a small table for a second time, making the dozen or so other occupants of the ancient stone-vaulted room jump.

None of were the witches she'd hoped would be here.

'We've been through this umpteen times.' The tubby man's loud theatrical drawl reverberated around the stone walls. 'That line needs to be whispered to the assassin, not spoken out loud for every sodding Tom, Dick and Harry to hear. These are the murderers Macbeth hired to kill his best friend, Banquo. They've just rocked up at a party the Macbeths are throwing for all the top bananas, and one of them has Banquo's blood all over his mush. Macbeth's not going to like that now, is he? He doesn't want anyone to know what he's been up to. All he wants is to know the deed is done and to send the murderers on their way, without his guests noticing. Now, does, that, make, sense? It bloody should, by now.'

A middle-aged man and a woman, clearly playing the Macbeths, nodded their heads and mumbled their agreement.

'Right. Once again from your bit, Macbeth: "*See, they encounter thee…*" blah, blah. And get it right this time. Only a week and a half left before you'll be doing all this for real. Off you go then.'

Tom Kirk spotted her.

Arms open wide, he made his way over to where she still stood by the door, 'Christine, I'm so glad you could come.'

She held up her hands to ward him off. Quite apart from not being the hugging type, particularly with someone she'd only met for the first time less than a week ago, she needed to keep this professional.

Getting the message, he took a step back.

'I wasn't sure I'd make it.' She tried to speak softly so as not to disturb Macbeth as he delivered the same passage again, with the last line coming over this time in an exaggerated strangled whisper.

'Of course. Come and meet everyone.'

'I'd just like to listen, if that's okay. I played a part in Macbeth myself at school.'

Kirk gave her a lop-sided look and waggled an inappropriate eyebrow. 'As Lady Macbeth, no doubt.'

'Hardly. I was never anyone's first choice for that big a part.'

He made a frame of his fingers and looked her up and down through it. 'One of the witches then?'

She laughed. 'As the fourth witch actually. Hecate. She's not always in it, apparently. And even when she is, she only has a few lines, which is why they gave the part to me. Even I couldn't muck them up.'

'Isn't there debate on whether Shakespeare actually wrote the part of Hecate? We don't have her in this one. No space for a big production. This is a slimmed down version. In fact much of the story will be told outside around the grounds, rather than in here. Immersive theatre, it's called, with the audience playing the part of cast members in crowd scenes, like this one, and the added advantage, if we're lucky with the weather, of showing off our grounds and the garden to all comers.'

'Don't think I've heard of immersive theatre.'

'It's not unique, but it could be the first time it's been done on this small a scale. It was Colin's idea. Colin Chirnside. He's been brilliant.'

She pointed towards the short tubby man with the sticky-up hair and raised her eyebrows.

'That's him. He's an excellent stage director.' Kirk pointed out a pair of canvas chairs along the stone wall to their right. 'Let's sit. We've borrowed Colin actually. He works for a progressive theatre production company in Newcastle, but he lives locally and so he's doing this as a volunteer.'

'Very noble of him.'

Sparks had never got the whole concept of volunteering. In an emergency, yes. Rescuing someone, helping disaster victims, that sort of thing. But not in the way they promote volunteering now. Why would anyone want to do something for nothing that they could get paid for elsewhere?

'It is. Most of the people here are volunteers. Except me. I get paid through a charity grant to manage the volunteers and raise the profile of the charity that looks after the tower. Part-time only though.'

'Did you know Ben Quinn or his daughter, Fleur?'

'Not Fleur, except in passing, but Ben yes. He's… he *was* on our committee, and Ursula is one of our garden volunteers. You know she was going to be one of the three witches, don't you?'

'Have you found anyone to take her place yet?'

'Not yet, and it's getting late. I might have to step up myself. I've heard all the lines often enough, so it shouldn't take too long to learn. Unless, of course…' He raised one eyebrow and gave her a cheeky grin.

Sparks held up her hands and snorted a laugh. 'Don't even think it. We're in the middle of an active investigation.'

They lapsed into silence, each concentrating on the actors, with Sparks recognising the part where King Macbeth first encounters Banquo's ghost; Macbeth staring at an empty chair, his face wearing an exaggerated fearful expression.

'Thou canst not say I did it – never shake thy gory locks at me.'

A tall man in his sixties stepped forward and waved his arms.

'Gentlemen, rise. His highness is not well.'

Then Lady Macbeth stood between the two men and spoke to the same imagined audience.

'Sit, worthy friends. My lord is often thus and hath been from his youth.

'Pray you, keep seat. The fit is momentary; upon a thought he will again be well. If much you note him—'

Everyone in the room heard the sound of a throat clearing in the doorway and turned in unison.

Sparks recognised Red, her long hair piled up into a loose bun, her eyes sweeping the interior until they found Kirk.

'I understand,' she announced, 'that you are in need of a witch.'

Kirk jumped up and dashed towards her, arms open wide – clearly a habit. 'Trinny! You're a lifesaver. Mwah, mwah!'

Red allowed him to clasp her hands in his and accepted his air kisses as her due.

CHAPTER 20

Keegan pushed his plate away and rubbed his hands to dislodge naan bread crumbs. 'So no-one saw anything, and no-one knows anything.'

'Not that we've discovered. Yet. You know how these things go.'

Massey's plan when he got home had been to put a frozen meal into the microwave, open himself a bottle of beer, and go through the preliminary postmortem report they'd received yesterday with a fine-tooth comb, and then give Helen a call back when he'd finished eating.

But when he pulled into the street at around half seven, he'd found Keegan's car parked outside his house and the man himself lying back in his reclined driver's seat with the window open, listening to an audio book.

'About bloody time. Sarah's away for the rest of the week for work and the girls are staying at her mother's, so I thought I'd come and pester you. I picked up a menu from that Bubhuksha Balti place in Shiremoor and told them they'd better still be open by the time I called. Thought we could order in, and I'd be saving you from starvation.' Keegan had made a point of looking at his watch. 'But we're pushing it a bit now.'

'What do you mean? I've got a house full of food.'

Although an Indian takeaway had sounded good, and Helen could wait a while longer.

He needed to talk to her – he'd been trying for long enough – but it wasn't a conversation he was looking forward to having.

Decision made, he'd ordered the chicken pathia with chilli coriander rice, while Keegan opted for a lamb vindaloo with garlic pilau. They added both peshwari and methi naans, a stack of papadums and a tray of pickles.

The order arrived in record time, probably so the staff could get locked up and away home. Wednesday could hardly be a busy night for them. Many takeaways only opened Thursday to Sunday these days.

They ate fast. Massey hadn't realised how hungry he was.

With their bellies full, Keegan finally got down to the real reason he'd come; to pump him for information on the investigation.

Massey rinsed the plates in the sink and stacked them in the dishwasher, while Keegan got fresh beers from the fridge and went through to the lounge, but not before poking his nose into the freezer and a couple of cupboards too, presumably to check his story about having plenty of food in. When Massey joined him in the lounge, he found Keegan staring at the big gap on the alcove shelves where his vinyl collection should be.

'I thought all those albums would have been yours. You seem the type.'

'They *are* mine, and I'll get them back.'

Keegan sucked his teeth. 'I feel a vicious custody battle coming on.'

'Whatever.' Somehow the man always knew how to get under his skin.

Sitting in the armchair by the window, Keegan took a long draw from his beer. 'Definitely murder then.'

Massey brought up the preliminary PM report on his phone and flicked through the main points. 'Not one hundred percent sure, according to this. The position of the body indicates that Ben made no attempt to escape the fire, so he was either dead or unconscious at the time, but no soot was found in what was left of the respiratory tract, which indicates he was no longer breathing when the fire took hold. But his body was terribly burnt, so they're waiting for the toxicology and histological analysis as confirmation. It looks like heat-induced fractures of the skull have complicated things a bit, and they haven't been able to come up with an accurate profile of the weapon, even with CT scans, but they're talking here about something heavy and club-like.'

'What, like a golf club?'

'Big, heavy and rounded, apparently. I'm picturing Fred Flintstone, but I'll speak to Lorraine and try to get a better picture.'

'She did the PM?'

'With the help of a specialist in burnt remains.'

It was after eleven when Keegan left. Probably too late to call Helen, but he tried anyway. No answer. He'd try again in the morning.

CHAPTER 21

Thursday, 17 October 2024

With his view of the blackened ruin of Stoneyriggs blocked by a stone-built public convenience block, Massey waited in the village hall car park for Sparks to arrive, gazing blankly out of the windscreen and turning the fraught conversation he'd had with Helen last night over in his head.

She'd called him not long after midnight, just as he was drifting off to sleep. 'How dare you refuse my calls,' she'd ranted.

'Only because we're in the middle of an active investigation,' he'd told her. 'And what about all the times you've ignored my calls and texts over the past five weeks?' How could she accuse him of refusing to speak to her when he'd been the one trying so hard to get in touch ever since she left? But clearly, as far as Helen was concerned, none of that counted.

She'd called to inform him that she'd found a new place to move into after staying with her parents since she'd left him and intended to collect all her things from the house at the weekend. She wanted him to make himself scarce while she was there.

'No chance,' he'd told her. 'You've already taken all your personal stuff. You're getting nothing else until I get my vinyl record collection back.'

Although, given the demands of a complicated murder investigation that could have him working all hours, how could he know now whether he'd be at home or not come the weekend? And having been married to him for fourteen years, she would realise that too, but still she'd slammed the phone down on him, and he'd had a shitty night's sleep.

He opened the car window now, hoping the sea breeze might perk him up a bit, but it was the smell of freshly baked bread that assailed his senses and took him right back to his childhood, just after his mother had married his stepfather, and his life had become happy and settled for the first time. There'd been a bakery just round the corner from their new home and he'd come to associate the delicious yeasty aroma with happiness and contentment.

Exactly what he needed this morning. An antidote to all the depressing thoughts about Helen and the breakdown of his marriage.

***

Driving through Cresswell, past the tower on the right and the blackened remains of Ben Quinn's house on the left, Sparks could see Massey's Hyundai in the village hall car park. It looked like he was sitting in the car waiting for her.

She still couldn't decide how she would broach the subject of her trip back here last night after having left him in Forest Hall. She'd have to tell him. With her luck, if she didn't, it would end up being pertinent to their investigation.

But the question was more about how she could tell him that she'd deliberately lied to him by omission. Because that was what it amounted to.

After all, she'd had ample opportunity before they'd parted yesterday to tell him she'd intended to come back to Cresswell, but she hadn't. She could have told him at any point during the afternoon that Tom Kirk had invited her to watch the first rehearsal at the tower, but she'd bottled it. She hadn't wanted him making anymore smart-arsed comments about her fancying Tom or two-timing Dazz for a start, neither of which were true.

Well, mostly not true.

She had found Tom attractive. At first. But not now. He'd lied about not knowing Red. Last night he'd given himself away. He knew her pretty well, it seemed.

Either way, she wasn't stupid enough to start any sort of relationship with someone even marginally involved in a case she was investigating.

Especially one so eager to throw her over as soon as Red hoved into view.

She found Dazz surprisingly attractive too, but she wasn't *seeing* him, so how could she be two-timing him, with Tom Kirk or anyone else?

It wasn't until she pulled into the space alongside Massey's car that she glanced over and realised he had his eyes closed and hadn't registered her arrival. She opened her car door and climbed out, closing it behind her as quietly as she could before rapping hard on his passenger window.

Massey jumped so hard his head hit the roof liner.

***

'Smell that,' he said, once he'd recovered and climbed out of the car. 'Fresh bread. Love that smell.'

He couldn't believe he'd drifted off for a few minutes.

Sparks remembered the sign she and Daz had seen. 'There's a Blue Moon Bakery somewhere along here. See the sign there? It must be around the back.'

'Maybe we should knock on the door and invite ourselves for breakfast.'

'Not seven o'clock yet. A bit early.'

'Whoever's baking the bread must be up.'

'Haven't we got somewhere else you want us to be?'

She had a point. The Barrons lived further south along Beach Road, beyond the Golden Sands Holiday Park towards Lynemouth. 'We might as well walk.'

Sparks had no objection. She'd have run it if she could.

'What's the plan when we get there,' she asked.

'To put them on the back foot and see where it takes us. But this is only a witness interview at this stage remember. After seeing them on the night of the fire and hearing what some people think about them, I'll be interested to see how they interact with each other as much as anything else.'

The Barrons' house stood on the far side of a small headland, on the right hand side of the road. Huge windows faced out onto an expanse of elaborately landscaped gravel garden stocked with what must be hardy salt-tolerant perennials. They'd need to be, this close to the sea.

Massey recalled their conversation with Ben Quinn and Michael Duffy on Saturday night, about the three men Durham had in the frame for Duncan's murder being those who'd landscaped the Kingsley's garden and had then gone to give Finn a quote on the afternoon Duncan died.

Had they ended up actually doing the work, or had the Barrons found someone else to do it?

As Sparks rang the doorbell, he turned to look back across the garden towards the road, the narrow bit of scrubland on the other side and the drop to the beach beyond.

The beach where Duncan's body had been discovered last year.

CHAPTER 22

Sparks had to ring again before they heard any movement inside, and even then it took an age before Verity Barron pulled open the front door, looking pale and ghostly in a long white robe.

'Good morning Mrs Barron,' Sparks said. 'This is DCI James Massey and I'm DS Christine Sparks. We'd like to talk to you and your husband.'

'Um... Finn isn't here. Only me, I'm afraid.' The woman's blue-veined eyelids fluttered. One hand, its knuckles red raw and cracked, clutched and unclutched the neckline of her robe.

'He must have left early,' Massey said, with an encouraging smile.

'Yes, he um... he goes along every Thursday morning to collect our order. Every week, without fail. Blue Moon.'

'Blue Moon Bakery?'

'That's right. Three dozen poppy seed rolls. They're delicious, the best you'll find. Um...' She bit her lip, then smiled in relief. 'Here's Finn now.'

A silver Audi SUV turned onto the drive and swept to a halt beside them.

'James Massey. What are you doing here?'

***

Clutching two large paper carriers bearing the bakery's logo in a chalky pale blue print, Barron led them into a stark lounge. Walls, ceiling, suite, a couple of side tables, everything white apart from a huge expanse of oatmeal carpet and some insipid coastal-themed watercolours in light wood frames dotted around the walls.

Still gripping the neck of her robe, Verity hovered in the doorway.

'Go and put some clothes on, woman. And make some damned coffee. Oh, and here, take these with you.' Barron thrust the carrier bags towards his wife, then turned back and addressed Massey, who'd moved over to the window to gaze out at the sea. 'Come to grill us on what we were doing on Sunday then?'

'Fabulous view you have here.' Although, in truth, if it hadn't been for the landscaped garden, Massey would have found it boring.

He loved the sea, but looking out only at a bit of scrub vegetation and that huge expanse of North Sea, day in, day out would soon wear thin. No wonder they'd wanted to landscape the front. From this angle, the garden looked like meandering streams of blue-grey slate chippings bubbling through sinuous beds of vegetation around angular paved jetties. It had taken considerable skill to create this gravel garden, and no doubt a lot of money.

'I like it,' Barron said. 'Very quiet at this end. We don't get many people at all on this little beach near. That's why I bought this piece of land and built on it.'

Massey smiled and allowed a pause to develop before speaking. 'Duncan Kingsley died down there on that beach, didn't he?'

Barron sighed impatiently and ran fidgeting fingers through his salt and pepper hair.

'A little further along actually. Just this side of Snab Point. It's more rocks than sand there. Anyway, I thought you were here about Ben.'

'Why did Kingsley go down there? You were having a barbecue here at the time, I understand.'

'He wanted to go as soon as the men arrived, but Elena wasn't ready, so he went for a walk on the beach.'

'The men?'

'Landscapers. They'd done his garden. He didn't know I'd asked them to quote for some work here. When they'd gone, I rejoined the rest of my guests out the back, while they must have gone looking for Duncan. End of.'

'Did they end up doing all this work?'

'Yes. They put in a competitive quote, and they made a bloody good job of it. As you can see.'

'Hard to believe they'd have even put the quote in if they'd just committed murder.'

'Yet that's exactly what they did. I think it would have looked more suspicious if they hadn't, don't you?'

Sparks had been making her way slowly around the room, examining all the watercolours. She stopped and looked directly at Barron, giving him her best shark smile. 'I thought the election for a new president would have been all done and dusted now. Why isn't it?'

'What?'

'The rugby club. The election to replace Duncan Kingsley as president. What's been holding it back?'

'What does that have to do with anything?'

'You're acting as a stand-in for Duncan now, aren't you? I'd have thought you'd have been keen to get everything settled as soon as possible, and yet here you are, more than a year later, still standing in.'

'First of all, young lady, I am not a stand-in for anyone. As Vice President, I have been fulfilling the role of the President since the day Duncan – may he rest in peace – was taken from us. I've done—'

'Are you concerned you might lose the vote? Is that why you keep delaying the election?'

'What? For God's sake Massey, are you going to let her carry on with this?'

Massey smiled. 'I'd like to know the reason for such a long delay too.'

'Why? That's club business.'

'Ben was standing against you, wasn't he? From what I've heard, he had a good chance of winning.'

'And now he's dead,' Sparks said.

His face puce, Barron rounded on her. 'How dare you. You're suggesting—'

They all heard the sound of clinking china. A moment later Verity Barron struggled into the room carrying a huge, heavily laden tray.

Her husband made no move to help, so Massey took it from her, his hands brushing hers, feeling the roughness of her skin. Eczema, perhaps? 'Where shall I put it?'

Verity lifted one of the side tables in front of a two-seater settee and he placed the tray on top, determined not to topple the cafetière, breathing in the delicious aroma of the four freshly baked poppy seed rolls that sat alongside four china cups and saucers, a butter dish and two cut crystal containers he assumed contained jam and marmalade.

'Our guests don't have time for any of that,' Barron snapped, aiming a withering look at Sparks. 'They have exactly two minutes to ask their questions and leave.'

Sparks put her head to one side and gave him another of her shark smiles. 'You were about to tell us why the election for president is taking so long.'

Barron emitted an impatient snort. 'If you hadn't already noticed, the club too has been caught up in the inquiry into Duncan's murder. Which, I might remind you, your own Northumbria force was barred from investigating, so what right do you have to interrogate me about it now?' He took a couple of paces towards the window and ran his fingers through his hair again. 'Look, it's tragic, and I'm devastated. Ben was my oldest friend. But his death has nothing to do with Duncan's murder. If it did, I'd have had Durham detectives hammering on my door this morning instead of you two. That investigation is all over bar the shouting. The election for a new president can go ahead now.'

'With one less candidate.' Sparks said, still smiling.

Barron looked fit to explode.

'Can you think of any reason why Ben or Fleur should have been targeted?' Massey asked.

'Of course not. Ben was the best of men. There's not a man alive who could have possibly wished him ill. If you ask me, it'll have been that Fleur they were after, and Ben just got in their way.'

'Why do you say that?'

'Well she's very… butch

'Are you saying you think she's gay? What difference does that make?'

'Well yes. Anyone can see that. Just look at that haircut; it's more short back and sides than mine. And the clothes she wears. I don't believe I've ever seen her in a dress. And she's so mad keen on playing men's sport, isn't she?'

Massey could see the disgust in his sergeant's eyes as she took another step towards Barron. He was about to say something to diffuse things, when Barron jumped in before him.

'Have you considered that Fleur might have wanted shot of her dad, knocked him unconscious and set that fire, but then couldn't quite get out of the house in time to save herself? Well, have you?'

Massey and Sparks looked at each other. No, that theory had not yet been floated, and it didn't make sense of Fleur's own injury, but they weren't about to tell Barron that.

'Why would she want rid of Ben?' Massey asked

A muscle clenched in Barron's jaw. 'Who knows? Could have been anything'

'When was the last time you saw or spoke to Ben or Fleur?' he asked.

'Oh for God's sake... It was after the charity night at the club on Saturday. That's the last time I saw Ben, I mean. I saw Fleur at the party early on, but not towards the end. I'd had a few by then mind, so she could have still been there. Didn't see either of them after Saturday night.'

'And you, Verity?'

Verity Barron jumped as if she'd been shot before raising watery-grey eyes to them. 'I um... I saw Ben at the party on Saturday, like Finn said. That was the last time. Fleur too.'

'I didn't see you there.' Massey said.

'Oh, she was there alright,' Barron said. 'Hiding in the corner, as usual. Now is that it?'

'Not quite. Can you tell us where you both were on Sunday before the fire?'

Barron looked fit to explode.

'These are routine questions we're asking of everyone,' Massey assured him, but he thought Barron might still refuse to answer.

'If you must know, we were both here, on our own, all day Sunday. We saw no-one and spoke to no-one. Just the two of us. Got that?'

By the time Barron bundled them to the door, once he could be absolutely sure they were leaving, he became more magnanimous. 'Did you know I'm chair of the Pele Tower Community Development Group, Massey?'

Massey raised his eyebrows. 'No, I didn't.'

'We're having an event tonight for the trustees and volunteers to thank them for all their hard work in helping to hit our funding target so much sooner than expected. Last minute thing. Obviously, with Ben's death, it'll be more subdued than we'd otherwise have had, but I think we need to do something to buck everyone up.' He paused for a moment on the doorstep. 'We'd have used the village hall, of course, but your lot are in there, so it'll be at the rugby club. If you drop by, you'll be able to get a look at us all in our natural habitat. Seven o'clock?'

'Thanks, we'll pop in.'

Barron looked at Sparks and scowled. Massey realised he'd meant the invitation for him alone.

***

'What a piece of work,' Sparks said as they started walking towards the village hall.

'You enjoyed setting him off.'

'Not like it was difficult. I just needed to be female and in a position of authority. That's all it takes with men like him. What do you reckon he does for a living if he can faff about at home on a weekday morning?'

'I've no idea. Maybe he works from home. Or maybe he's on the sick. He doesn't look exactly healthy.'

'Hmm. Can't see Verity having a job. Looks too fragile. Did you see the state of her hands? Do you think she could have some sort of illness too, or just the effects of being married to such a misogynistic bastard?'

Massey laughed.

'By the way...' Sparks looked down at the ground as they walked. '... I need to tell you something, before we go to the rugby club tonight.'

Hands in pockets, Massey half turned towards her as he walked. 'Fire away.'

'I um... I went to the tower last night to watch a rehearsal of Cresswell Macbeth.'

'And?'

'And not a great deal. Talked to that Tom Kirk bloke for a while...'

Massey raised his eyebrows but said nothing.

'... until Red turned up.'

'Who?' he asked, although he knew immediately who she meant.

'That Trinny-what's-her-face.'

He sighed. 'Is she in the play?'

'She came to volunteer her services as one of the three witches now that Ursula Kyteler is out of the running – a role that I'm sure will suit her down to the ground, by the way. Clearly fancies herself an actor. What's Trinny short for?'

Massey gave her a look from under his brows. 'Trinity, I think. Why?'

Sparks snorted. 'Not the Holy Trinity, that's for sure.'

'Anything else I need to know before we go tonight? And would you have even told me at all that you'd been there if Barron hadn't invited us?'

But Sparks had her eyes fixed ahead of them. 'Speak of the devil – which is so much more appropriate – that looks like Red along there.' She pointed towards a small figure standing at the road, just beyond the first houses of the village proper. 'If we're speaking to people who might have seen or spoken to Ben before the fire, don't you think we should be speaking to her too? And, by the way, it was you Barron invited, not me.'

Massey grunted. Sparks was right, they did need to speak to Trinny, but he'd have preferred some time to prepare himself first. 'You're coming tonight too. Don't think you're getting out of it that easily.'

CHAPTER 23

A big stone-built house stood on their right – modern but in keeping with the much older building coming up, beyond which lay the South Side cottages where Margaret Charlton lived. And beyond that, Trinny stood at the kerb, talking to a young boy, both seemingly oblivious to their approach. The boy wore school uniform, a backpack over one shoulder, and held a lunch box. Trinny straightened the collar of his jacket and smoothed his thick red-brown hair.

Such maternal gestures. The boy could only be her son. Massey's heart stopped. His steps faltered.

Steaming ahead, her focus on Trinny, Sparks hadn't noticed his hesitation. 'Hey there,' she called, when she was still some distance away.

Both Trinny and the boy turned. Two faces, the boy's still soft features almost a mirror of hers.

Jesus, how old is he?

Trinny gave them a brief smile, just as a car pulled up at the kerb and the boy climbed in, then waved him off until the car turned left up the hill, past the blackened remains of Stoneyriggs.

'Your son?' Massey asked.

'He is, yes. Off to school. Good morning James. And Christine, isn't it? Tom told me your name last night.'

Sparks lifted her chin and glared. 'Detective Sergeant Christine Sparks.'

Trinny's smile didn't quite reach her eyes. 'Of course. So is this an official visit?'

'It wasn't going to be a visit at all,' Massey said. 'But now we've run into you, we might as well get it out of the way. We're talking again to everyone in the village who might have spoken to Ben or Fleur Quinn in the days and hours before the fire.'

'You'd best come in then.' She led them down a narrow lane and round the back of the old cottages.

The yeasty aroma still in the air, coupled with a white powdery mark on Trinny's sleeve sparked a connection in Massey's brain. 'Blue Moon Bakery. That's you then?'

Trinny turned towards them and smiled. 'It is. My own little local enterprise.'

Where they might have expected to see back gardens belonging to the cottages on Beach Road, they saw two stone buildings facing them, one behind the other – possibly holiday lets, and beyond that an area that might have once been a small boatyard.

'Here we are.' Trinny led them around the back of the furthest of the two buildings and through a small glass-canopied courtyard, sheltered from the sea breeze by a high stone wall and filled with greenery. They entered a sleek modern kitchen extension, every surface in the room sparkling clean. Heat still radiated from twin glass-fronted double ovens, their last load cooling on a stainless steel bench to one side.

Massey breathed in the aroma.

In a tall rack on his left, plastic trays laden with produce and ready for delivery had been covered in white paper sheets bearing the Blue Moon Bakery logo in the same chalky blue print they'd seen on Finn Barron's carrier bags.

'I hope this isn't going to take long. I have deliveries to make.'

'So I see,' Massey said. 'Where to?'

'Most of it's going to the Drift Café along the road. I do a sandwich shop in Amble and a couple of cafés in Morpeth too, but I don't bake a great amount – I don't have the space – and I only bake three days a week.'

Which accounted for the fact he hadn't noticed the smell before this morning.

'You must have some private customers too. We've heard good things about your seeded rolls.'

'Ah, that's why you were walking from that direction. You've been to see Finn.' Trinny made a point of looking at the clock on the wall. 'Finn prefers to buy direct, so I make a special order just for him every Thursday. Can we get down to business now? Ask away. Whatever it is you need to know.'

Massey took a moment before speaking; this new Trinny disconcerted him. Casually dressed, yet brisk and business-like, her luscious copper hair pinned up into a tight bun and all the passionate sensuality he associated with her buttoned up. So different to the Trinny he'd shared such a heated encounter with all those years ago, and then met again less than a week ago. Today's contrast to the sultry images he'd carried in his head for so long unnerved him. And now he had to think of her as a mother too.

How old is the boy?

He felt rather than saw the look Sparks sent him that told him to get on with it.

'We won't keep you long,' he said. 'Firstly, can you tell us how well you knew Ben and Fleur?'

'Not that well. Obviously, in a small village you can't help but know your fellow residents, up to a point. So I knew Ben to say hello to, and I knew he was involved in the rugby club and the Pele Tower, and the local history society, and on and on. He was that sort of man.'

'What do you mean by that?' Sparks asked.

'Just that he was a typical committee man. He had a finger in every slice of the community pie.'

'Is that a bad thing?'

Trinny laughed. 'Not my cup of tea, but it was clearly his.'

Sparks cocked her head to one side and smiled her dangerous smile. 'And what is your cup of tea?'

Amused, Trinny glanced up at Massey through lowered lashes. 'Is that relevant?'

'What about Fleur?' he said. 'How well do you know her?'

'Not well at all. Completely different interests. How is she, by the way? I heard she was pretty badly injured in the fire. A couple of people are saying she isn't going to survive.'

'She's hanging in there at the moment,' he said.

'I imagine Ursula will be up at the hospital pretty much all the time with her.'

'I imagine so,' Sparks said. 'You know Ursula?'

'Better than I do Ben or Fleur.'

'Ever been in the house, Stoneyriggs?'

Trinny flicked another look at the wall clock. 'No, I haven't.'

Massey sucked his teeth, not liking the direction Sparks was taking the conversation, suspecting her motives in doing so. 'Can you tell us when you last saw or spoke to Ben or Fleur?'

'I'm not sure I've ever spoken to Fleur, but I did see her at the rugby club on Saturday. Early on at least. The last time I saw or spoke to Ben was when you were also there, later that same night. Whatever he said, you'd have heard too.'

'Do you know of any reason why either Ben or Fleur would have been targeted, or of anyone who might hold a grudge against them?'

'Not at all.' She looked at her wrist, and then at a clock on the wall. 'Now, if you don't mind, I really must go. I should have delivered The Drift's order already by now.'

She manoeuvred them towards the back door, which still stood open. The morning sun lit up the glassed-in courtyard, highlighting one particular huge and luxuriant climbing plant that Massey hadn't noticed when they went in; heart-shaped leaves, brilliant blue flowers.

'What's this?' he asked.

'Morning Glory, Heavenly Blue. Beautiful, aren't they? Not many flowers left now it's October, but I plant them every year. The white-flowered version is known as the Moon Flower, which is pretty apt, given my surname is Moon. But I prefer this blue one, hence my business name: Blue Moon Bakery. This little courtyard is ideal for them, so long as I keep them well watered.'

'Where were you on Sunday,' Sparks asked.

Trinny looked at her. 'Here. All day. Staying out of the way of day-trippers.'

'How long have you lived in Cresswell?' Massey asked. 'I seem to remember you come from further south somewhere.'

She cocked an eyebrow at him. 'I don't come from anywhere really. I'm a nomad at heart. We've been here a few years now. On and off at first, renting a holiday home mostly. I'd been looking for somewhere in the village to bring up my son, and this place became vacant just at the right time, right when he was due to start school.'

They'd reached the narrow lane that led back to the front of the cottages. Trinny was about to turn back when Sparks stopped her. 'How old is your son? I'm sorry, I don't know his name.'

Trinny looked from Sparks to Massey and smiled. 'No reason you should. His name is Max and he's ten.'

***

'Do you think he's yours then?' Sparks asked, as Trinny walked away.

'What?'

'Could Max be your son?'

'Jesus Christine, you don't mince your words, do you?'

'It's what you're thinking though, isn't it?'

He couldn't deny it. He didn't. Instead he turned and strode, head down, towards the village hall. Trinny would have told him back then, surely, if she'd got pregnant as a result of their one night stand. But would she, really? The last impression she'd ever had of him was of how he'd sneaked away in the night like a coward while she slept. Why would she have wanted a father like that for her child? And even if she had, how could she have found him anyway?

He thought of his daughter, miscarried when Helen had found out about his single act of unfaithfulness. Had he fathered a son at the same time as condemning his unborn daughter to death?

CHAPTER 24

If anyone had asked, Massey could not have said how he'd managed to get through the rest of the day. On autopilot mostly, although he'd had to sharpen his wits while talking to Superintendent Lou Portas.

She'd called at around midday about the test results Lorraine French had sent through to them both. Toxicology analysis had shown a COHb concentration of only three percent in Ben Quinn's blood, and histology found no inflammatory reaction in tissue samples, both results clear indications that Ben was dead before the fire started, thus significantly raising the likelihood his death was a homicide that the fire had been set to conceal, rather than arson having been the main motive.

'So what do we have?' Portas had asked.

'As you'd expect, no-one is saying they were anywhere near Ben's house before the fire on Sunday, and there's no way we'll be able to speak to Fleur in the near future. She's going to be in an induced coma for six weeks or more. And she may have no idea who attacked her, since she was hit from behind. Ursula still lived at Stoneyriggs despite the split, although she'd stayed with Betsy Halliwell – one of the other witches – on Saturday night and they'd both got the bus to the Metrocentre on Sunday morning. Michael Duffy called and told her about the fire.'

'We know that for a fact?'

'Not yet, but easy enough to check. Andrew and Phil are going through alibis. Odds on Ursula's is sound. Madge has launched an appeal for dash-cam footage or photos taken in Cresswell on Sunday. There's an outside chance, at best, we'll get anything from that, but it was a hot day at the seaside, there were more people than usual around for an October weekend, and villains have been caught out that way before.'

'More outsiders around, you mean. They're not going to have noticed anything different to the norm.'

'They don't need to have noticed anything themselves to have caught something in the background. We might just get lucky. We're talking to

Ben's work colleagues too. He managed a wholesale butchery place, and Ursula works in the office there. But, so far, we've found no trouble with staff or customers that could be relevant.'

They'd talked for a while longer about other cases they had on the go, although nothing could banish the thought of a little boy called Max from his mind. Even when Donaldson brought back sandwiches from The Drift Café for lunch and they ate them together in the conservatory, with Phil Jackson playing the fool, he could think of nothing else but the little boy who looked like his mother but could well be his son too.

The afternoon dragged as he caught up with his growing mountain of admin tasks – the most onerous aspect of his role as DCI. He was glad when the clock ticked round to half five and Donaldson and Jackson finished for the day. He and Sparks stayed back for another hour, before locking up the village hall.

***

The club's small car park was full already when they arrived, so they each parked outside the grounds at the kerb beneath a row of trees in the throes of shrugging off their red and gold autumnal finery.

The weather might have remained generally fine and warm during the day but, with the sun having long gone down, they felt a decided wintery nip in the air. Sparks, like a child, kicked her feet in the drifts of dried leaves on the pavement and he couldn't help but join in, making him smile for the first time since his encounter with Trinny this morning as they made their way to the main entrance.

Barron had arranged the use of the club's upstairs lounge bar for the evening, where a new brass plate above the door bore the engraving 'Kingsley's' in black lettering.

Massey felt moved. He wondered if Elena and her sons knew about the dedication, or would even appreciate it now that the boys were no longer welcome to play for the club, which was Barron's doing, if what he'd heard was true.

Inside, his eyes were drawn to a wall of huge plate glass windows that looked out over the club's two grass pitches and to the open farmland beyond. All they lacked were sliding glass doors out onto a terrace balcony, like at Morpeth's ground.

The noise level was high; thirty to forty people engaged in animated chatter. Probably the first time they'd been able to gather in such numbers to discuss Sunday's tragedy. As a Cresswell Pele Tower committee member, Ben would have been here himself tonight. He must have been a committee member here at the rugby club too, if he was standing for president.

Trinny had called Ben a typical committee man. But the same could be said of Finn Barron. He was chair for the Pele Tower, acting president at the rugby club, and involved somehow with the village hall too.

Sparks went to the bar to get them both a coke, while Massey spoke to Michael Duffy, who'd made a bee line across the room as soon as he'd spotted them.

'Didn't expect to see you here, James.'

'Michael. Are you involved at the Pele Tower too?'

'Not anymore, but the wife is. She's one of the garden volunteers. That's her over there with the short red hair.' Duffy pointed to a little plump woman with a pixie-cut cap of hair dyed more a brilliant orange than red. She sat in a group, all talking earnestly to each other. Ursula Kyteler may not be there, but Massey recognised the other two who'd accosted him on Saturday night, who he now knew to be playing the parts of witches in the tower's Cresswell Macbeth performance. Wasn't the buxom one Betsy Halliwell, who Ursula had gone to the Metrocentre with on Sunday? The one who had a psychologist or psychotherapist business going on somewhere in the village?

'Did you know,' Duffy continued, 'that there's the remains of an old walled kitchen garden at the tower? Used to belong to the old mansion house that the local bigwigs built right next door. This was centuries after the tower was built, of course, and now the house is gone, and most of the garden too, but the tower is still standing strong.'

'Sounds like you have a great interest in the place yourself. Maybe you should volunteer there too.'

'Oh, I used to. I was one of the original members when the restoration appeal was first set up. I love the history of the place, so I was happy to do it, until bloody Finn Barron stuck his oar in. The man insinuates himself everywhere; he's like a disease, although Ben could never see that. So, when he became Chair, that was it for me. I resigned. Look at him lording it over there. Full of himself. After what he's done. And she's just as bad. If I…' Duffy's hands had become fists. He glowered at the Barrons, but he refrained from saying more.

'We don't know they've done anything yet,' Massey said, as Sparks joined them and handed him hid drink. Duffy had been about to say something more about the Barrons. He might still do, if he could get the man alone for a few moments, but this was hardly the best place. He'd make a point of talking to the man tomorrow.

Finn and Verity Barron sat with a group of men and women Massey mostly didn't recognise, apart from Tom Kirk who sat on Verity's far side. Kirk caught sight of someone by the door and his face lit up. He said something to Verity, got to his feet and started to move across the room. About to look round to see where he was off to, Massey saw Finn surge to his feet too.

Verity reached out a hand to hold him back but, shaking his head, he ignored her while the people around them gave him quizzical looks.

'What's the point of all this tonight then?' Sparks asked Duffy.

'Apparently Finn Barron thinks we all need cheering up, and that giving everyone the pleasure of watching him lording it over us will do nicely.' He snorted a bitter laugh. 'I think not.'

Massey had the impression that all the conversations going on around the room were touching on the same subject. 'At least this room is a little more salubrious for the volunteers than the village hall,' he said.

'Sorry?'

'Finn said something about this event having originally been planned at the village hall.'

'Was it, bollocks. There *was* nothing planned before Ben was killed. The meeting wasn't called until Monday afternoon. Originally, it was meant to be just the remaining trustees hammering out with Tom Kirk and Colin Chirnside whatever changes need to be made to the Halloween event following Ben's death. Yes, in the normal course of events, they'd have used the hall for that sort of meeting, but then this celebration thing was tacked on. Completely inappropriate, if you ask me. The whole thing is a joke.

Duffy lifted his hands, realising he'd clenched his fists again. He flexed his fingers twice and lowered his hands to his side.

'There was nothing even mentioned about Ben in the email Finn sent round on Monday, you know. It should have at least mentioned him. Why wouldn't it? You tell me? I couldn't think of anything else *but* Ben that day, and every day since. And if you ask me, most of these people feel the same. They've only turned up tonight because they want to know what's going on. Two suspicious deaths in a small village in just over a year? Everyone's worrying about what's coming next.'

'I assume Barron's planning on making some sort of speech,' Sparks said.

'Oh, he'll be spouting off about something and nothing, that's for sure. But he'd better honour Ben or I'll be having words. That's the only reason I came tonight, to make sure that he does honour Ben.'

Sparks nudged Massey and nodded across the room. 'What's up with Barron? He looks like he's about to keel over.'

Even from here, they could see sweat standing out on Barron's brow. As they watched, he shook himself and stood up straight, shrugging Verity off as she fussed around him. He clapped his hands. 'Ladies and gentlemen…'

Conversations carried on until Barron rattled a silver pen on the side of his pint glass. Gradually, the hubbub petered out and all eyes turned in his direction. But, by then, Barron himself had been distracted by something over by the door. He paused for a moment, mouth open and pen suspended in the air.

Massey, Sparks and Duffy turned to look. Massey felt a shiver run through his insides as he spotted Trinny Moon standing near the door of the lounge, arm in arm with Tom Kirk.

'Jesus,' Sparks murmured. 'That bloody woman gets everywhere.'

Barron tore his eyes away from the door and cast a panicked look towards Verity, who whispered something that could have been encouragement or a warning, because Barron rapped the pen on his glass again.

Reluctantly, Massey dragged his own focus back to the proceedings, but Barron appeared to be struggling to do the same.

Clearly, the man was trying to concentrate on the task in hand, but he couldn't prevent his eyes from flicking back and forth towards the door. Eventually, he got a grip of himself and raised his glass. '…I'd like to make a toast to our dear friend Ben Quinn, who died so tragically on Sunday. Ben was a great supporter of Cresswell Pele Tower, and of this club, as well as being my own closest friend ever since I arrived here from Scotland when I was a boy, and he should—'

Barron's eyes bulged.

Massey heard Michael Duffy's impatient mutter beside him.

'He should… he should not have—'

Barron's chin trembled. He clutched his chest and took a couple of involuntary steps backwards.

Christ, was he having a heart attack?

Verity grabbed her husband by the shoulders, her lips moving, saying something into his ear.

Massey and Sparks both dumped their drinks on the nearest table and rushed across the room. Most people sat shocked and unmoving, except for one woman.

'First aider,' she yelled, and dashed across in front of them.

'Stop this!' Massey heard Verity hiss into her husband's ear. 'You're ruining the evening.'

'We need to lie him down,' Massey said. 'Christine, call an ambulance.'

'*No!*' The venom in Verity's tone shocked him.

A tall older man with a full head of grey hair turned with authority to the congregation. 'I'm afraid Finn is not well. If you could all—'

'*I said, no!*' Verity glared as she helped Barron down into a chair, her eyes coal black holes that would have shot daggers and felled the man if they could.

Massey stopped in his tracks and held a hand up to hold back Sparks and the first aider. He watched in appalled fascination as Verity forced her face into as calm an expression as she could muster, until she was able to stand and address the room herself in a voice much stronger and clearer than Massey had heard from her before.

'It's alright everyone.' She warded off the eager first aider with one outstretched arm. 'Everyone stay, please. Enjoy yourselves. Finn will be fine if we just give him a moment. This happens now and then.'

As she spoke, Finn raised his groggy head. His breath ragged, he waved a hand and gritted his teeth in a semblance of a smile. 'I'm fine, I'm fine. Verity's right, this has happened before. Sorry folks, I just need… a moment and we can get back to business.' He turned to the tall older man. 'Len, tell the barman to serve everyone another drink on the house, will you? I'll sort it out with him later.'

'Jesus,' Sparks said as she and Massey made their way back over to the table where they'd left their drinks. 'It's like we're in the middle of a performance of Macbeth right here. I bet, if we asked him, Barron would say it was Ben's ghost he'd just seen over by the door talking to Red.'

Massey glanced over there now; only Tom Kirk remained. His eyes searched the room but couldn't find Trinny. She'd disappeared as quickly as she'd arrived.

'And did you see how dilated her pupils were?' Sparks said. 'Verity, I mean. She must be on something.'

Massey *had* noticed. 'Finn's too.'

Neither Michael Duffy, nor his wife were anywhere to be seen either now, although Mrs Duffy's two friends – his own Saturday night tormentors – still stared intently across the room towards Finn Barron.

***

Sparks tooted her horn as she drove away. Massey checked his emails. He'd paid a premium for same day delivery, and the parcel he'd ordered online first thing had been delivered in the last hour to a locker at his local supermarket, which would be open until ten, and it wasn't yet nine. He'd be there before half past and home by ten. It meant he was in for another late night, but that was okay. Rather that, than leave the situation to chance.

On the way, he tried to make sense of what had happened at the club. The way Finn Barron had clutched his chest, it certainly looked as if he was having a heart attack. But Verity had been adamant, he didn't need an ambulance, or a first aider. Whatever it was would pass, she'd insisted. It had happened before, and he'd been fine then.

And it *had* passed. After a few minutes, Finn had got up, restarted his speech and delivered it faultlessly. He'd repeated what he'd said originally about Ben and thanked everyone for their contribution in reaching the funding target. He'd even thrown in the odd joke for good measure. Then he'd gone on to talk about how the money raised would be used as match funding for a grant to help develop the tower further as a community resource. He'd ended with an appeal for anyone not playing a part in Cresswell Macbeth to be sure to buy their tickets before they sold out.

As soon as Barron had announced that last part, Sparks had nudged him in the ribs. 'You see,' she'd said. 'Told you.'

He still had no idea what she'd meant.

CHAPTER 25

Shivering, Verity pulled the collar of her white quilted coat up around her ears and stared across the ramparts and out to sea until the cold breeze forced her to blink. From up here she could see for miles. She could feel... separated from all her worries; from the horror of everything that had been happening around her down there. Usually, up here on the roof of the pele tower, she could rise above it all and see clearly everything that felt so hazy down below. With Finn on the sick from work for months now she'd hardly had a moment on her own, so nights like tonight were precious because she knew he'd sleep for hours. He always did after one of his episodes. It had taken three of them for her to realise they gave her treasured time alone, to take his keys, let herself into the tower, and climb up to the roof. Usually, it calmed her. But with tonight's events running through her head on a loop, her muscles refused to relax.

Finn had insisted on driving them home from the club, however much she'd protested. He still hadn't looked himself by then, and she'd told him so. But, as usual, he wouldn't listen. He should never have even got behind the wheel. Not before he'd properly recovered. It was pure luck he'd got them home in one piece.

She hadn't lied at the club when she'd announced that tonight wasn't the first time he'd taken a turn like that, although it *was* the first time he'd almost collapsed with it. And in public this time too. Yet the stupid man still refused to go back to see the doctor. The episodes could be mini heart attacks, she'd insisted. She'd heard that could happen. What if the next one turned out to be the big one?

She should have let those two detectives call an ambulance. But instead, she'd done as she'd promised; she'd refused to let anyone near her pig-headed husband. And then, as soon as they got home, he would not *shut up* about the whole rigmarole. The same thing, over and over. How the club wouldn't want a president who might peg out at any moment. How it was bad enough he was having to take time away from work, and he couldn't allow himself to look any weaker than he already did before the election, not when there were so many who'd be pleased to see the back of him.

'But Ben's gone now,' she'd said. 'And how can you ever get well enough to go back to work if you refuse to tell your GP everything?'

'How can I tell him,' he'd shot back, 'when he's a member of the club?'

'The doctor can't tell anyone. He'd be struck off if he did.'

'But by then, everyone will know.'

She'd shaken her head in frustration. Why couldn't he see what he was doing to himself? The more ill he felt, the more he refused to see the doctor and the more he self-medicated, which – as far as she could see – only made him more ill. He'd even begun ordering tablets and powders online after their nearest two pharmacies had queried why he was buying so much of the medication he was convinced he needed.

'So set a date for the election then,' she'd reasoned, as if talking to a child. 'And as soon as it's over, go to the bloody GP.'

'Things need to settle. Since Ben's death. The members blame me. I know they do.'

'For what?'

'For his *death*.'

And so it went on. A vicious circle. The same argument over and over, with one overwhelming thought running through her head. That if it was anyone's fault Ben had died, it was hers. She'd wished him gone, and it had happened. Just like with Duncan. She'd wished him gone too, and he'd been murdered.

She'd felt a huge wave of hysteria rise up inside her. Hands clenched, shaking from head to foot, she'd screamed in his face that she *could not not do this anymore*.

Leaning out from the battlements now, she laughed into the wind, remembering how his mouth had fallen open in shock. Finally silent, he'd stared at her in disbelief.

'What if the next time kills you?' she'd demanded, still shaking with anger. 'What then?'

'Don't be stupid, woman. I'm not going to die.'

'How do you know? You have no idea what's wrong with you, because you're too *pathetic* to go to the GP. You're—'

She'd clamped her mouth shut when his mobile chimed. But with all the anger she'd carried for too long still seething inside, she'd let rip another scream and stormed out of the room, slamming the door behind her.

His next episode *might* well kill him, and he refused to do anything to help himself.

What would happen to her then? She couldn't imagine being without him. Not when she felt so unwell herself?

And yet now, up here, with the wind blowing her hair across her face, her whole body finally began to relax, and she wondered *why* her husband felt people blamed him for Ben's death. Did he blame himself? But no, that couldn't be it. He'd never been one to take the blame for anything. She stared across towards the blackened ruins of Stoneyriggs. Did Finn *know* what had happened in that house? Was he *actually* responsible?

CHAPTER 26

'What are you doing still out of bed at this time,' Keegan demanded, 'You need your beauty sleep in the middle of an active murder investigation.'

Massey put down his cordless screwdriver. 'How do you know I'm not in bed? You could have just woken me up. How late is it?'

'A few minutes before midnight. What are you up to?'

'Just finished. Why the hell are you ringing now anyway? A social call, at this time?'

'Maybe. Maybe not. I've had a call. You need to know about it.'

'And it couldn't wait until morning?'

'No it sodding couldn't. I'm bored. Sarah and the girls are still away, and I can't hack the silence.'

'So watch the telly, or put on some music.'

Keegan snorted. 'At least I have music I can put on.'

'So have I. Just not on vinyl. For now.'

'Yeah right.'

'Are you going to tell me who called, and why?'

'Michael Duffy. He thinks your lot aren't taking his concerns seriously enough. He's considering going above your head.'

'Lou will love that. So what are we talking about, his belief that Finn Barron killed Ben Quinn and probably Duncan Kingsley?'

'Got it in one.'

'So what am I supposed to do about that? We have nothing on Barron at this point. He and Verity claim they were home alone in the hours leading up to the fire at Stoneyriggs, and we have nothing to disprove that. We have to assume that Durham couldn't make a hole in his alibi for Duncan's murder either, but I have no access to that inquiry. Although it looks like it would have been nigh on impossible for him or Verity to have followed Duncan onto the beach without being seen. I've left messages for DCI Flint, who's SIO on the case, but he hasn't got back to me yet.'

'I know Terry Flint. I'll give him a friendly call. Encourage him to get in touch. In the meantime, I think you need to make time tomorrow morning to go and see Duffy. Have a chat with him. Otherwise you're going to have Lou breathing down your neck.'

'We had a chat with him earlier tonight actually. He started to say something but then stopped. He'd disappeared before I got the chance to ask him about it.'

'Before or after Finn Barron collapsed?'

'Before. Duffy disappeared in the middle of all that. And if you know about that, then he's called you since.'

'Probably just mouthing off. He and Ben had known each other all their lives.'

'I know. I'll make a point of speaking to him tomorrow.'

They chatted for a while longer about nothing much. Massey was glad to talk, every minute of their chat being another when he wouldn't have to count polka-dot pixies. But then, just when he thought Keegan had run out of things to say, the man came out with a belter.

'What's that redhead's name again? The one from the party on Saturday. Word is you've been sniffing after her lately.'

'Oh yes? Who did you get that from?'

'A confidential source. Come on then, who is she?'

'Nope. Not getting into that.'

***

Massey put away his tools and tidied the mess he'd made, then sat for a while downstairs watching the news, determined not to succumb to the lure of the whisky bottle.

He'd given in a few too many times lately in an effort to find sleep, but it had to stop. No way was he going down that road; he had more than enough bad memories from childhood of the damage alcohol could wreak. And besides, he had some thinking to do.

It wouldn't have been Sparks, so it had to have been Duffy who'd said something to Keegan about him being distracted by Trinny. Had his thoughts been so transparent earlier at the club when he'd spotted her in the doorway? If Duffy had noticed, what else might he have read into it? Had other people noticed too?

Not that there was anything *to* read into it. But he'd need to be more careful in the future. Everyone in Cresswell was a potential suspect at this point. He couldn't afford for it to appear he was favouring a possible suspect, even when he knew in his heart she couldn't possibly be involved. But she *had* spoken to Ben at the party the night before the fire, therefore she had to be counted in as both a witness and a possible suspect. For the moment anyway. Which would make it difficult for him to do what he had to.

He needed to talk to her about Max. He had to know if the boy was his son, and couldn't bear having to wait until she'd been officially ruled out of their inquiry.

But then what would he do if she confirmed that yes, he was Max's biological father. How could he deal with that. Because, quite apart from the fact he'd have no choice but to inform Portas, who'd immediately take him off the investigation, he'd also have to deal with the knowledge that a single surreptitious act of infidelity had condemned his unborn daughter to death, while simultaneously creating another new life.

But he couldn't wait. Somehow, he was going to have to have that talk with Trinny.

CHAPTER 27

Friday, 18 October 2024

Never usually troubled by dreams, Sparks' sleep that night was beset by dark images of raging wildfires devouring an army of black-eyed wraiths and chasing her and Massey across moorland towards looming medieval castle walls. Trinity bloody Moon featured prominently, glaring down at her from battlements, denying her access to the castle while at the same time rising up from a gaping hole in the ground – her long red hair hanging loose, and thick with mud and dead leaves – to drag Massey to her lair in the dungeons, leaving her outside at the mercy of the flames, alone.

She awoke in a cold sweat not long after 3 am, got up for a drink of water and decided not to go back to bed and risk a repeat performance. Instead, she sat in an armchair by the window with her laptop, searching online for the full script of Macbeth. It had to be out there somewhere in the ether, but all she could find in her eagerness to explore the outlandish theory her brain had presented her with were scene-by-scene summaries and study guides. She clicked on the Royal Shakespeare Company's Learning Zone and started reading, because who could possibly know better about Macbeth than the RSC?

At five, with her eyes smarting, she went for a moonlit run along the length of Whitley Bay beach and back. By the time she'd showered and got ready for work, she'd made half a dozen pages of notes and texted Massey, saying she had a new theory she needed to discuss ASAP.

When he arrived at the village hall ten minutes after her, he looked as if he'd hardly slept himself. She outlined her theory while they waited for the kettle to boil, but for all she'd girded herself already for the ridicule she knew would be coming her way, she still wasn't prepared for his huge guffaw of laughter in the enclosed space of the tiny kitchen.

'Jesus, you nearly burst my ear drums!'

'This is what you've dragged me in here early for? You think our murderer is acting out scenes from bloody Macbeth?'

With his mouth still gaping open in disbelief seconds later and his eyebrows seemingly stuck to his hairline with Velcro, Sparks knew she had a battle on her hands. But she'd show him.

***

Massey insisted they should wait until Donaldson and Jackson arrived, so Sparks would only need to embarrass herself the once, and he struggled to keep a straight face until they were all settled around the table in the conservatory with coffees and bacon rolls that Donaldson had picked up at a Greggs shop on his way in.

'Okay,' she said. 'I have a new theory, but I need you all to hear me out first without saying a word. Are you all cool with that? Yes? Alright then. So first, here's the plot of Macbeth in a nutshell...'

Phil Jackson groaned.

'... and I promise I'll make it quick. Here goes. Macbeth and his mate Banquo are returning from a big battle when three witches make three prophesies for them. The first says Macbeth will become Thane of Cawdor, which comes true. The second is that Macbeth will become King of Scotland. When Banquo asked for a prophesy for himself, they tell him that while he wouldn't become king, his descendants *would*.

'Back home, Macbeth tells his wife all about it. Of course, she loves the idea of becoming queen and, being the impatient type, she tells him it could happen sooner if he'd be prepared to kill the existing king, Duncan. In fact she decides to help him by pushing him into committing murder when the king visits their castle, even when Macbeth might have backed out. She drugs King Duncan's guards while Macbeth does the deed, and then she smears the guards in Duncan's blood, so they get the blame.

'So now King Duncan is dead, his two sons have run away to England, and Macbeth becomes King of Scotland. But then he starts to worry about the third prophesy and so plots the murder of both Banquo and his only son, Fleance. He sends assassins to kill them. They succeed with Banquo, but Fleance escapes and is never heard from again. Are you all with me so far?'

Phil Jackson could hold it in no longer.

'Is this for real, sarge? Shakespeare for breakfast in the middle of a homicide investigation? I thought I was the comedian on this team.'

Sparks pinned him to his seat with a glare. He held up his hands in surrender, zipped his lips closed and mimed throwing away the key.

'Okay, so that's enough Shakespeare for the moment, and now—'

'You're telling me.' Jackson couldn't help himself. 'I detested all this shit in school.'

'And now I'm going to show you how I believe this is relevant to our inquiry.'

'Before we go there,' Massey said, standing up to leave her no room to protest, 'can we get another coffee first? I'm parched.'

Donaldson volunteered to make it for everyone, but Massey and Jackson followed him – all three proving to be way too many cooks in such a small kitchen – while Sparks set up a flip chart and stand she'd found in the cupboard.

'Are you sure about this?' Massey asked her, as they all made their way back to the conservatory.

'I am. It needs saying. There's too much here that fits what we're dealing with for it not to be at least discussed.'

He grimaced. 'If you're sure…'

Back at the table, she scrawled the names of the characters in Macbeth in order of their appearance in the play. 'Alright, so we have the three witches, often referred to collectively as the weird sisters. They like spinning predictions for people.' One finger on her chin, head to one side, she stared at Massey. 'And who have we seen locally who likes doing just that?'

'That video from Saturday,' Jackson shouted.

'Gold star. And all three of them happen to be playing the parts of the weird sisters in Cresswell Macbeth for Halloween. Or at least they were. Ben Quinn's wife, Ursula has backed out for obvious reasons and her place has been filled by another… local resident. Alright then, Macbeth himself might be a little more difficult, so we'll gloss over him for now and look at some of the others first? King Duncan, anyone?'

'That's obvious,' Donaldson said. 'Duncan Kingsley.'

'Another gold star. How about Banquo?'

'Ben Quinn,' Massey said.

Sparks could see it in his eyes, and in the way he sat forward and placed his elbows on the table. He'd begun to get her theory now.

Jackson raised one index finger. 'He didn't have a son though,'

'No, but he had a daughter called Fleur, who escaped the fire that killed her father, while Banquo had a son called Fleance, who escaped the men sent to assassinate them both.'

'This is mad,' Jackson said. 'So who are you saying Macbeth is then, and what would he have to gain?'

'Macbeth was one of King Duncan's thanes. And a thane is like an Anglo-Saxon equivalent of a Baron.'

'Finn Barron,' Massey said. 'Whose wife Verity, so we've been told, always wants more, just like Lady Macbeth, although we've seen precious little evidence of that.'

'Exactly, and the Macbeths blamed King Duncan's guards for his murder, while here we have Duncan's three landscapers, who'd gone to give Finn Barron a quote for some work and then followed Duncan down to the beach to kill him. Allegedly.'

'Isn't there someone called Macduff in the play too?' Donaldson said. 'Who's he?'

'He's another thane. He starts suspecting Macbeth of Duncan's murder, and Banquo's.'

Phil Jackson's hand shot up again. 'Got it. That has to be Michael Duffy.'

'So we know Macbeth committed murder to become king and then to protect his throne,' Donaldson said. 'But what would Barron's motive be? The presidency of the rugby club? That really is madness.'

Massey sat further forward. 'You're saying that Finn or Verity Barron noticed the similarity of their friends' names to the characters in Shakespeare's Macbeth and decided to use the play to plot their own murders. All in order for Finn to become president of a tuppenny league rugby club? I can't believe that.'

'Now, now,' Sparks said. 'It's a bloody good club. So I'm told.'

***

They batted the theory back and forth for another hour or so, with Donaldson typing notes into a mind mapping tool on his laptop for them to study later, while Sparks scrawled connections on flipchart paper. Massey would need something more persuasive than just a wild, off-the-wall theory before he could take this to Lou Portas.

They all jumped when they heard a knock on the conservatory window.

Jackson, sitting closest, leant over and twisted the rod to open the blinds on the car park side, while Sparks turned another page on the flip chart pad to conceal what they'd been discussing.

Donaldson raised his hand to acknowledge the man outside, hands cupped against the glass, peering in at them. 'That's Len Stafford,' he said. 'Chair of the hall's management committee. He's the one who agreed we could use this place.' Gesturing Stafford towards the front of the building, he got up to go and open the main door to let him in.

'He's also in Cresswell Macbeth,' Sparks said. 'I saw him at the rehearsal the other night.'

Massey too recognised the tall grey-haired man, but from the Pele Tower event at the rugby club last night. Hadn't Michael Duffy said he was one of the committee members for the tower too. This village was proving to have more tangled connections than the cables behind his TV.

He followed Donaldson towards the front door. 'Andrew, see what crossovers you can find between all the different club and charity committees around here, please? Christine and I will have a chat with Mr Stafford.'

Stafford peered in towards the row of pull-up banner stands he could see through the glass partition of the entrance lobby. Clearly expecting to be invited further into the building, he paced back and forth across the floor, but Massey had no intention of letting him through until he had the nod from the others that all trace of their recent discussion had been cleared away. 'I um, knocked on the door a few times. I knew you must be in the conservatory. How are you finding the place?'

'Thank you for allowing us to use the hall, Mr Stafford. It's convenient. For us, that is. I appreciate it's inconvenient for the people who use your facilities normally and have had to find somewhere else.'

'Yes, quite. But we all do what we can, don't we? I understand this is now a murder inquiry, and of course, we all want the perpetrator caught. So um…'

He paused for a tad too long and Massey, who'd usually prefer to see where silence took them, decided to put him out of his misery. 'So how can we help you this morning, sir?'

'Ah, well um…' Stafford sucked his teeth and grimaced. 'It's a little difficult, actually.'

Through the glass, Massey spotted Sparks. She gave a brief nod.

'Why don't you come through to the conservatory for a chat? Would you like a cup of tea, or coffee?'

CHAPTER 28

Stafford talked about the weather until his tea arrived, about how wonderful it had been for the time of year, and how marvellous it would be if it stayed that way, at least until they'd got Cresswell Macbeth out of the way.

'I hear you have a part in the play?' Massey said.

'Um, yes. I'm playing Ross. He's a nobleman, a messenger of sorts. Macbeth's cousin. He pops up now and then to deliver news that moves the play forward. It's a vital role actually. Particularly in the way Colin has us doing it. You see, we'll be performing different scenes from the play in different parts of the tower and the grounds. The tower's not massive inside. There isn't room for a huge stage production, and the winding staircase to the upper floor, where we do have a bit of a raised area, well, it's steep and narrow, so um, it's not suitable for everyone. But then Colin came to us with this marvellous idea to maximise our audience, and the amount of tickets we can sell of course, by making the performance... what does he call it? Immersive, that's right, immersive theatre.

'You see,' he continued, 'the audience members become active participants in some scenes. They don't have to say anything of course, they'll be more like extras in a film, if you see what I mean. If everything goes the way it should, the cast and volunteers will be able to move people around in groups from one scene to another. There's a lot more to it, of course, but um... well, that's the nub of it.'

Massey reopened the conservatory door for Sparks, who carried a cup of tea in one hand and a packet of biscuits in the other.

'I didn't think you'd want another coffee.'

'You were right. Come and join us. Mr Stafford has just been telling me about the Cresswell Macbeth play they're doing soon up at the tower, and how it'll be an immersive experience.'

Sparks took her notebook out of a back pocket before joining them at the table. 'Yes, so I heard. It sounds intriguing.'

Massey rubbed his hands together. 'So then, Mr Stafford. What brings you here to see us this morning.'

'Um…' Stafford picked up his tea cup and put it down again. 'Well, it's just… Good heavens, I feel as if I'm telling tales out of school here.'

Sparks smiled. 'In what way, sir?'

'Look, um… It's just… This could be nothing, of course. It's just that, well, he could be putting himself in danger, I think, if there's a murderer about. And there's the question of slander too. I wouldn't like to see him getting himself into trouble with the police, if a complaint were to be made.'

'Who are we talking about,' Massey asked.

'Michael Duffy of course. He's going around saying some dreadful things, and I um… Well, I thought you should know, that's all. I'm concerned, you see. I called at his house this morning to have a few words myself. Suggest he call in to see you instead of shouting about things in public. But he was out, and the more I thought about it, I um… I thought I should tell you myself.'

'And what has Mr Duffy said that concerns you?

'Um…'

This time, Massey let the ensuing silence run on for a few moments, knowing Stafford would fill it eventually. He did.

'Look, he's going around telling everyone that it was Finn Barron who set the fire that killed Ben Quinn. And not only that. He's accusing Finn of killing Duncan Kingsley too. And of course, that can't be true, because you're going to arrest those three men for that.'

Massey blew out a sigh. 'Not Northumbria Police. The Durham force has been dealing with that inquiry.'

Stafford looked at him as if he'd grown two heads. 'How can they investigate something that happened in Northumberland? And how did I not know this?'

'There were persuasive operational reasons at the time for Durham taking over the investigation. Now, I'd like you to tell us exactly what Mr Duffy has said to you.'

'I've already told you. He said that Finn Barron killed both Duncan and Ben. And it's not just me he's told. He's said the same thing to several people and now it's going around the whole village. I'm not sure whether Finn himself has heard yet, or Verity, but they will soon enough. Gossip spreads like a disease in this village.'

'As in most villages I'm afraid, Mr Stafford.'

***

'I think we need to go and have a few words with Mr Duffy,' Massey said, as soon as they'd closed the front door on Stafford. 'I'd intended to anyway. I got the impression last night he had more to say. And then when I got home, I had a call from Guy Keegan, who told me Duffy had called him to accuse us of not taking his concerns seriously and that he's thinking of going above my head.'

'What? You're joking. What a tosser. We definitely need a word.'

Donaldson loomed towards them, a silhouette against the bright light through the conservatory. 'I've emailed that info you asked me for.'

'Thanks Andrew.' Massey opened the document on his phone. 'This confirms what we were talking about. Finn Barron is vice president, standing in as president at the rugby club, he's chair of the Cresswell Pele Tower Community Development Fund, and he's also a trustee for the village hall committee. Gets around, doesn't he?'

'He does. But look at Ben Quinn. He was a trustee for both the hall and the tower, and also for the Cresswell History Society that I'm sure someone told me sparked the whole tower restoration thing off in the first place. He was on the committee at the rugby club too, and standing for election against Finn. As is Len Stafford, who is also the chair for the committee here at the hall and vice chair at the tower.'

'What about Duffy? Ah, here he is. Looks like he's never been involved with the village hall, but he used to be a trustee at the tower, until he stood down at the last general meeting. He told us last night he'd left because of Finn.'

'What was it Red said yesterday morning about Ben Quinn being your typical committee man? Looks to me like they all are.'

***

On the drive to the Duffy's house, Massey tried to think of ways he could possibly engineer seeing Trinny again. Because he really needed to know. About the boy.

The couple lived in a bungalow on the main road at the top of the village. A boundary map might put it in Ellington rather than Cresswell. A waist-high stone wall, topped by a tall, recently manicured yew hedge concealed the building from the road. They pulled up at the kerb and let themselves into the garden through a double set of wrought-iron gates that hung on stone pillars almost as tall as the hedge, hearing clamouring howls as soon as they clicked the latch closed behind them. They waited for a moment to make sure no dogs were loose, but decided the sound was coming from inside the house, and intensified with every step they took up the wide gravel drive.

Mrs Duffy answered the door. A plump and vivacious fifty-something, with her gleaming cap of impossibly orange hair glowing in the bright sun, she had to shout to be heard above the cacophony of howls from behind a solid door at the end of a long hallway, the wood thudding ominously in its frame.

'Don't mind them,' she said. 'They might sound like a pack of wolves, but they're big softies really. My babies.'

'What are they?' Sparks asked. 'Aside from just being dogs, I mean. They must be big, the way that door's moving.'

'White Siberian Huskies. Oh I know, it sounds like there's a dozen of them, but really, there are only two, honestly. Beautiful creatures. Big fluffy white bundles with the most fabulous blue eyes. You should see them.'

'No thanks.'

'Is Mr Duffy in?' Massey asked.

'I'm sorry, no. He went out first thing. I'd expected him back before now, but—'

'Do you have any idea where he might be?'

'I'm afraid not. I zone him out half the time. He might have mentioned Milo Kingsley, but that won't be it. Milo will be in college now. Is this about all those awful things he's been saying? I told him he shouldn't go shouting his mouth off left, right and centre. It'll come back and bite you, I said, but did he listen? No, he didn't. And now he's got the police after him.'

'We'd just like a chat, that's all.'

'Oh, I'll tell him you were here, don't you worry.'

'Ask him to give me a call, please.' Massey handed over one of his cards.

Back in the car, he sighed. 'I'd have liked a word with Duffy before I speak to Portas.' He clicked on her name in his phone contacts, but his call dropped out without being answered. He rattled off a text instead, asking her to call him.

'Maybe he's over there now, talking to her.'

'Great. Big help, Christine.'

'On the other hand, if he really has gone to see Milo, then that's another parallel with the play. Macduff travels to England to meet up with King Duncan's son, Malcolm. And here we have Michael Duffy travelling to see Duncan Kingsley's son, Milo. And there's another name similarity: Malcolm, Milo…'

Massey rolled his eyes. 'Well they both start with an M and have an L in them. And we're already in England.'

'A figurative parallel, not a literal one, you plank. I wish I had a copy of the bloody play.'

CHAPTER 29

On the drive back down Cresswell Road, Sparks spotted the tower gates standing open. 'Can we pop in there for a moment. There might be someone around who can lend us a copy of Macbeth. And you've never seen the place, have you?'

Massey swerved to the kerb and parked up; thankful he had no traffic close behind him. No, he hadn't been anywhere near the place yet and it was about time he had a look. Quite apart from anything else, Trinny might be there.

Not that he'd get the opportunity to have the sort of chat he wanted with her though, if there were other people hanging around, and Sparks of course.

They walked up a wide reinforced grit path. No one in sight, but lots of sawing and banging noises from somewhere.

Built in the fourteenth century, he'd read online, to protect against raids by the infamous Border Reivers, the imposing tower stood at the top of the path, with the sun in a clear sky behind it. Its stone walls, surmounted by battlements all around and a turret in the left corner closest to them, looked dark against a sky as blue as the Morning Glory in Trinny's little courtyard.

He imagined a soldier standing guard up there, eyes peeled for signs of attack from the sea, as well as up and down the coast.

As they moved closer, he noticed the diagonal marks in the stonework and recognised them as the scars of where the local Cresswell family had butted a Mansion House against the tower in the mid seventeen hundreds. A house that had survived for less than a century before being replaced by a grander residence further inland and demolished. Yet the tower still stood proud. Although it may not have done for much longer if it hadn't been for a huge community archaeological and rescue effort over at least five years, that resulted in the restored tower being opened to the public to help generate the funds to maintain it into the future.

They followed the sounds of hammering round to the rear of the tower, where they found three men building some sort of wooden framework.

'Christine.' The voice came from behind them. They turned to find Tom Kirk hurrying towards them. 'I thought it was you. And DI Massey. Come to give us all a grilling, have you?'

Massey smiled and noticed Sparks' fingers curl, although in annoyance or embarrassment, he couldn't tell. 'Not at all, Mr Kirk. We dropped in to—'

'Tom, please. We're busy making some scenery for the play. Believe it or not, these bits of wood will look just like stone walls by next weekend. Once they're painted, of course.'

'We've been hearing about it from one of the cast. Immersive theatre, I understand it's called.'

'That's right. We'll have little stage sets dotted about inside and outside of the tower, and the cast will flit about from one to another, involving the audience and carrying them along to the next scene, and the next. To tell the truth, I'm terrified it'll all go to hell on the day. I wake up in the night dreaming about it – nightmares mostly. What if the pop-up stages don't turn up next Friday, or I can't find a fog machine, or another of the witches drops out. Or, horror of horrors, what if one of the main players is arrested for murder in the middle of a performance. But hey-ho. Nothing ventured and all that.'

'I'm sure it'll all turn out fine,' Sparks said.

Massey had no such conviction. 'Have all the tickets gone now?'

'Just a couple left, for the evening performance. Are you buying?'

'Perhaps.' He couldn't ask Trinny to go with him, and Sparks was already supposed to be going with Dazz Albright. Maybe he'd buy both anyway and give them away. 'Alright. I'll take them.'

'Good man. You won't regret it.'

'Actually,' Sparks said. 'We've come to ask if you have a spare copy of Macbeth lying around that we could borrow.'

Kirk gave her a puzzled look but chose not to enquire why they wanted it. 'Possibly. Colin will know if we have. He's inside. Follow me. We've got a bit of a dress parade going on in there at the moment.'

***

The first people they saw as Kirk pushed open the heavy wooden door were the three witches, inspecting each other's appearance and cackling like the Shakespearean weird sisters they'd play. They wore ragged black robes and pointed hats, straggly grey wigs and heavy stage make-up, complete with long spidery white eyelashes. Massey couldn't help but be reminded of his ordeal at the hands of two of them – and their friend Ursula – less than a week ago.

Of course, Trinny had taken Ursula's role now and still managed to look beautiful, despite a cluster of prosthetic warts on her chin. Their eyes met and she gave a maniacal screeching laugh, revealing a row of artificially blackened teeth.

'They look good, don't they?' Kirk said. 'And Trinny's done wonders, standing in for poor Ursula at the last minute. It's as if she's played the part before. But Colin's had to alter Ursula's costume a bit for her. He's even sewn an extra layer to the bottom, look.'

Trinny raised a leg to display Colin's handiwork. 'Happy to help out. It's good fun.' Her eyes lingered on Massey's for a moment, before sliding towards Sparks. 'Tom tells me you've played the part of one of the witches yourself, Detective Sergeant.'

Sparks' smile didn't reach her eyes. 'That's right. A long time ago.'

'Hecate, I heard. Who probably didn't exist in the original play written by The Bard himself. Isn't that right, Colin?'

A plump untidy man knelt in front of a middle-aged woman standing on a box, who Massey took to be playing Lady Macbeth. It took a moment for the man to realise Trinny had addressed him, but eventually he stopped pinning, lifted his head and peered over the top of his spectacles, somehow managing to retain the half dozen dressmaking pins clamped between his lips.

'What's that, Trinity darling?'

'The police are here to arrest us.'

Tom Kirk looked embarrassed. 'What? No, no. Not at all. They've just come to borrow a copy of the play, if you've got one spare. Chief Inspector, this is Colin Chirnside. Colin is our stage director, production manager, wardrobe person and all-round indispensable expert on anything Shakespearian. Colin, this is DCI Massey. I think you met DS Sparks on Wednesday evening.'

'Did I? Oh yes, I did see you hanging about I think, but we were never introduced, isn't that right dear?'

Sparks agreed that yes, it was. 'We were hoping you might have a copy of Macbeth we can borrow.'

Chirnside winced. 'You really shouldn't say that word out loud in here, you know. It's unlucky. Do you mean the full play, or the woefully abridged version we're performing here next week?'

'The full play, if you have it please.'

'Hmm.' He spat the pins out into his hand. 'Bloody things. Sorry. I'll cut my lips to bits one of these days and I'll be a shoo-in for Count Dracula. I've got my own copy of Macbeth out in the car, dear. I suppose you can borrow that; on condition you bring it back in the same state you find it. I'll get it for you if you can wait a few minutes. Anything to help catch the beast who did for Ben and his daughter. Lovely man, Ben. Did you know he was a trustee here? Great supporter of the arts, was Ben.'

'Yes sir, we did.'

'Right. Good then. Just give me five to finish pinning this lady's frock and I'll go and get that book for you.'

Sparks smiled her thanks, but Massey's attention was elsewhere.

Trinny ignored him, or at least she pretended to, although he knew she was conscious of his continued gaze on her. He could tell in the subtly flirtatious arching movements of her body as she and her fellow witches moved across the floor to the right of the door, where the huge cauldron that Kirk had collected from the village hall stood. He'd have sworn no-one else could possibly pick up on the invisible thread between them, until Sparks leant in closer.

'Get a room,' she whispered.

As soon as the witches got themselves settled on rickety three-legged stools, which could easily have been a previous woodworking project of the three men making the scenery outside, they began chanting their lines in wild cackles.

So far, Betsy and Scarlett had avoided looking in his direction.

Donaldson and Jackson had interviewed them both, and he'd read through their statements as a matter of course.

Particularly that of Betsy, the buxom one, to ensure her account of Sunday matched Ursula's.

He'd like to have interviewed them himself, but he'd held back. For a start, neither had said anything that warranted further investigation, and he worried that his motivation lay more in what they'd done to him at the party than how they related to the murder inquiry.

'You know we had three witches here for Halloween last year, right?'

He hadn't noticed Tom Kirk creeping up close to him.

'Just them. Down by the gate with their cauldron, spinning prophesies for all the visitors. They were a great success. That's what gave Colin the idea for doing Macbeth this year.'

'The same three women?'

'Well, partly. Not the lovely Trinny, of course. She's only ridden to our rescue this year as a stand-in for Ursula, after, you know, what happened. And not Scarlett either, now I think about it. But Betsy and Ursula, yes. And Maureen Duffy—'

'Really? Michael Duffy's wife? Massey tried to imagine the perky woman they'd just met dressed as a witch, and failed. He certainly couldn't see her being part of accosting a strange man in the rugby club in such a provocative manner.

'That's the one. Didn't fancy it again this year, she said. Still one of our best garden volunteers though.'

'Don't suppose you've seen anything of Michael today, have you?'

'No, sorry. Don't see much of him at all since he resigned as a trustee.'

'Why did he resign?'

Kirk sucked in a mouthful of air then puffed it out. 'You'll have to ask him that.'

So there was a story to be told. Duffy said he'd left because of Barron, but why? 'When was this?'

'Oh, a year or so ago.'

A flurry of waving arms and loud cackling over by the door drew their attention as someone else approached up the path. The bright daylight streaming in through the open door acted like a spotlight. Kirk opened his arms wide and abandoned them. 'Verity, what a lovely surprise. And where's that man of yours?'

***

Her face as pale as ever, Verity Barron wore the same white padded coat she wore on the night of the fire, Sparks noticed.

The woman looked ghostly in the doorway and gave the three witches a wide birth, looking more than a little uncomfortable accepting Tom Kirk's theatrical embrace.

'Finn's gone round the back to check on the scenery they're making,' Verity said, wringing her hands together. 'Brr, it's cold today, don't you think? Winter's on its way.'

'At least the sun's still shining,' Kirk said. 'And long may that last.'

Attracted by the sight of Lady Macbeth standing on the box, with Colin Chirnside kneeling on the stone floor beside her, Verity edged further into the stone vaulted space, while Kirk went outside to look for Finn.

'As cold as a witch's tit,' Chirnside said. 'It's a lot bloody colder inside than out, dear. And for heaven's sake, don't anyone wish bad weather on us until after next weekend.' He struggled to his feet and reached up for Lady Macbeth's hand. 'Down you come, my love. Go and get changed and I'll run the hem up on the machine tonight. Don't want you tripping over it on the big day, do we?'

Sparks watched Lady Macbeth gather the skirts of her robe over one arm and shuffle over to the steep winding staircase in the north east corner.

They must be using the upper floor as a changing room.

Having moved from bright sunlight into cavernous gloom, attracted by the dress alteration activity going on, Verity must not have spotted them, for she jumped and laid a hand on her chest when Massey shifted position. 'Chief Inspector, Sergeant, I didn't see you.'

'How's your husband this morning, Mrs Barron,' Massey asked. 'Is he recovered?'

'Oh um… yes, completely. He's fine now. He's um…' She cast her eyes right, then left, as if desperately searching for something worth saying, but failed and wandered off towards the door instead.

Sparks noticed someone else was watching too. From beneath her spooky white eyelashes, through the cover provided by her still raucous fellow witches, Red's eyes followed Verity's every move, just as they'd followed Massey's at the charity night party. Yet Red's whole demeanour changed as soon as she heard Finn's voice outside.

Sparks would have liked to observe what happened, but Colin Chirnside tapped her arm. 'Come along dearie, I'll get you that book.'

CHAPTER 30

Finn Barron and Tom Kirk paused outside, allowing Sparks and Chirnside to pass through the door.

'They haven't got far, have they?' she heard Finn grumble. 'Are you sure it'll all be finished in time?

'Absolutely,' Kirk replied. 'All the pieces will be built, and they'll all have had at least their first coat of paint before this weekend's finished. We have every volunteer down to come in tomorrow and Sunday to get everything ready, and…'

Along with the cackling of witches, their words faded as Sparks followed Chirnside down the path towards the gate.

'Am I allowed to know why you need a copy of The Scottish Play, dear?'

As he said the words, Sparks recalled some superstition about the name of the play bringing bad luck if spoken within a theatre. She'd look it up later. 'I'm sorry, no.'

'Hmm. All mightily intriguing dear. Here we are then.' Chirnside stopped at a boxy Volvo estate that was so ancient it needed an actual key to unlock it. He opened the driver's door and reached across to the glove box.

'Now I want you to treat this book like a holy relic, dear. It's a precious object. To me anyway.'

He handed her a ragged brown paper package – an old A4 envelope folded in half.

'This is the full text of the original play, with a lot of my own scrawls included in the margins. It's probably fifty years old if it's a day, so it has seen better days. Just like it's owner. I trust you'll make sure it finds its way back to me when you're finished with it.'

'I'll return it to you myself as soon as possible.' She unfolded the top of the envelope and was about to reach inside to pull out the book, when Chirnside patted her hand.

'Best leave that until you're back at the hall. Don't want you dropping it in the muck.'

***

'Double, double, toil and trouble; fire burn and cauldron bubble.'

Three loud chanting voices reached them from inside the tower as they walked back up the path. The witches launching into their lines.

Chirnside gave an uncomfortable laugh. 'There they go again; rehearse, rehearse. Trinity needs the practice though, although she's slotted well into Ursula's place and hardly needs any direction. She's a natural. Could have been a great actress, I think, if she'd had a mind to go down that route…'

Sparks had no doubt at all that the woman had been born to play the part of a witch.

'…and I've yet to thank her for giving me the idea of doing this whole immersive theatre thing in the first place.'

About to ask him what he meant; Sparks was distracted by a single voice ringing out from inside. Not Red's voice.

'Cool it with a baboon's blood, then the charm is firm and good.'

The lines acted like a prompt, opening up a wormhole directly back to her old school assembly hall stage. '*O well done. I commend your pains,*' she chanted, the words coming automatically. '*And every one shall share i' the gains. And now about the cauldron sing, like elves and fairies in a ring, enchanting all that you put in.*'

Colin Chirnside stopped in his tracks. 'You know the part of Hecate. Good heavens girl.'

Sparks felt a flush mount in her cheeks. 'I um... played her at school.'

'She clearly made a big impression on you if you can still remember the lines at the drop of a hat.'

'It's not like she had a lot to say.'

'True, but still. Well done, dear. I did hear Trinny's comment before, but I don't agree with her. I believe Shakespeare not only wrote Hecate in himself, but borrowed her from Greek mythology. Did you know that?'

'I think I probably did, back then, but I'd forgotten.'

'Hecate is a goddess often depicted with three faces: the maiden, the mother and the crone. Or sometimes with the heads of three different animals; dog, snake and horse. Take your pick, whatever you fancy. I prefer the former.'

Sparks laughed. 'Me too.'

'Historically, there's an unholy symbolism to the number three, you know. Bad things come in threes; people still say that now. And good old Will took advantage of that fear in his plays, particularly in Macbeth. Three witches, three prophesies, three murders, another three prophesies, the three faces of Hecate, and on it goes.

She couldn't help but like this tubby, untidy man. She imagined they'd never be short of something to talk about. In fact a few minutes of chat passed before the voices from inside the tower intruded again.

A man's voice, Macbeth's lines.

Where the hell had he come from? No-one had passed them on the path.

'Whatever thou art, for thy good caution, thanks. Thou hast harped my fear aright, but one.'

Then, unmistakably, the voice of Red.

'He will not be commanded. Here's another, more potent than the first.'

Then immediately, the voice that had spoken the first solo line; the plump one? Betsy Halliwell, the physiotherapist or psychotherapist, or whatever the hell she called herself.

'Macbeth, Macbeth, Macbeth.'

Beside her, Chirnside winced. Then the male voice inside spoke again.

'Had I three ears, I'd hear thee.'

They'd reached the doorway now and could see a slice of inside. Finn and Verity Barron, Lady Macbeth, Tom Kirk and Massey, all in a loose circle around the three witches and the man playing Macbeth, who Sparks now recognised as one of the men who'd been banging and sawing around the back of the tower.

Betsy delivered the next line.

'Be bloody, bold, and resolute. Laugh to scorn the power of man, for none of woman born shall harm Macbeth.'

Chirnside leant in close and whispered. 'We've got the witches themselves saying these lines. You'll see in the book that it should have been ghostly apparitions conjured up by the witches, but we only have so much space here, and only so much interest among the locals for speaking parts.'

Sparks noticed Massey trying to catch her eye. He gave an infinitesimal nod towards Finn Barron, who was leaning in unnaturally towards the cauldron, listening to the lines spoken by the witches with a concentration that burned as fiercely as Stoneyriggs had. She wondered if Massey had also noticed the stare Red continued to level on Verity Barron.

She held up the book in its brown paper envelope and he nodded. They made their excuses to leave but Finn Barron, still entranced by the lines being spoken by the cast, barely acknowledged them.

As they walked down the path together, Sparks noticed Scarlett Crowley's voice for the first time as she delivered the third witch's prophesy that had faded away to nothing by the time they reached the gate, but she remembered the words anyway.

'Be lion-mettled, proud; and take no care who chafes, who frets, or where conspirers are. Macbeth shall never vanquished be, until Great Birnam wood to high Dunsinane Hill shall come against him.'

CHAPTER 31

The Drift Cafe was busy with a late lunch crowd. But then, it seemed to be a busy place all day, every day, inside and out. Co-incidentally, the only table available inside was the same one Sparks and Dazz had sat at last Sunday. How long ago did that seem now? And to think, all she'd been concerned about then had been the identities of Red and her little gang. But now they had arson and murder to investigate, and possibly a double murder if Fleur didn't survive.

While Massey went to the counter to order, Sparks unfolded the envelope and reached inside, her fingers encountering another wrapping. Polythene. She saw why as soon as she pulled the book clear. A little tatty, Chirnside had said, but Jesus what a sodding mess. The bloody thing looked like it had spent its whole fifty years on the floor being trampled on. The size of a slim modern paperback novel, the cloth-bound hardbacked volume had been slipped inside what looked like a freezer bag to stop it falling apart. The front cover was ripped and tattered and the broken spine looked as if it was clinging on by just a couple of threads, revealing cracked and crumbling glue no longer capable of holding together the motley arrangement of tattered and dog-eared pages that had yellowed with age.

She'd wanted to check something before Massey came back to the table, but didn't dare take the book out of its bag in here. With her luck, someone would jolt her elbow and the whole thing could go flying. It would have to wait until they got back to the village hall.

Anyway, Massey had something else on his mind when he returned. 'Did you notice, at the tower? Those two are definitely on something. I'm sure of it.'

'The Barrons. I agree.' It would certainly explain the pair's strange behaviour, and Verity's weirdly dilated pupils last night.

'If they weren't such middle-aged pillars of the community, I'd swear they spent their downtime sharing... Bugger.' He patted his pocket and pulled out his phone just as the ringtone finished its first chime. 'It's Portas. I'll take it outside.'

Through the window, Sparks watched him sidestep a peloton of cyclists in vivid Lycra dismounting and balancing their sleek mounts in a neat row on kickstands. With his mobile clamped to his ear, he wandered across the road towards the dunes and only halted when he could be sure no-one was within earshot.

A waiter deposited their order on the table just as he returned. Sparks prodded the stuffed roll on her plate. 'What the hell is this?'

'Exactly what you asked for, but in one of Trinny's poppy seed rolls. Thought we might as well try them, while we're here.'

'Did you now?'

'And we need to shove them down quick, because Portas is expecting us at HQ in an hour.'

***

Sparks hated to admit it, but Red's poppy seed roll had tasted divine. The woman had a talent. Another one, that was, as well as being an expert, calculating, man-eating bitch.

They called in at the village hall to drop off sandwiches for Donaldson and Jackson, and to ask Donaldson to email them the latest version of the Macbeth theory that they'd continued to work on. While Massey drove, she read it through and related new points to him. Donaldson had also sent her a link to the full text of Macbeth online. If he'd managed to track it down so easily, why the hell had she been unable to find it herself this morning? They hadn't needed to have gone to the tower earlier after all, although she was glad they had.

'Did Portas say whether Michael Duffy had been in touch with her?'

Frowning, he gave her a sideway look. 'I didn't ask. I think she'd have mentioned something if he had. Why?'

'It's another parallel to the play. We haven't been able to find him. His wife doesn't know where he is—'

'Or she chose not to tell us.'

'Perhaps, but I believed her. She had no idea where he was.'

'He could be home by now. Give them a ring.'

Sparks let the number ring until it cut out, unanswered. 'Maybe she's out with the dogs.'

'Or he has come home, and they both are.'

Sparks gave an exasperated sigh. 'Right, okay then. Have it your way. He came home, they've taken the dogs for a walk, and everything is hunky sodding dory.'

'Why are you so concerned?'

She thought of the lines she'd heard the three witches chanting in the tower. 'Because, in the play the witches give Macbeth a new set of prophesies. They tell him to beware Macduff, which makes Macbeth send men to kill him. But he isn't there, so they butcher his wife and children instead. And not just that. Like I told you before, Macduff had actually gone to England to see King Duncan's son Malcolm. He wants his help to raise an army that will defeat Macbeth and put Malcolm on the throne. But here's the thing. He didn't tell his wife where he was going.' She allowed her eyes to bore into the side of his head until he became uncomfortable.

'And?'

'And didn't Maureen Duffy tell us she thought Michael might be going to see Milo, Duncan Kingsley's son?'

'Why would she think that if he hadn't told her about it? Think about it for a moment. If Michael told his wife that much, then it sort of disproves your theory, doesn't it?'

CHAPTER 32

Portas had her vintage coffee percolator already bubbling when they arrived.

'Sit,' she told them, nodding to her little table by the window that looked out onto the back of a huge DIY outlet. 'I've been trying to make sense of the information Andrew Donaldson sent over for me. It's um… interesting. Although you're still going to have to lay it all out for me.'

Massey and Sparks sat side by side in silence at the table while Portas finished what she was doing. Sparks knew Massey would never throw her under a bus, but this was *her* theory when it came down to it, not his. Any flak was hers to take. But what if Portas refused to entertain the links that were to her glaring, and someone else was murdered?

'Alright then.' Portas strode across the room and dropped an A4 hard-backed notebook onto the table beside them. 'I'll pour the coffees while you two start explaining why you think we have a murderous Shakespeare fan on the rampage in Cresswell.'

Massey laid the palms of his hands on his knees. 'Well, you see—'

'I've got this,' Sparks said. 'If anyone's going to be shot down, it should be me, since I came up with the theory.'

Portas raised one eyebrow. 'I'm surprised. I thought wacky ideas were your department, James.'

Sparks took a bracing breath. 'We need to go back to last year—'

'Is this going to upset Durham?'

'Yes, I think it might, ma'am.'

'Oh goody. Fun times ahead.'

'I have no idea how much you know about Macbeth, ma'am, so if it's alright by you, I'll lay it out pretty much the way I did this morning. Just the essentials of the play so you can see where I'm coming from.'

Portas nodded. 'Go ahead.'

'You see, in the first act Macbeth demonstrates his bravery in helping King Duncan to win a great victory in battle. Later, on the heath, he and his best mate Banquo come across three witches, who make three prophesies.'

Sparks began counting on her fingers.

'One, they tell Macbeth that he'll be awarded a new title in honour of his bravery and, two, that he will later become king. Banquo asks them to tell his future too, so they make a third prophesy. They say that while Banquo won't be king himself, his decendants would be.

'So anyway, when Macbeth is awarded the title Thane of Cawdor, he sees that the first prophesy has come true, and he tells his wife that the witches also said he'll become king. She really fancies the idea of being queen, so she encourages him to believe he could take the throne straight away if only he'd be prepared to murder King Duncan. She'd even help him to do it. And that's what they do. When the king visits their castle, she drugs his guards, Macbeth kills the king, and then she plants the knives Macbeth used on the sleeping guards and makes sure they have the king's blood on them, so they'll be blamed for the murder.

'Now then, last year our old Chief Super Duncan Kingsley, who was also president of the Ellington & Cresswell Rugby Football Club, was murdered while walking on the beach next to Finn Barron's house. Three landscapers, who went to give Barron a quote for work at his own house, are getting the blame. These blokes had already done some work for Kingsley. Now you have to bear in mind that Barron is ambitious, in his own little world. Back then, he was the rugby club's vice president. Technically he still is, although he's been acting as president since Kingsley's death, and he'd made no secret of the fact he intended to stand against Duncan for the presidency once his term came to an end. We've been told by more than one person that Barron's wife Verity, is also ambitious, although that's not what comes across to us—'

Portas held up a hand and opened her notebook.

'Alright then, let me write this down. You're equating Finn and Verity Barron with Macbeth and Lady Macbeth. And yes, I get that a thane in the play is a bit like a baron, so you have the link with the name. You've also got Duncan Kingsley as King Duncan, and Ben Quinn as this Banquo fellow, and both actual names are markedly similar to those of the characters.'

'That's right, ma'am. And Banquo had a son called Fleance who, according to the witches, might well become king. While Ben Quinn's daughter is called…'

'Fleur.'

'Right, ma'am. And Fleur has been pushing for women's rugby at the club, which Barron doesn't like at all and might have seen as a challenge to his bid for presidency. So in the play, Macbeth – now a murderer – fears he'll eventually be bumped off by Banquo or Fleance so that Fleance, or another as yet unborn son can take the throne, and so he sends some assassins to kill them. They manage to kill Banquo, but Fleance escapes.'

'And you think that's synonymous with Quinn's murder.'

'Yes, ma'am. I know Fleur didn't exactly escape, but she's survived so far.'

'On the night of the charity match party,' Massey said, 'both Ben Quinn and Michael Duffy told me and Guy Keegan that they believe Durham are about to charge the wrong men for Duncan Kingsley's murder and that Finn Barron is desperate to be elected club president. I don't remember either of them actually putting those two beliefs together and coming up with Barron being responsible for Kingsley's murder though. Not then at least, although Duffy is now going round telling anyone who will listen that Barron *is* responsible for the deaths of both Kingsley and Quinn.'

Portas turned to Sparks. 'And this Michael Duffy, in your theory, is Macduff?'

'Yes, ma'am.'

'And what happens to him in the play?'

'Macbeth becomes angry once he realises Macduff suspects him. He sends men to Macduff's castle to kill him and his family, but Macduff isn't there and Lady Macduff doesn't know where he is. She and her children are then murdered.'

Portas looked at the ceiling. 'Isn't it all too convenient though? Who'd even consider basing two murders on a famous play by William Shakespeare, in a small community that's busily rehearsing their performance of the exact same play, and expect no-one to put it together?'

'Ma'am, about Duffy—'

'Why on earth would someone like Barron incriminate himself in such a way? It's his own counterpart in the play who is the villain, so why would he draw attention to himself like that. I think it's much more likely that whoever is doing this is trying to frame him.'

'You do believe all this then?' Massey asked.

'I think it has to be considered seriously.' She gave a short laugh. 'But I'd rather not be the one who has to lay it out for Durham just when they're about to tie the Duncan Kingsley inquiry up in a bow.'

'Ma'am, I think we need—'

'I mean, can you imagine their faces when they hear all this?

'*Ma'am.*'

Portas gave Sparks her full attention. 'You have something more to say, Christine?'

'I do, ma'am. I'm concerned about Mr and Mrs Duffy. We went to his address this morning to speak to him. His wife said he wasn't in, and she didn't know where he was. On the way here I tried to call the house, but no-one answered.'

'And you're saying what? That this relates to the play where Macduff disappears, and his wife doesn't know where he's gone?'

'Yes ma'am, and then she and her family are murdered.'

'Do the Duffy's have children?'

'If they have, I don't believe they live at home now. They have two dogs though, who Maureen Duffy described this morning as her babies.'

'And who would raise the roof, like they did with us this morning,' Massey said, 'if a stranger turned up.'

'But what if the murderer is not a stranger?'

***

When Massey and Sparks called in at the Duffy's house on their way back to Cresswell, they found both at home in the garden.

'Thank God for that.' Sparks looked nervously towards the open front door as they climbed out of the car. 'But where are the dogs?'

Michael Duffy spotted them first.

He strode over to the gate. 'Come to arrest me?'

'Just an unofficial warning at this point,' Massey said, 'against making any more defamatory statements.'

'Don't worry,' Duffy gave them both a wry grin. 'I've had an official warning already from the missus to keep my big trap shut. And she's told me in no uncertain terms exactly what will happen if I disobey.'

Massey laughed.

'Where are the dogs?' Sparks still expected them to come flying around the corner of the bungalow at any moment, howling like wolves.

'Out. Maureen pays a dogwalker to give them a nice long run two or three times a week.'

On the far side of the garden, Maureen Duffy dropped an armful of autumn leaves into a wheelbarrow and waved. Massey waved back. 'Shame, I'd like to have seen them. Siberian Huskies, I understand.'

'That's right, big vicious buggers, they are.' Duffy looked directly at Sparks, then laughed. 'Not.'

'Have you had any strange visitors recently, Michael, or noticed anyone hanging around?'

'You mean besides yourselves? No, no-one. And Maureen would have said if anyone had called while I was out. Why?'

'Just enquiring.'

'Oh yes? Just idle curiosity then. My backside, it is. Well you don't need to worry about us. The dogs would let us know as soon as anyone set foot through the gate.'

Massey hoped Duffy was right. He'd had a bad feeling in his gut ever since Sparks had convinced him of the links between their investigation and the play; not least because he knew it meant he was going to have to read the bloody thing for himself.

CHAPTER 33

Since they'd got back from checking on the Duffy's, Massey had been fielding questions from Sparks as best he could. He knew she could tell something was up with him. He could see she had a good idea it concerned Trinny, but he had no intention of actually getting into a conversation with her about it, particularly not with others around. But by 6 pm, she gave up on their standoff and went home, leaving him alone. He suspected she had a date with Dazz. He could have ribbed her about it and made their standoff a Mexican one, but he knew the whole concept of 'going out' with a man, particularly a father of small children who'd only recently split from his wife, still made her uncomfortable, and he couldn't do that to her.

If only she felt the same when it came to *his* private life.

Donaldson and Jackson had left at around five thirty after a discussion about whether it was worth depriving the community of their village hall for any longer. All the witness interviews they'd wanted to carry out with locals had been done, but the hall wasn't suitable for anything more formal. Anyone pulled in as a suspect would need to be taken to their main base in Wallsend, with all of its facilities. Or, at a push, to the nearest 24-hour access station at Hartington, since that was much closer to Cresswell. But he was loath to hand back the keys just yet, since it would take him away from Trinny, and from a little boy who could be his son.

He'd agonised all day about how, or even if he should go and knock on her door. And how he could possibly broach the subject if he did? Should he use the pretence of wanting to ask more questions relating to the case, or just be honest and ask her outright if he was the father of her ten-year-old boy? He still couldn't decide. He suspected it would all depend on whatever words came tumbling out of his mouth when, *if,* he found himself alone with her.

He looked at his watch. Not half six yet. Any boy Max's age would surely still be up watching television or doing homework, if kids even got homework at that age. He couldn't exactly have the sort of conversation he needed with Trinny in front of him. And besides, technically she hadn't yet been cleared of any involvement in their case. And until she was, he'd be playing with fire in exploring any sort of personal connection with her. Even the teeniest possibility there could be, or previously had been something personal between them should be reported to Portas. But if he did that, he could be removed from the case. And then he'd have even less of an excuse to see her, or her boy, who could be his too.

Christ's sake, was he going to hang around here all evening until he could be sure a ten-year-old would be asleep in bed? No he bloody wasn't. And he wasn't going to do any more reading of Macbeth either. He was going home to catch up on his own sleep. He needed to be up and out early, before Helen turned up with a van. She hadn't said exactly when she was coming over, but he wasn't about to leave it to chance.

***

Massey checked the hall's front door a final time and slipped the keys into his pocket. Looking up at the twilight sky, he made his way around the side of the building to the small car park, where the slow rhythm of the tide rattled pebbles over the rocks only metres away. Hard to believe this peaceful little village could harbour a murdering arsonist.

Backing out of his space in the small car park, with the merest sliver of dark shadow marring the circular perfection of last night's full Hunter's Moon, still low in the sky, he thought of Trinny. Of course he did. He hadn't known eleven years ago that her surname was Moon, but now he'd think of her every time he saw the blasted thing up there in the sky.

But then he had another thought. Max Moon? His son's name was Max bloody Moon? Somewhere in the back of his mind a bell rang. Was Max Moon a fantasy character maybe, from his own childhood?

He laughed at himself. Max might not even *be* his son. The fact the boy looked so much like his mother gave him no clues. If he'd had dark hair and was a head taller than your average ten-year-old, then he could have been—

Jesus!

Trinny Moon planted both hands on the bonnet of his car in shock. She'd stepped right out in front of him, for Christ's sake. She could have got herself killed.

Although, at less than ten miles an hour, he couldn't have done her too much damage. But for God's sake, he'd heard the impact as he'd hit her.

He flung open the car door and rushed over. 'Are you alright?'

Trinny put one hand over her mouth and the other on his chest. Blinking hard in his headlights, she nodded. 'I'm okay, I think.'

He saw a dark patch near her lower lip, where her hand had been.

'You're bleeding. Here, let me see.'

He tried to take hold of her hand, but she pulled it away.

'It's nothing. I'm fine.'

'What the hell were you doing, walking out in front of the car like that?'

'I… I wanted to catch you before you left. I needed to see you.'

He felt her melting against him. He wanted so much to take her in his arms and kiss her. Every single nerve in his body tingled with desire. Eleven whole years hadn't dimmed the flame even one iota. But this couldn't happen. He pushed her away. Held her for a moment at arm's length to make sure she was steady on her feet before dropping his arms to his side. He couldn't allow any more speculation to arise if someone happened to be watching them. Yes, he wanted to talk to her. He *needed* to talk to her so much it ached. But not here, and not like this.

She reached out her uninjured hand, grasped the lapel of his jacket and took a step closer, trying to draw him back into her embrace.

'No.' He brushed her away and stepped back. 'We can't do this.'

'You want it as much as I do. I can see the lust in your eyes. Remember that night, James? I do. I've never—'

'*No.*' This felt so wrong. He put both hands up, warding her off. 'We can't do this. That was then, this is now. I'm investigating a murder and you're—'

Her face twisted. 'I'm what? Involved? A suspect? You bastard.'

'No, not that. But I can't get involved with you now. You must see that.'

Jesus, this was so not the way he'd wanted this conversation to go. He almost suggested he unlock the hall again so they could talk properly inside, but he didn't think he'd be able to keep his hands off her, or hers off him. And that absolutely could not happen. She was a single mother in a community he was investigating for murder. Anything between them now could only ever be seen by others as an abuse of his powers of office over her.

Just a moment. She was a mother…

'Where's Max?'

'Watching the TV, or playing on his Nintendo. I knew you were about to leave. I wanted to—'

'You've left him on his own?'

'He's ten-years-old, not two. He's perfectly alright on his own for half an hour.'

'I can't believe you've left him—'

'Why, because you think he's yours?' She laughed out loud. 'I could have shagged half a dozen blokes on that holiday, James. You might not even have been the first. Any one of them could be Max's father.'

Shock hit him like a left hook to the jaw. Sparks' words on the subject of this woman flooded his brain. He grabbed Trinny's arms and shook her. 'And did you? Was I just one of many poor suckers you lured to your caravan?'

Trinny's mouth twisted into a sneer. 'Oh, don't worry. You made it perfectly clear what you thought of me back then. A quick leg over and then not even a goodbye. Sneaking away like that. Leaving me with—'

'You mean he *is* my son?'

'Max is *my* son. He's never had a father. You had no rights then and you have none now.' She shook off his hands and ran.

He let her go; his blood pounding too hard in his veins for him to process her words. He felt dizzy. He needed to sit down before he fell down.

Back behind the wheel, he waited for all the raw emotions to abate.

Elation. Despair. *Grief.*

He had a son, but he'd lost a daughter. Max would have been just a little younger than his half-sister, if she hadn't died through miscarriage *because* he'd been conceived.

And perhaps his marriage could have been happy, if he'd never met Trinny, if he hadn't given in to his baser impulses.

But then he wouldn't now be finding out he was the father of a ten-year-old boy.

He had a son.

He felt sick. Tears welled in his eyes.

Christ's sake, he needed to pull himself together. He glanced around, wondering if they'd been spotted. But there was no-one in sight outside, any houses facing in this direction were much too far away for anyone inside to have been able to see them clearly anyway, and none of the nearby buildings had windows overlooking the village hall car park. Except the dwelling attached to the ice cream shop. Maybe someone could have spotted them from there, but that was all.

In which case… how did Trinny know to come along at precisely that moment, exactly as he was leaving?

That's what she'd said, wasn't it? That she'd wanted to catch him before he left.

But how could she have known he was still here?

CHAPTER 34

Massey cooked himself a huge plate of chips and ate them with two steak and ale pies. For some reason, he felt ravenous. Way too hungry to want to spend the time cooking something more nutritious. He felt a need to share his news with someone, but couldn't think who.

Sparks was the obvious person, since she already had more than an inkling. But that wasn't happening. Not with her current opinion of Trinny. And, besides, she'd probably be with Dazz.

He couldn't tell his mother. Not without some preparation work first, that she'd suddenly become a grandmother to a ten-year-old boy. Nor any other member of his family come to that. Not yet.

So Keegan then? He'd become as good a friend as he'd ever had over the last year or so. But wasn't Keegan's wife due back sometime today?

And should he really be wanting to celebrate his sudden acquisition of a son anyway, when the boy's very existence was so closely linked to the death of his unborn daughter and the collapse of his marriage?

His stomach still churned, but not with hunger. It was all the emotions inside him warring with each other.

He paced the room, picking things up, then putting them down. He flopped down on the settee and flicked through the channels on the TV, finding nothing capable of holding his attention.

No way would he be getting much sleep tonight.

He looked at the whisky bottle. Nope. The last thing he wanted was to go down that route tonight. And, particularly when he might have to deal with Helen tomorrow.

She'll be livid once she finds out.

He heard his mobile beep. A text; from Terry Flint. Keegan's promise to have a word with the DCI had paid dividends.

He was just about to open the message when his phone rang in his hand. Control. He accepted the call.

A suspicious death. In Cresswell.

CHAPTER 35

What had they missed? This could have been prevented. They should have prevented it, somehow.

But if they'd shared with the Duffys the reasons for their concern, would they have listened?

Michael certainly wouldn't have.

The initial investigator had established an outer perimeter by blocking Cresswell Road in both directions until CSIs could take a close look at the road and pavement surfaces and gather any evidence. Tyre track impressions, footprints, discarded litter, anything at all.

From the gate, which formed the inner perimeter, he could see that a forensic tent had already been erected against the front door. The deceased, still inside, would remain there until permission was given by the pathologist to remove the body, which could take some time. He hoped they'd get Lorraine French, but that wasn't a given.

He'd requested Zafar Davani as Crime Scene Manager, and had been gratified to see him already there when he arrived.

'I just live in Pegswood,' Davani told him. 'No distance away.'

'Glad to have you here.' And he was. Davani was the best CSM they had.

'The husband made the call,' Davani said. 'Michael Duffy.'

'We just spoke to him here this afternoon.'

'He must have gone out later then. He found his wife slaughtered and their two dogs missing when he came back. He managed to call 999 but then collapsed with a suspected heart attack inside. Responding officers had to get an ambulance for him.'

'Jesus, so we've had medics tramping their size twelves all over inside then?'

'Afraid so. They were still here when I arrived. It's going to make our job difficult.'

'If there's anything to find, Zafar,' Massey said. 'I know your team will find it.'

Davani laughed. 'It's a miracle you're looking for then?'

'How long since the ambulance left?'

Davani stroked the screen of his tablet then looked at his watch. 'Not even ten minutes. They've taken him to NSEC.' Massey clicked a number on his phone and raised it to his ear. They needed someone at the hospital as soon as possible in case Duffy had anything to tell them when he came round. If he came round at all. He also wanted to know why the man had gone out again, and where to.

***

There were other houses dotted around, but the Duffys' bungalow, already sheltered on all sides by a high hedge, had no immediate neighbours. He hadn't held out much hope of anyone having spotted any unusual activity but, on the off chance, he'd sent officers to call at every house further up this end of the road, and a couple in the other direction. He'd also asked Donaldson to check with local bus companies about what services would have run to and from Cresswell on this road over the past few hours. With luck there'll have been a double-decker going past, with someone observant sitting upstairs. That would be the only way anyone might have got a glimpse of the killer from over the hedge.

There was no certainty though that the killer had gained access to the property from the front. The first responder, a native of Ellington, had told him that when he was a kid, there'd always been an accessible gate in the hedge at the rear of the property that led out into woodland.

After checking with Davani, he'd sent Sparks round there with a uniformed officer and a CSI to see if it still existed and establish security on it.

She should have been back by now. Once the CSIs had marked out and cleared an ingress route to the front door, Davani had promised to let him know, and he wanted her with him when he went inside.

Sparks slid up beside him while he was looking in the other direction and made him jump. 'It looks well-used. Opens onto a path which leads into that woodland over there.' She pointed over his shoulder at the tree line that ran parallel to the east boundary of the bungalow. 'Looks like that's probably the way they go when they take the dogs out. The murderer could easily have entered and escaped that way.'

'Any signs of that?'

'Hard to tell. We were careful. The CSI did his bit in the immediate vicinity outside of the gate and was happy to leave the constable round there. He'll let Zafar know about the path, so it gets included.'

Massey pulled up a map on his phone and stroked his finger slowly on the screen.

'According to this, there's an access road to Golden Sands Caravan Park through those woods. It starts on Cresswell Road just a little further down from here, and runs down to that big entrance on Beach Road, just before Finn Barron's house. So anyone cutting through the woods could have gone that way.'

'Maybe someone needs to get over to the Barrons' house ASAP then. See if we can catch the bastard before he can dispose of the weapon or any of the clothes he wore.'

'Even if the killer went that way, it doesn't have to mean it was him, but I agree, we need to check. I'll get Madge onto it.'

'Who's at the hospital with Duffy?'

'Phil Jackson. He went straight over and met the ambulance there.'

'Will Duffy pull through, do you think?'

'Still hanging in there last time Phil called. But it wasn't looking good.'

'I hate to say this—'

'I know. You told me so.'

'That's right. I did. It's the plot of Macbeth all over again. Except in Macbeth, Macduff survives and helps King Duncan's son raise an army against Macbeth.'

'Maybe this killer meant for Duffy to survive too,' he said. 'They couldn't possibly have known he'd have a heart attack.'

'He's not dead yet. And if the killer *is* Barron, regardless of the play, surely Duffy would have been his main target. The bloke's been accusing him in public of two other murders.'

'Maybe he expected him to be home too. However it went down, Durham are going to have to reconsider their case against the three landscapers for Duncan Kingsley's murder now.'

'Sir?' The voice came from one of the CSIs. 'You can go in, just as soon as you're suited up.'

Massey nodded his thanks.

***

Walking up the drive, single file, keeping between the tapes, Massey felt the familiar clench in his belly. He'd be concerned for his own humanity if he didn't feel apprehension at what he was about to witness: the horror that one human being could inflict on another.

They stepped through the forensic tent onto metal treadplates in a hallway lit by a crime scene tripod lamp. The same hallway he and Sparks had looked into on their first visit, with the door at the end that had thumped and rattled in its frame with the weight of the baying dogs behind it. The one and only time either of them had actually spoken to Maureen Duffy.

The floor was a mess of smeared and overlapping bloody footprints, trailed through from the room at the end. Duffy's prints initially, most likely, which had then been trampled over repeatedly by the paramedics who'd attended him. Intent on saving his life, they wouldn't have given a thought to the detritus they'd scattered in their wake. The wrappings and backing from the electrodes they'd attached to his chest, a narrow torn-off strip of electronic printout paper.

Davani was right. They needed a miracle.

On the other side of the door lay a cramped multi-functional space that must operate not only as kitchen diner, but as a snug too. In the doorway a large patch of moulted white fur matted the carpet; clearly the preferred sleeping place of at least one of the missing dogs, and marred now by Maureen Duffy's blood. Arterial spray, they saw, from a huge gaping wound in Maureen's neck.

Attacked from behind while sitting, she'd slid forward in an armchair, feet splayed and knees almost touching the pool of blood on the floor;

her back arched across its seat, and her head lodged unnaturally between two crochet-covered cushions. At least that was the most likely explanation for her position.

His eyes were drawn to a pucker right at the edge of the blood pool, a forensic marker just to one side of it. The edge of a shoe print perhaps?

Maureen had changed for bed and her blood-soaked nightdress had rucked up around plump bare thighs. Massey's belly turned cold at the thought she might have been sexually assaulted, but after a second look he didn't believe she had. It looked more as if her nightdress had clung to the pile of the chair's fabric as her body slid forward in death.

With one gloved hand over his facemask, he examined Maureen's lifeless body for other injuries but saw none. He found this so much harder to do when he'd previously met the victim in life. The fact he'd only been having a conversation with Maureen this morning made it ten times worse. She'd been so vivacious, so full of life.

He felt sick.

CHAPTER 36

Saturday, 19 October 2024

Three in the morning, and Massey's eyes burned with the tiredness of a multitude of sleepless nights. They'd left Davani and his team to it a couple of hours ago when Lou Portas had arrived, and had adjourned to the village hall. Just the three of them at the table in the conservatory for now, with strong coffees and a packet of chocolate biscuits, and Colin Chirnside's tattered copy of Macbeth open before Sparks.

'Here, this is the bit we heard up at the tower this morning. It's where the three witches meet Macbeth again to give him three more prophesies. In the full play the witches show him three apparitions, and it's the apparitions who deliver the prophesies, but here in Cresswell we have the witches themselves delivering them. So, the first apparition – some sort of armed head – tells Macbeth he needs to "beware Macduff". Then a bloody child appears to deliver the second one, telling him that "none of woman born shall harm Macbeth". There's a twist at the end related to that one. Do you want to hear it.'

Massey felt the nerves in his jaw tingle and scrubbed his face. 'Christ sake, Christine, it's not the punchline of the latest blockbuster. Just tell us.'

She sniffed. 'Okay. So it *is* a man who kills Macbeth in the end. It's Macduff, who it turns out was delivered by caesarean section, so not technically born of woman. Now do you want to hear the third prophesy, or not?'

Portas sighed and raised one eyebrow.

Sparks huffed. 'The third apparition is a crowned child, who tells Macbeth he'll never be defeated "until Great Birnam Wood to high Dunsinane Hill shall come against him", which of course he believes could never happen because trees don't move. Do you want to hear the punchline for that one too?'

Before Massey could respond, Portas jumped in. 'We're none of us here at this time in the morning for the hell of it.'

Sparks jutted her chin. 'Macduff has gone to England to find King Duncan's son, Malcolm. They raise an army and march back to Scotland. As they approach Macbeth's castle at Dunsinane Hill, they disguise themselves with cut branches from the trees of Great Birnam Wood as they pass through, so that it looks to the people inside the castle as if the woods themselves are moving.'

Portas leant back in her chair and rubbed her head hard with both hands. 'How is this relevant to Maureen Duffy.'

Delicately, Sparks leafed through loose pages.

'Earlier in the play, Macbeth is upset because he knows Macduff is suspicious and can never be loyal to him. He's even refused to come to their banquet, where Macbeth sees the ghost of Banquo. That's why Macbeth goes back to the witches for more prophesies. And look what's happened in real life. How could Finn Barron not be upset about the way Michael Duffy has been ranting about him being a murderer?

'Yes, unlike Macduff, Duffy *did* go to the banquet – or at least to the fund-raising celebration do at the rugby club – but he had a right grumble about Barron, and he disappeared as soon as the bloke fell ill.'

Portas' pen scratched as she jotted down notes.

'The first apparition tells Macbeth to beware Macduff, and this afternoon Barron heard one of the witches say that same line at the tower. James, you saw his face. He was acting really weird, wasn't he?'

Massey had to admit that he was.

'So then Macbeth sends people to kill the Macduff family, but Macduff himself isn't there. They still kill Lady Macduff and their children though. And look what's happened tonight; someone has murdered Maureen Duffy. And look who wasn't there. Michael bloody Duffy.'

Portas dropped her pen on the table and rubbed her temples with steepled fingers. 'You've got my head done in with all this. What are you saying here? That Finn Barron sent someone to kill the Duffys? Who?'

'Or he did it himself. The killer's most likely route away from the bungalow leads almost to his door.'

'Don't he and his wife have alibis for the Ben Quinn and Duncan Kingsley murders?'

'Not for Ben's,' Massey said. 'They claim they were both at home, but we've found no-one to prove or disprove that.'

'And where else could that path from the bungalow lead to?'

The weakest point in their story.

Massey pushed through the door to grab an Ordnance Survey map from Donaldson's makeshift desk.

'Fill the kettle and switch it on while you're through there,' Portas shouted.

'Yes, ma'am,' he grumbled.

***

The map, once unfolded and spread across the table, gave Massey a much clearer sense of the terrain than the limited what3words app view he'd been looking at on his phone screen. Immediately, they could see that the killer's probable escape route from the back of the Duffy's bungalow could just as easily have taken them to any one of the five hundred or so caravans and lodges spread over both Cresswell Towers and Golden Sands holiday parks or, with a little deviation, to pretty much anywhere else in the village.

'As soon as it's light, I want those woods searched,' Portas said, getting to her feet and peering through the blinds towards the sea.

'Already sorted.'

It was one of the first things Massey had arranged as soon as they knew about the gate, and the Police Search Adviser had already been in communication with Zafar before they'd left the scene.

'We've got Jodie O'Neill as PolSA. Her team should be arriving around half six, seven-ish.' He looked at his watch. 'Jesus, in less than two hours. It won't be light enough under the tree canopy until around eight for a proper search.'

'Good. And we need to be talking to Durham, as soon as.'

'Actually, I got a text from DCI Terry Flint just before we got this call out. He's the SIO on the case over there. Haven't had time to even read it yet.' He pulled his phone out of his pocket and scrolled, looking for the text.

'Never mind a bloody text, we need a proper conversation with him, and we need access to…' Nose in the air, Portas turned around. 'Is that fresh bread I can smell?'

Sparks rolled her eyes.

Massey turned away in case the flush he felt inside had spread across his face. 'That's the Blue Moon Bakery. It's a small enterprise at the back of South Side cottages along the road.'

Eyes closed; Portas inhaled deeply. 'God, it's got my belly feeling as if my throat's been cut.'

Massey glanced at the empty chocolate biscuit packet scrunched up on the table. Portas had eaten more than her fair share of those.'

'Is it too early to buy some?' she asked.

'It's not a shop. She supplies local cafés.'

'Might she make an exception, do you think? I'm sure you could sweet talk her.'

Sparks snorted, but clamped her lips together when he gave her a warning look. After Trinny's vicious response to him almost running her over last night, he didn't think he could sweet talk her into anything.

'I think that's a great idea,' Sparks said with a wicked twinkle. 'I'm a bit peckish myself. How about you and me both go round there now, James?'

CHAPTER 37

'Good morning,' Sparks said.

Trinny jumped, sending a plastic container and its contents clattering to the ground in the little covered courtyard. She got down on her knees. 'What the hell do you two want,' she hissed, 'at this time in the morning?'

Massey had no idea what to say to her. He crouched down to help her pick up clusters of little dried seed pods.

'Our boss has got a whiff of your baking,' Sparks said, matching her own voice to Trinny's muted tone. 'She's hoping you might be able to spare a few buns. She's hungry.'

'I um… Yes, I could probably do that. I always make extra.'

'How about the poppy seed rolls? They're delicious. We tried them at The Drift.'

Trinny's hand bumped into Massey's, and she flinched, almost overturning the tub again. 'I think so. Yes, I have enough of those. Will a dozen do you?'

'More than enough,' Massey said. He twirled a sprig of the brown pods in his fingers as Trinny jumped to her feet. 'What are these?'

'They're um… They're seeds from the Morning Glory over there. It's become a sort of emblem for my business, I suppose. But it's an annual, so I need to collect the seeds if I want to regrow them next year. Please, just leave them. I'll get your rolls.'

They followed her into the kitchen. She crossed straight to a small sink and washed her hands.

On one of the counters stood an open Kilner jar, part filled with small black seeds and surrounded by papery fragments. From the pods, presumably.

Further along, below a shelf of flour containers – four different varieties, according to the labels – and a row of glass jars holding seeds of all sizes, they saw a small grinder, empty now, next to a jar of what looked like black grit.

Trinny turned from the sink just as Sparks bent forward to get a whiff of the grinder. 'You'll not smell much in there. It's ground poppy seeds. I do a seeded batch loaf too, and I always put some ground seeds into the flour, as well as the whole ones. I go through kilos of all kinds of seeds.'

She lined a paper carrier with a large sheet of crinkly paper and carefully laid twelve rolls inside.

Massey reached into his pocket for his wallet and pulled out a ten pound note. 'How much do we owe you.'

'You don't. I don't have any change. Buy me a drink if you see me out again.'

Sparks jumped in before he could spout whatever nonsense would have come out of his mouth. 'Thank you. That's very generous.'

CHAPTER 38

Clutching her hands beneath her chin, feeling the rough skin on her knuckles, still greasy from the hydrocortisone ointment she'd applied, Verity stared through the back bedroom window at the pale figures in the tree line. Mere specks in the distance, like ghosts against the darkness of the woods.

'Forensic suits.'

She flinched. Finn had crept right up close. She hadn't heard a thing, but now every nerve jangled. She'd thought he was still downstairs.

'They're searching for something.'

She could see that herself. She didn't need him to point it out, as if she were stupid. She'd spotted them earlier from the landing window. They must have started as soon as it was light. Something else dreadful must have happened through the night.

'There'll be police at our door again before long.' Finn said. 'They'll already be speaking to people on the holiday parks.'

Verity realised she'd begun wringing her hands again, smearing the ointment away from where it needed to be. She tried to still them.

She had an appointment this afternoon. Without Finn.

Yesterday, he'd gone out without telling her. When he came back, he told her he'd been to the doctor's, like she'd wanted him to, and his GP was sending him for an emergency appointment at Wansbeck Hospital, today, and he did not want her with him.

It had felt like a slap in the face at the time; an attempt to punish her for losing her temper, which had come as much of a shock to her as it had to him.

It had taken a while to realise it gave her an opportunity to do something she'd been considering lately, so she'd sent a text to Betsy asking if she could possibly fit her in for an initial session at the same time as Finn's appointment. Betsy agreed, and Verity had spent the time since then worrying if she'd done the right thing.

She had no intention of telling Finn. If he knew, he'd try to stop her going. He'd turned her into a quivering wreck over the years, and it suited him to keep her that way, despite all the rubbish he told his friends about her being so demanding.

But, since staring into that pulsing black void in the midst of the Stoneyriggs flames, she'd finally realised what he'd done to her.

He'd spent their entire marriage disempowering and manipulating her. All the bullying and the affairs. Why had it taken her so long to realise she'd married a monster? And just how big a monster was he? Could he really be guilty of the terrible things she now suspected him of?

She'd told the police he was here with her all afternoon on the day of the fire, but he'd gone out. Not for long, but he *had* gone out.

Still behind her, Finn grabbed her arms in a vice-like grip and she clamped her lips together to prevent a yelp of pain from escaping. 'You won't forget what you need to tell them,' he said, 'will you?'

Fresh tears squeezed their way between lashes she'd screwed shut.

Finn shook her. 'Will you?'

She jerked her head in agreement. 'I... I won't.'

'Good. Now, I think it's time we had breakfast, don't you? You remembered to take the rolls out of the freezer, didn't you?'

CHAPTER 39

Massey handed some keys for the village hall to Inspector Brian Truman of the NPT for his team and the search team to use. By seven, he'd decamped his own team to Area Command. The first thing he did on arrival was to call Terry Flint, who didn't sound overjoyed to hear from him.

'Heard you caught another one in Cresswell last night.'

'We did, so we need a conversation about Duncan Kingsley's murder.'

'You think we've got it wrong.'

Massey didn't respond,

Flint gave a bitter laugh. 'I assume you've come up with an alternative theory.'

'Oh, you're going to love it. How about if I come over there this morning and we can discuss it.'

'No chance. The press are on high alert. I don't want them spotting Northumbria coppers and publishing another load of crap. You won't have had time to notice, but we caught a big one of our own last night. A farmer near Sacriston went ape-shit and slaughtered his family, then came and turned himself in, as calm as you like. Not my case, but the journos are swarming. So I'll come to you if you don't mind.'

That suited Massey. Travelling to and from Durham would have eaten into what was doubtless going to be a ball-breaker of a day. It gave him time to go home for a quick shower and shave before Helen turned up. Not that he expected her being early – she'd never been early for anything in her life. And since she couldn't fail to know he was leading the investigation in Cresswell, she'd probably assume he'd be out all day and night anyway. So why hurry? But still, he pulled out his mobile and set it to silent while he remembered, so he wouldn't have to deal with her calls later when she found out what he'd done.

He looked over to Ana's desk, where Sparks was using her hands as a talking aid as she attempted to explain their theory so Ana could add the essentials to a presentation. More than once, Ana's eyebrows almost shot off the top of her head. They'd be getting a lot of that kind of reaction before everyone got their outlandish Macbeth theory.

Portas had already informed Chief Superintendent Crowder of the latest developments and how they could relate to Duncan Kingsley's murder. Rather her, Massey had thought, than him. The Chief already considered him a magnet for weirdness.

Then she'd summoned him an hour ago to tell him Keegan would be moving over to the team temporarily. 'You could do with more bodies on this one,' she'd said. 'He's already been involved peripherally anyway, and he has a good depth of knowledge on the rugby club and the characters we're dealing with. And besides, he's ready for a break from all those cold cases for a while.'

Massey wasn't going to argue. He and Keegan worked well together, and he'd like to see him brought back into the fold again. In his opinion, Keegan had done enough penance since his fall from grace last year that had almost finished his career. His exemplary work since then on the Operation Casper cold case files should have been enough to cancel out all his bad press.

And here he was now, teeth bared in a huge grin that almost split his bearded face in two, raising his insulated coffee mug towards him. 'Nice one, mate.'

Massey raised his own mug. It had been Portas' idea, not his. But a good one. Particularly when they were about to lose Madge Brown to retirement. Maybe this was exactly the right solution for the team in the long run, never mind just for this case. He still needed another sergeant though, and he'd had a thought about that. But that was for another day. It was half nine now, and this would be the first time even some of his own team had heard the Macbeth theory laid out in full, let alone Terry Flint.

***

Flint looked nothing like Massey had imagined him. He'd pictured a stocky, no-nonsense bruiser, not this scrawny stick insect of a man, who looked ill. A dogtooth jacket hung on narrow shoulders as it would on a coat hanger and, with so little meat on the man, his black trousers threatened to slide to the floor at any moment.

But Flint's deep-set eyes betrayed no weakness. A piercing pale blue, like sun-bleached denim, they squinted as if he'd spent his whole life riding the Arizona plains. The man's handshake was firm too.

'It would be a lie to say good to meet you,' he said, his accent a thick nasal Teesside. 'The last thing we need is you lot pulling our case to bits. But, you know, in other circumstances...'

Keegan joined them. 'Good to see you, Terry.'

'You too mate. I've just come up to hear whatever wild theory you've cooked up.'

'It's a doozy,' Keegan said.

Massey looked at his watch, spotted the door opening to admit not just Portas but Crowder too. Time to get started. After introducing Flint and announcing Keegan's temporary transfer, he took a deep breath.

'Alright folks. Ears pinned back? They'll need to be, because our new theory is like nothing you'll have seen or heard of before. Now, for the purposes of this briefing at least...'

He directed a brief smile towards Flint.

'...we'll be talking about the two current murders in Cresswell, *and* last year's murder of retired Chief Superintendent Duncan Kingsley as one inquiry. That does *not* mean we've stolen the Kingsley inquiry back from Durham Constabulary, and it does not mean that any formal decision has yet been taken to link the arson and murder of Ben Quinn to last night's slaying of Maureen Duffy.'

They would be officially linked before the day ended though. He was sure of it.

'Ana, if you would, please. Now everyone, all I ask of you for the next however long it takes is that you suspend your inevitable disbelief, because...' He waited while Ana clicked to bring up a table, four columns, seven or eight rows. '... I'm going to take you back to Will Shakespeare's time.'

Terry Flint surged to his feet. 'Bloody fairy tales? I don't have time for this.'

Crowder didn't move, but his voice boomed from the back of the room. 'Sit down and listen, DCI Flint. You might learn something.'

With bad grace, Flint sat.

Next to him, Keegan leant back in his chair, clasped his hands over his beer belly, and stretched his long legs out in front of him. His eyes twinkled and his bared teeth grin became wider. 'Once upon a time…' he said.

Everyone laughed, even Flint.

'Okay,' Massey began. 'You'll see that this table lists the characters in Macbeth alongside victims and persons of interest in all three murders. They're not necessarily in the order that the characters appear in the play.'

He gave everyone a moment to read the information on the screen before continuing.

'First up, we have King Duncan of Scotland, who is murdered at the beginning of the second act by his thane, Macbeth. I'll get into what a thane is in a moment. Over here, we have the name of our first victim, Duncan Kingsley. So, King Duncan, Duncan Kingsley, a bit of a coincidence, but nothing much on its own. You'll all know that Duncan Kingsley's murder inquiry was handed over to Durham Constabulary, which is why we have DCI Flint with us today. According to the press – and we all know how reliable they are – DCI Flint's team are close to charging three men with Kingsley's murder.'

He paused to give Flint an opportunity to say something.

He didn't.

'Next up, we have the king's thane Macbeth who, with his wife, murdered King Duncan when he visited them and framed the king's guards. I have it on good authority from DS Sparks, who acted a part in Macbeth at school, that a thane is like the Anglo-Saxon equivalent of a baron. She is now our resident expert on all things Shakespeare.'

Several people laughed.

Sparks grimaced.

'By coincidence, we have here a Finn Barron, resident of Cresswell. In fact on the day he was murdered, Duncan Kingsley had gone to a barbecue at the home of Finn Barron and his wife, Verity. He was stabbed to death on the beach very close to the Barrons' house.'

He looked at item three on the list and paced a few steps back and forward. Everyone in the room, with the exception of Flint, knew what was coming. Phil Jackson started a chant and a couple of others joined in.

'We'll have less of that please. I know you've all seen the video.'

Terry Flint looked confused.

'I'll send it to you later,' Keegan told him.

'No you sodding won't,' Massey said. 'Right then, if you've all finished, we have the three witches. But I can't go into them any further without first introducing the next on the list: Macbeth's friend and fellow warrior, Banquo. You see, Macbeth and Banquo come across the three witches after a big battle. The witches make three prophesies. The first is that the king will give Macbeth a new title, Thane of Cawdor, to reward him for his bravery in battle. The second is that Macbeth will later become king. But when Banquo asks them for a prophesy too, they tell him that although he wouldn't ever become king himself, his descendants will.

'Now, onto real life, last year, at the time of Kingsley's murder. A local charity that runs Cresswell Pele Tower was planning a Halloween fundraising event and had recruited three local women to play witches to add a bit of atmosphere. No mention of Macbeth back then though. However, these women took to the task with gusto and got into practice by spouting spooky prophesies for people as a laugh. Now this year, the charity is actually planning to stage a version of Macbeth at the tower on the weekend before Halloween. A week today in fact. Both performances are sold out. Again they have the three witches, although this time they are specifically meant to be the witches in Macbeth, And again, they're getting into practice by handing out prophesies to anyone who'll listen, and – as I found to my own expense – even to those who don't want to listen.'

Phil Jackson instigated a round of whoops and hollers.

Flint banged his hand on the table. 'This is a joke. Bloody Macbeth? None of this challenges the case we've built.' He huffed in disgust. 'I can see why we ended up holding the shitty end of the stick on the Kingsley investigation last year, because every fucker over here has got their head screwed on back to front.'

Crowder looked fit to explode.

Determined not to bite, Massey headed him off at the pass. 'You're entitled to your opinion, DCI Flint, and we can talk about that later, in private. But for now, we need to get on with this briefing.'

Flint muttered under his breath. Massey could have sworn he said, 'Briefing, my arse.'

'Okay, where are we. Banquo. That's right. The witches told him that his descendants would be kings. At that time Banquo had only one son, whose name was Fleance. But after Macbeth had murdered Duncan and was made King in his place, he didn't like the thought that Fleance, or any other children Banquo might have in the future could take the crown from him, so he plots to kill both of them too. He sends assassins, who manage to kill Banquo, but Fleance escapes.

'Present day, we have Ben Quinn, who was murdered less than a week ago and his house set on fire. His daughter was in the house at the time and was also attacked. Although she is so far surviving, she was badly burned and is in an induced coma, so is incapable of telling us what she may or may not have seen or heard. Her name is Fleur. So Banquo, Ben Quinn. Fleance, Fleur.' He stared at Flint. 'Still coincidence?

'And that's not all, because last night's murder fits with the play too. Another thane, Macduff grows suspicious of Macbeth, convinced he'd killed both Duncan and Banquo, so he rides to England to find Duncan's exiled son Malcolm and raise an army against Macbeth. Oh, and by the way, Duncan Kingsley's eldest son is called Milo.

'So, while Macduff is away, Macbeth sends assassins to his castle. They don't find him, but they murder his wife and children anyway. Now, back to reality. Last night in Cresswell, another local resident Michael Duffy, who had recently been going round shouting his mouth off that Finn Barron murdered Duncan Kingsley and Ben Quinn, went out when he would normally have been expected to be at home. When he came back, he found his wife Maureen slaughtered and their two dogs missing. So we have Macduff and Michael Duffy, and we have Malcolm and Milo.' Massey faced Flint again. Balancing imaginary weights in the palms of his hands, he cocked his head. 'Still a fairy tale?'

CHAPTER 40

Massey had a quick look at his phone when they took a quick break. Eleven missed calls from Helen. He didn't listen to his voicemails. He knew exactly what she'd have said, and didn't have time for the abuse.

He wanted to collar Flint, but Crowder got there before him and drew Flint out into the corridor. He could understand how the man felt. This Macbeth theory was so off the wall that anyone would be sceptical, particularly the man in charge of building the case that their theory might just disprove. But hopefully, when they all came back to the table, he'd be more receptive. They needed Durham to share details of their investigation. Full access.

Flint looked subdued when he returned, but hardly chastened or receptive.

Massey jumped straight in. 'So we all now know who the relevant characters are, both in the play and in reality. Let's talk about possible motivations behind these real murders, and for now let's assume that firstly, these murders *are* all connected; secondly, that the same person, or persons, is responsible for all of them; and thirdly, that, for some insane reason, they're exploiting the similarities between the names of the people involved to those of the characters in Macbeth. DCI Flint, I'm not asking you to lay out your case against the three landscapers, but feel free to chip in once I've explained what we have so far.'

Eyes on the table, Flint gave a stiff nod.

'Good. Now I'll be the first to admit that the only motives we've uncovered so far are thin to the point of being transparent. Firstly, we have our own retired Chief Superintendent Duncan Kingsley, who was also president of the Ellington & Cresswell RFC. Finn Barron was, and still is Vice President, although he's been acting up as president since Kingsley's death. On the day of the murder, Kingsley and his wife attended a barbecue at Barron's house. Several other local residents were there too, including both of our later victims. Now, Kingsley had recently had some landscaping work done at his own home and was delighted with the result, to the point that he asked the workmen to do regular maintenance for him.'

Although Flint's eyes were fixed firmly downwards, Massey felt sure he was listening intently. This was sensitive ground.

'At some point during the barbecue, those same workmen turned up at Barron's house. He'd arranged for them to come to quote for work to his own property. But why make such an arrangement for a time he knew he had lots of people coming over, including Duncan and Elena Kingsley? According to Ben Quinn and Michael Duffy at the post-charity match party last Saturday night – and DI Keegan will bear me out on this – Finn Barron has always been envious of Duncan Kingsley. Whatever Kingsley had, Barron had to have too, only bigger and better. And—'

'Just a moment.' Flint butted in. 'How come the pair of you were having cosy chats with Quinn and Duffy about Kingsley the night before the fire?'

'Ah, right,' Keegan said. 'You wouldn't know. It's because our Northumbria Police fifteen played against the Ellington & Cresswell RFC – the club Kingsley was president of – in a charity match last Saturday, in aid of the Cresswell Pele Tower Community Development Fund. Kingsley arranged the match originally for last summer, on the tenth anniversary of a previous charity match between the two teams. But after his murder, it was postponed. Barron eventually rearranged it for last week. There was a fund-raising party in the clubhouse afterwards. That's when the conversation took place. Can't remember if it was Quinn or Duffy who brought it up in the first place, but they were talking about the news report on the three landscapers. Neither thought you'd got the right men.'

'That information should never have got out,' Flint said. 'We weren't ready. We still aren't ready to charge them, but our case is sound. I stand by it one hundred percent.'

Keegan gave a sage nod. 'Well, how about you try to set that aside and keep an open mind for the next half an hour. Give the man a chance.'

Flint rolled his eyes and crossed his arms. He nodded to Massey. 'On you go.'

Massey paced as he talked. 'Okay, so we've heard that Finn Barron has always been jealous of Duncan Kingsley. Let's assume he arranged for those landscapers to come around right in the middle of the barbecue precisely because he wanted to piss Kingsley off. And Kingsley, rather than make a scene in front of everyone, went for a walk on the beach across the road from the house. The men would have been there at the house with Barron for some time. Why would they then have gone down to the beach after Kingsley, whose beef was with Barron anyway, not with them? Why would they want to further piss off an ongoing customer? How would they have even known he was still on the beach? He could have walked along to the village. What motive could they have had for murder? And where could they have parked their van so that it wasn't visible from the house and didn't stick out like a sore thumb to anyone else. Surely someone would have seen it.'

He stopped in front of Flint, inviting a response.

Flint flushed. 'You want to know what we have against them? I'll tell you. We have Kingsley's blood in their sodding van.'

With his mouth open, Massey rocked back on his heels.

Keegan jumped into the void. 'In what form?'

'What do you mean, what form? In the form of blood for fuck's sake. Irrefutable DNA evidence. In their sodding van.'

'But on what? On the inside of the van itself?'

'On a cloth that one of them must have used to wipe the knife or their hands.'

Keegan considered for a second, before responding. 'That could have had nothing to do with the murder. If I knew Kingsley – and I did know him, by the way, pretty well – then I know exactly what he'll have been like when those men were doing his garden. He'd have been right in there with them, getting his hands dirty and being a pain in the arse. He could have cut himself while—'

'In which case he'd have used something at home, wouldn't he?'

Flint had a point, but so did Keegan. Durham's case could hardly hold up on this alone. 'You have to have more than that.'

'Timings. They told us they went straight to Killingworth after leaving Barron's house. But if they had, they'd have been picked up on camera on the A189 a good fifteen minutes sooner than they were. So where did they go? And why did they have Kingsley's blood on a cloth in their van? If they had an alibi for that time, at least one of them would be shouting it from the rooftops by now. And let's not forget, they do all have previous.'

'How long after the murder was it before you searched their van?'

Flint scrunched his eyes closed and gritted his teeth. Massey thought for a moment he was going to refuse to answer, but eventually he responded. Grudgingly. 'Five weeks.'

'How many? Jesus. Inside the back of a van during all that hot weather last summer? Surely it's impossible to know exactly when the cloth was put there? And wouldn't the guy you say wiped his hands on it not have made it his business to get rid of it?'

'On the balance of probability—'

Massey threw his hands up in the air. 'How the hell…?'

'Is it possible anyone else could have slipped away from the party and followed Kingsley to the beach?' Sparks asked.

Flint looked glad of the change of direction. 'No-one admitted to it or said they'd seen anyone leave during the crucial time.'

'That doesn't mean no-one did.'

'No-one else had a motive.'

'That you've found. What's supposed to be the motive of the three landscapers?'

'They fell out with Kingsley when he saw them turn up to quote for work at the home of his—'

'His what? His rival?' Massey gave a harsh laugh. 'Really? You think the Kingsleys would have attended a barbecue at the Barron's house if the animosity between the two men was that bad? Could the fact that Kingsley didn't like the idea of the landscapers doing work for Barron ever have been enough for them to hunt him down on the beach and stab him to death?'

'Or they realised he was upset, and they went looking for him on the beach to set things right, to protect the maintenance contract he'd just given them. Maybe he wouldn't accept that. He had a go at them and things got out of hand.'

Massey glared at Flint. He wasn't the only one. They all knew Duncan Kingsley's reputation on the force as a decent and fair man. What Flint was describing did not ring true with any of them.

With all eyes on him, Flint slammed his hands on the table. 'I've had enough of this shite.'

This time, Crowder let him go. His exit would have been more dramatic had his efforts to slam the door behind him not been frustrated by the overhead soft-close spring.

'Tetchy,' said Keegan, shaking his head.

***

Flint's anger would likely cause problems in getting access to Durham's investigation, but that was a worry for later. Massey still needed to get the rest of his own team behind their bizarre theory first. He wiped his hands down his face and took a few moments to organise his thoughts before continuing.

'Alright. Back to business. We have Barron arranging for the landscapers to come round at the same time he knows he'll have a garden full of people there for a barbecue, including the Kingsleys. Possibly, he arranged for them to come then in order to get up Kingsley's nose, or maybe the arrangement was more fluid than that and they just happened to arrive at the most inconvenient time. However it happened, Kingsley took himself out of the way by going for a walk on the beach, where he met his murderer.' He stroked his chin and sighed. 'It would be good to know who else was at that party.'

'We will,' Keegan said. 'Flint will calm down. Just give him time.'

Massey glanced at the set expressions on the faces of Crowder and Portas. Perhaps a decision on whether Durham would open up their case to them would be taken at a higher level, regardless of DCI Flint's opinion.

'Alright then, let's summarise. In the play, the king is dead, killed by his thane Macbeth, with the support of Lady Macbeth. The king's guards are accused of his murder and slain. Duncan's sons go into exile and Macbeth is crowned the new King of Scotland, but he worries that Banquo's prophesy will come true too and that Banquo's son will try to take the throne from him.

'In Cresswell, Duncan Kingsley, president of the local rugby club is dead. His landscapers are looking good for it, and Durham look set to charge them. Elena Kingsley has sold up and moved with their sons away from the area. Finn Barron is standing in as president of the rugby club, and you'd think he'd push for an election as soon as possible, but he doesn't. Maybe because he can't be sure he'll be voted in. He has two rivals standing against him. His old friend Ben Quinn and Len Stafford, chair of the village hall. And since he's not actually Macbeth, he can't just bump off anyone who gets in his way. Not quite so easily anyway.

'Now, as well as being egotistical, apparently Barron is a misogynist. Hates the thought of women "invading" the world of rugby and is fiercely resisting the further development of women's teams at the club. However, Ben Quinn's daughter Fleur is a staunch proponent of women's rugby. Barron can see what it's like at other clubs, where not only is women's rugby on the rise, but women also make up a good proportion of the senior positions on management and trustee boards, and he's determined to stop this happening at *his* club. What if Fleur ended up on the board? She could even end up as president one day.' He looked around at the faces of his team. 'Has everyone got the parallels so far?'

A murmur of assent rippled around the room.

'Good. Back to the play. Banquo has only one son at that time – Fleance, and Macbeth is determined to ensure that neither he nor any of Banquo's as yet unborn children can challenge him. He decides Banquo and Fleance must die. He sends assassins to do the job. Banquo is killed but Fleance survives and escapes, never to be heard of in the play again.

'In Cresswell, it's more than a year since Kingsley's murder. During that time perhaps the threat of women's rugby at the club, posed primarily by Fleur's activities, has risen. Barron is delaying the election for a new president but, in effect, he *is* president. Then Ben Quinn is murdered, Fleur is attacked and left for dead, and a fire set to cover up the crime. Badly injured, Fleur survives but is put into a coma potentially for weeks. She can't tell us anything about what happened. Like Fleance, she is out of the story. Any thoughts anyone?'

Phil Jackson raised his hand. 'When's the ice-cream and popcorn coming round?'

The room erupted in loud groans and laughter.

'Flint should have stayed to hear this.' Keegan said. 'There's way too much here to ignore.'

Massey grinned. 'I haven't finished yet. There's more. So back to the play, Macbeth has had Banquo killed and Fleance is at least out of the way. However, Banquo was his best friend. He's feeling a load of guilt and starts seeing Banquo's ghost – in particular, at a banquet that another thane, Macduff has refused to attend. To his guests, Macbeth looks like he's going mad when he starts raving at Banquo's ghost. They think he's ill, but Lady Macbeth tells them everything is fine, this happens to him sometimes and it'll pass.

'In Cresswell, on Thursday, the rugby club hosted an event for the trustees and volunteers of the Cresswell Pele Tower, and guess who chairs the committee. Finn Barron. He invited me and Christine along— '

'Barron invited *you*.' Sparks said. 'I just tagged along.'

'True. Anyway, we went. And while Macduff might not have attended Macbeth's banquet, Michael Duffy *did* go to Barron's, but under sufferance. Claimed he'd only gone to ensure Barron honoured Quinn, who also happened to be on the Pele Tower charity committee, in his speech. I suspect it had more to do with his wife needing a lift. She's a… she *was* a volunteer in the tower garden.

'Duffy told us he'd been one of the first trustees of the charity, but had resigned when Finn Barron became chair. He insinuated that Finn *and* Verity Barron were guilty of some wrongdoing, but then clammed up. We know he believed it was Barron who killed Kingsley and Quinn, but whether that's what he was referring to again then, we never found out. I'd intended to take him aside to follow it up, but never got a chance because Finn Barron took ill. He started sweating and mumbling to himself. It looked like he was having a heart attack, but Verity refused to let anyone near him. The same thing had happened before, she said, and he'd be alright in a moment. Just like Lady Macbeth when her husband started ranting at the banquet.

He allowed that one to sink in for a moment before continuing.

'Now, back to the play. Last time, I promise. Macduff refused to go to the banquet, because he suspected Macbeth of horrific crimes. But he makes his feelings on the subject known and, of course, Macbeth gets to know about it and wants him dead too. He sends assassins to Macduff's castle, but Macduff isn't there. Lady Macduff tells them she doesn't know where he was, but they kill her and her family anyway. It turns out that Macduff has gone to England to find King Duncan's son Malcolm to help him raise an army against Macbeth. He wants Malcolm to claim the throne that should have been rightfully his when his father died.

'Back in Cresswell, last night someone gained access to the Duffy's bungalow while Michael was out. They slaughtered Maureen. Their two dogs, who'd have raised the roof barking at strangers, are missing. They raised hell when Christine and I called earlier yesterday and spoke to Maureen, who incidentally told us she had no idea where her husband had gone, although he'd mentioned something about Duncan Kingsley's son, Milo. So far, we have no idea whether the dogs barked last night. Certainly, no-one we've spoken to so far heard then, but the houses aren't exactly jammed together. I can think of two scenarios. Either the killer took the dogs, or the dogs never returned from wherever it was they'd gone in the afternoon with the dog-walker.

'So, Michael discovered Maureen dead when he returned home. He managed to call it in but then had a heart attack before anyone arrived. We haven't been able to speak to him yet, but I'd be interested to know if he *had* been to see Milo.

CHAPTER 41

Crowder and Portas left them to it. Most of the team were on-board now. As off-the-wall as it was, there were too many similarities for them not to be. The biggest issue was with motive. In the play, Macbeth was the villain of the piece. He murdered King Duncan and sent assassins to see off his other victims. In life though, they had to assume Durham had found nothing to contradict the Barrons' alibis for Kingsley's murder. So, unless Barron too had assassins he could send to do his dirty work, then he and Verity must be innocent. Of that murder at least.

Keegan stroked his beard. 'What do we have on the landscapers?'

Andrew Donaldson rattled the keypad of his laptop. 'Aggravated assault for brothers Ryan and Justin Blacklock. Common assault for their nephew, Callum Wyatt.'

'Is it possible,' Madge Brown asked, 'that Durham have the right men, but the wrong motive?'

'What if they'd been paid by Barron to kill Kingsley?' Laidler suggested.

Sparks snorted. 'What, just so he could be head honcho in a poxy rugby club?'

'That's where the theory falls down,' Massey admitted. 'Unless we've suddenly migrated to Midsomer, nothing we've found so far should be enough motive for murder. And if the killer *is* Barron, he is surely not so stupid he'd stick a signpost on his own head by pointing us at every turn towards Macbeth, is he?'

'Depends on his opinion of our intelligence,' Keegan said.

Throwing himself into a chair, Massey winced when the corner of his mobile phone dug into his leg.

He pulled it out, wondering how many missed calls and messages it held now from Helen. Too many. Just as well electronic communications had no significant weight, or his phone would have ripped a hole in his pocket by now.

He'd read somewhere that the whole internet weighed no more than a single strawberry.

'So if not Barron, then who? And why point us to Barron?'

Brown sat up straighter. 'Verity. Their marriage can't have been a bed of roses for her if he's that bad. Maybe he's been playing around.'

'Good point. We need to find out, without stepping on Flint's toes.'

'Flint will come around,' Keegan said. 'He'll have chewed it over on the drive back and spoken to his boss by now. You've probably got something from him already on that phone you're treating like a hot potato.'

Trust Keegan to notice.

Out of curiosity, ignoring the growing count of unopened texts and missed call alerts he knew would be from Helen, he opened up his secure email app.

'Good call. Flint says he's sorry for being a prick and his DCS is to speak to ours ASAP. And look. He says, "btw, FB shagged half of Cresswell." Good one, Madge. Verity might well have a motive for framing her husband if he's a serial cheat, but would she be willing to kill innocent people to achieve that?'

'Looks like they're off their faces half the time,' Sparks said. 'You said it yourself. High as kites, the pair of them. Druggies don't reason things out the same as normal people.'

'A girlfriend could have a motive too,' Ana suggested.

'Or...' Rob Laidler shuffled his tall bony frame in his seat. '... what about if it *was* Barron who killed Duncan Kingsley, and the rest is Elena or one of the sons looking for revenge by framing him for another murder. After all, Ben Quinn wasn't killed until the press claimed Durham were going to charge the landscapers. So maybe the thought of Barron getting away with Duncan's murder set them off.'

Massey considered it. 'Barron *had* barred Duncan's sons from playing in the charity match their dad had originally organised.'

Keegan shook his shaggy head. 'Why not just kill Barron then? Surely, if they're prepared to kill at all, they'd be better just going for Barron himself rather than trying to frame him by killing innocent people.'

'Or maybe it *is* about the presidency of the rugby club after all,' Sparks said. 'But we're looking at the wrong candidate. That Len Stafford was very keen to come telling tales about Duffy. Maybe that was more about pushing us towards the similarities to Macbeth. Cresswell might not be Midsomer, but it's still a small village, so likely pretty insular. Grievances that might seem petty to outsiders could end up looking enormous to someone like Stafford.'

'Another thing we need to consider,' Massey said. 'Even in a village where several of the residents are busy rehearsing their parts in a production of Macbeth, there can't be many with the in-depth knowledge of the play necessary to even conceive of such a plan. I mean, yeah, Mr and Mrs Average would probably know Shakespeare wrote Macbeth, and maybe that it's supposed to be cursed, but that's where it would end for the majority of people.'

CHAPTER 42

After 2 pm, back in Cresswell, Massey and Sparks caught up on the search of the woods and the house to house enquiries. What Massey really needed was a couple of hours to get his head down, but that wasn't about to happen any time soon.

They'd arranged to meet Jodie O'Neill, Brian Truman, and Zafar Davani at the Village Hall and were late arriving. Still only hours since he'd handed the keys over, yet entering the hall felt like the first time again. At least half of the pull-up banners had been packed back into their cases and stacked against a wall. From the lobby door, he could see straight through to the conservatory at the back, and out to the sparkling sea beyond.

His breath caught when he saw crumbs and tiny black seeds scattered on the table. Screwed up in the middle lay the paper bag Trinny's rolls had come in this morning. He had no problem at all with the remaining rolls having been filched. It was the rush of emotion he felt that made him pause. He leant on the back of a chair until the feeling passed, a voice ringing loud in his head.

I have a son.

He shook his head to dislodge the voice. Much as he wanted to revel in the feeling, he had a job to do here.

'Y'alright?' Truman asked in his Mackem twang.

It might have been just a casual greeting, or perhaps Truman had spotted his moment of weakness. Massey shook the man's hand. 'I'm good. You?'

'Bearing up. Considering.' A typical ironic response in the North.

Jodie O'Neill lifted her dark eyes from her tablet and grinned, her shorn hairstyle accentuating Grace Jones cheekbones. 'Massey. Long time no see.'

He returned her grin. They'd worked a couple of cases together in the past, four years or so ago. 'O'Neill. Congratulations on the promotion.'

'Thanks. You too. Looks like another off-the-wall case. Your speciality, I hear.'

'A couple of simple domestics next time wouldn't go amiss.'

'Get away. You love it. The weirder the better. Isn't that right, Christine?'

Sparks rolled her eyes. 'He attracts the weirdos.'

'Like iron filings to a magnet.' O'Neill's raucous cackle filled the room.

For all he was glad to see her, he had no energy for lots of banter. The sooner they finished here, the sooner he could find somewhere to shut his eyes for a spell.

He had no intention of going home though until he was certain Helen wasn't camped outside waiting to pounce. His batteries needed to recharge before he waded into that battle.

***

Truman confirmed that none of the Duffys' closest neighbours had heard the dogs bark during the relevant time, yet huskies were generally a vocal breed.

'You're thinking whoever did this was known to the dogs, and therefore to the Duffys.' Sparks said.

'Even if they were, I can't see two big dogs going anywhere with someone who'd just killed their owner.'

'So either they weren't there at all, or they'd been incapacitated.'

Davani considered his words carefully before speaking. 'There were no signs around the perimeter of the property that anyone had thrown anything like drugged meat into the garden. And why would a killer remove incapacitated dogs from the scene afterwards?'

'Do we know which dog walking service they used?' Sparks asked. 'Were the dogs brought back? If not, why?' She stroked the screen of her phone, tapped it, then began typing with her thumbs. 'They could even be the killer.'

She had a point.

'Anything else from the house to house?' Massey asked.

'More like caravan to caravan,' Truman said. 'A couple of families at Golden Sands were sat outside drinking with their neighbours until late. Said they heard noises in the tree line that separates the site from that field below the tower at around six thirty last night. Too dark for them to see whatever it was, but they assumed deer or badgers. Until our lot turned up, that is. And now they're convinced they heard the killer. Their vans stand next to each other, end-on to that boundary line, so it could well have been our perp they heard. Unfortunately, all they could give us was that approximate time.'

Massey sighed. He glanced at Sparks, still scrolling. 'Anything?'

'Five dog-walkers advertised online within a few miles, but none in Cresswell itself.'

'They'll all need contacting.'

'On it.'

He nodded towards Truman. 'Anything else, Brian?'

'Not yet. The team is still out there. It'll take time to get through all of those sodding caravans. At least the parks aren't full at this time of year.'

Massey sighed again. 'How about the search of the woods, Jodie?'

'Slow, but the conditions are dry, so that's a positive. Means anything we find will more likely have retained decent evidentiary traces. If we find anything, and it's a big if.'

He'd been banking on the searchers finding something.

'But never say never,' she continued. 'Someone has definitely been through there recently. Kept to the deepest cover too. That means there's more likelihood they got snagged up on branches or tripped on tree roots. So my gut tells me we *will* find something, but how useful it'll be is anyone's guess.'

'Okay. Thanks Jodie. How about you Zafar, anything?'

'Sorry, nothing yet.'

CHAPTER 43

With no room in the hall car park when they'd arrived, Massey and Sparks walked side by side towards the far end of the South Side cottages, where he'd had to park.

Crossing the narrow turn-off that led to Trinny's tiny home, Massey wondered if she was there now, with his son Max. The boy was of an age surely to have asked why he had no father. What would Trinny have told him? That his dad was dead, or had run out on them when she was pregnant?

When he found out, would the boy resent him for not being around before now?

Only a few vehicles remained at the kerb now, with long gaps in between. Massey walked on the outside of the pavement until it petered out to grass verge. He then led the way while Sparks fell in behind him. Neither noticed a car pulling level from behind. Not until the passenger window whirred open and the first vinyl album in its cardboard sleeve hit Massey squarely on the shoulder, followed by two more.

'You *fucking bastard*,' Helen screeched. 'How *fucking dare* you do that. You want your pathetic albums back. Here they fucking are. Catch this, you *bastard*.'

As he bent to the level of Helen's car window, the next one caught him smack on the temple, less than an inch from his eye. 'Jesus, Helen…'

'I was prepared to be reasonable,' she screamed, launching three albums at once through the window straight at his face. 'But not now. No fucking way, you *bastard*. You—'

'Out of the car!' Sparks yelled.

He hadn't noticed her rushing round to the driver's door and wrenching it open.

Helen ignored her and threw another album at his face.

'I said out. *Now!*' Sparks dragged her out and rammed her against the rear passenger door, pinning her arms behind her.

Nostrils flared, teeth bared in a snarl, Helen panted with unspent fury; the glare she aimed at him across the car roof murderous enough to drop a charging buffalo. 'The fucking gloves are off now, James. Better get yourself the best solicitor you can find, because I'm going to take you for *everything*.'

'You left me, Helen. Remember? And I still have no idea why.'

'Are you going to behave now,' Sparks said, 'or shall I arrest you for assaulting a police officer?'

Helen struggled, trying to shrug her off. She had the height advantage, but she was no match for Sparks.

Massey lifted the last of his albums from Helen's car onto the pavement, then began gathering up the ones she'd thrown. He knew anything he said now could only fan the flames, so he kept his mouth shut.

'Well?' Sparks demanded. 'Are you going to behave?'

Helen's expression told him she hadn't finished with him, but she knew she wouldn't get any further here, now.

'I'm done,' she muttered.

Sparks cocked her head and grinned her shark smile. 'What was that?'

'I said I'm done. Alright?'

'Good. And now you're going to get back into your car and drive away. And if you try something like this again, I'll have you arrested and in court so quick you won't know what's hit you. Do you understand?'

Helen sneered across the roof at him. 'Another one of your faithful posse of bimbos, is she James?'

Sparks rammed her against the car door again. 'I said, *do you understand?*'

'Yes, right. I understand. Let go.'

Sparks released her.

Helen threw a last contemptuous look over her shoulder before climbing into her car, slamming the door and speeding off.

'Do you want me to write her up?' Sparks said.

He noticed faces at the windows of the house closest and knew the news would go around the village like smallpox. 'Nah, just let it go.'

'So are you going to tell me what brought all that on?'

Handing a third of the albums to her to carry and bending down to pick up the rest, he started laughing. He couldn't help it. 'I knew she was coming round with a van today… to take what she wanted from…' His laughter turned into an uncontrollable roar. '…from the house.'

'And?'

'And I… changed the locks.'

Sparks lips twitched. Then she laughed too.

They deposited the albums on the back seat of his car, but then he noticed Sparks staring back towards the village hall. Straightening up and stepping back for a better look, he almost knocked Verity Barron off her feet. The woman gave a frightened little scream and scuttled through the garden gate of the nearest house. Only then did he spot what Sparks had been looking at. Trinny Moon and her son – *his* son – staring along Beach Road towards them.

CHAPTER 44

Once inside, Verity gasped her relief. Simply getting here today had been unbelievably stressful. For a start, she hadn't been able to find her keys to even get out of the house. But eventually, she found them shoved behind the microwave, so she knew Finn must have hidden them there.

Had he discovered her nocturnal wanderings?

He couldn't have, surely. He'd have said something. And he'd certainly have started to hide his own keys, as well as hers. Perhaps he hid hers every time he left the house without her, and this was just the first time she'd actually gone looking for them. After all, today was probably the first time since the Covid lockdowns that she'd managed to pluck up enough courage to leave the house on her own in daylight. It felt stressful. Completely different to being out at night, when everyone else was tucked up in bed.

So, as well as all her usual nervous hang-ups, she'd begun worrying whether he'd hidden the keys as a test. Was his hospital appointment even real, or just a ploy so he could watch her from somewhere to see where she went? He'd refused for months to see his GP, yet he expected her to believe that, in the space of just two days, he'd made and attended an appointment at the surgery without her, which he'd never done before, and been given an emergency hospital appointment that he'd banned her from attending with him. Of course he wouldn't want her with him. It was all a ploy to bring her back to heel. Or to watch her and see what she'd do. Or… A terrifying thought hit her. What if he was creating an alibi for another murder? Hers!

Yet if it *was* real, and his GP *had* sent him for an emergency hospital appointment, he must suspect something awful. Like cancer!

She should have realised that before.

She was his wife. She should have insisted on going with him, but instead she'd seized the opportunity to make this appointment of her own.

All the way along Beach Road, having left the house later than planned because of her missing keys, these thoughts had turned over and over in her head. She'd found herself sneaking surreptitious glances behind, well aware of how furtive she must look, while at the same time desperate not to betray how terrified she felt inside simply by being out of the house on her own in daylight.

Especially not to the two people she saw walking towards her on the other side of the road. Those two detectives who'd upset Finn the other morning.

Were they going to Betsy's house too?

Please God, no.

And then, just as she prepared to cross the road towards Betsy's house, that car had pulled level with them and the woman driver had begun yelling and throwing things out of the window. Then the female detective had dragged her screaming out of her car, like they do on TV. A tall, slim woman with long dark hair; not local.

She'd hung back, too terrified to run in front of them, which she'd have had to do to reach Betsy's. They'd have seen her. They'd have wanted her to make a witness statement. She'd have been even later for her appointment. Finn might have come past and seen her.

She'd almost turned tail and run back home there and then. But the detectives had let the screaming woman drive away, and then they'd started laughing, for goodness sake. How could anyone find something like that funny?

It had taken all her remaining courage to run across the road and through Betsy's gate. She'd probably never be brave enough, or have the opportunity to do it again if she hadn't.

***

Betsy led her into an airy room at the back with a picture window looking out to sea, talking calmly, steering her jangling nerves away from the unsettling episode outside. She relinquished her coat and sat down on a heather-coloured sofa filled with squishy pastel-patterned cushions, then stared around her at sea green walls hung with sunrise seascapes in pinks, purples, blues and greens, listening to the distant sigh of the sea against the rocks beyond gently undulating voile curtains.

'Comfortable? Would you like your feet up?'

Verity nodded, preoccupied by wondering *why* she felt so quieted and relaxed as soon as she walked into this space, so full of soft colour and texture, the complete opposite of the sterile tundra of her own white living room?

She felt her feet slowly rising, and realised that Betsy had activated an electric recliner function on the side of the sofa.

'We can lie you further back, if you like, once we've got some essentials out of the way. You're a new client, so we need to go through a couple of things first. Just basic stuff. It won't take long.'

Verity nodded again. 'Whatever you need.'

'Thank you. Once that's done, the rest of the session will be all about what *you* need.'

Betsy sat facing her at an oblique angle, with a large notebook open on her lap. She talked about confidentiality and potential safeguarding issues, or at least they were the words Verity, impatient to get to the meat of this session, managed to pick out. Then it was full name, address and medical history.

'Medications?' Betsy asked.

'Only hydrocortisone cream for my hands,' she replied. But Betsy asked again to be sure.

Eventually, they talked about her aims for the session. Verity wanted to say that she hoped she could just stay in this beautiful room for ever, but instead, she held out her hands. 'I want to learn how to control the constant anxiety that causes this horrible eczema rash. It blights my life.'

She said nothing about the behaviour of her husband, which she believed to be the source of that anxiety, or the terrible things she now felt convinced he'd done. Not yet.

Eventually, Betsy set the notebook aside and lowered the back of the sofa.

Verity sank further into the cushioned cradle, relaxing in a way she couldn't remember ever having been able to do since she was young, not even on the roof of the pele tower.

She barely heard the soporific words, but simply followed Betsy's instructions, counting the steps down to an imaginary deserted beach, where the sun shone, a gentle breeze ruffled her hair, and nothing could ever harm her.

It felt like no time at all before Betsy asked her to climb the steps again, bringing her back to the room with the sea green walls, where she lay on the reclined sofa, feeling as if she'd shifted position and now lay a little crooked, although still relaxed.

She glanced at her watch. It was later than she'd thought. She had to rush.

Before she could escape, Betsy laid a hand gently on her arm and looked into her eyes. 'Are you going to be alright, Verity?' she asked.

***

Conflicted, Betsy watched Verity hurry away. At any initial session, she always assured her client of the high standard of confidentiality they could expect from her. That was one of the most sacred tenet's of any therapy practice. Clients needed to feel secure in the knowledge that nothing they said in their session would be repeated outside of their conversations. However, she always covered safeguarding too, and the limited circumstances under which she may have no option but to break confidentiality. It was good practice to do so, although she'd never had a case before where she had to debate with herself the ethics of breaching confidentiality in order to protect someone.

Could she be overreacting? Was she seeing things here that weren't there? She would never do anything that could endanger her client without serious thought. But what about anyone else who could be at risk if she did nothing?

CHAPTER 45

He might have known that when he got home Keegan would be sat outside in his car waiting. 'Last thing I want is to go for a beer,' he warned him. 'I just need to get my head down for a while.'

Keegan studied his face and shrugged. He had to have seen the suitcases under his eyes, but still he climbed out of his own car and peered at the three stacks of vinyl albums on the back seat of his. 'They're a bit scuffed. Those ones on the top especially. You need to start taking better care of your property. Like that front door that's had a shiny new lock installed since I was last here, and now has footprints all over it. A woman's, I'd say. Marital hostilities heating up, are they?'

Massey grimaced, imagining Helen's rage when she discovered he'd changed the locks. 'You could say that. You can help me carry the albums inside, if you want.'

He inspected the door for damage and glanced along the street, checking Helen was nowhere in sight before unlocking the door.

Keegan followed him in, arms full, kicking the door closed behind him and sliding the albums onto their allotted shelf in the alcove. 'I'll bet you're one of those who can't relax until you've put this lot back into alphabetical order. I'll even help you sort them out. A beer would go down nicely, while we're on.'

Keegan was right. No amount of polka-dot pixies would send him to sleep until his music was arranged exactly the way he liked it. 'Better bring one for both of us then.'

Listening to Eric Clapton singing the blues, They'd reached the bottom of their bottles before Keegan told him why he'd come.

'Something I need to tell you. You're not going to like it, and you'll probably hate me for not telling you sooner.'

Massey placed his empty bottle on a side table. 'Go on.'

'It's something I saw. Months ago. But telling you then could have caused untold problems for you. At work, as well as home. The fact I didn't has bothered me. It goes back to January, before your permanent promotion to DCI, when your mother went missing…'

'I remember.' How could he not? 'Go on.'

Keegan puffed out his cheeks.

'Bloody hell, Guy. Spit it out.'

'I saw your wife out with another man. Arm in arm, eyes only for each other.'

Massey jerked his head back. 'What? With who?'

'You won't like it.'

'You're right. I won't. But I need to know.'

'Ray Flowers.'

Massey's heart jumped. His mouth fell open. 'Fucking what? But…'

'He was on the sick. Supposed to have still been ill with the flu.'

'But you've never met Helen. How did you know it was her?'

'Shit, I didn't want to have to tell you this… I was with someone who recognised her.'

'Who? Who were you with.'

Keegan closed his eyes and gritted his teeth. 'It was Lou. We were—'

'You mean Portas knows too, and she didn't tell me either?'

He knew he was shouting, but for Christ's sake…

'Think of the trouble it would have caused. You'd have planted him one. You could have lost your job.'

Massey shook his head. This was some kind of sick joke. 'Fucking Ray Flowers? He's the biggest dick I know. How could she… With him? No. I don't believe it.'

'It's true. They were out for a meal.'

'Where? And why were you there, with Lou Portas?'

'At the Shiremoor House Farm. We'd gone for a quick bite to eat while you and Sparks were trying to find your mother. We saw a couple leaving. I recognised Flowers. I was narked he was out and about when he was on the sick, while you were having to do his job. I assumed the woman was his wife, until Lou told me she was *yours*.'

Massey thought back. Portas had called in here to see him one evening. She'd met Helen then, only a couple of days before they must have seen her out with Flowers.

'Sodding Flowers? The man's more concerned with the cut of his suits than with his work. How the hell could Helen stand that?'

'No idea. I just know that you've been so wrapped up in wondering what the hell you could have done wrong to make her leave you,' Keegan said, 'that I just had to put you out of your misery. It's not you at all. It's her.'

'So that was when? Ten months ago? Jesus wept!'

He remembered his first day on Operation Bryony after being turfed off the investigation into the death of Sonia Wragg because his own mother knew her and was a witness. Flowers had been on his mobile talking sweet nothings to someone when he'd walked in. That must have been Helen. The bastard. All those times Helen had claimed to be working late with a group from church, had she actually been out with that prat? He'd have realised, surely. Although she had been acting strangely back then.

'She left me for him?'

'Another bottle?' Keegan asked.

'Fuck, yes.'

***

Keegan drained his second bottle, checked Massey was going to be alright, and then saw himself out.

Of course he'd be alright. What was there not to be alright about. He'd just discovered that for ten months at least his wife had been creeping around with the biggest prat to walk the earth. Had it been going on before then too?

He tried to recall when he'd first noticed a change in Helen's behaviour. But the changes had been so subtle it was impossible to pin down one particular time.

How the hell had she met Flowers in the first place? Had she deliberately set out to seduce someone she knew he'd detest to get him back for what he'd subjected her to all those years ago? She couldn't have made a better choice. Flowers was the most obnoxious, lazy, conceited prick he'd ever met. And he was married, for fuck's sake. With children.

Had he left his family for Helen? Was he moving into this new place Helen had found too?

But she was a devout Catholic. Or so she claimed. Surely the church frowned upon extramarital affairs. Although, in his view, the church – any faith, not just that lot – was disgustingly two-faced about everything else, so why not that? Then it hit him. He recalled Flowers shooting the cuffs of a lilac designer shirt one day during the hunt for Musk Man, his fingers straightening a gold cufflink, in the shape of a tiny crucifix.

Jesus wept. Flowers was a Catholic too. Helen must have met him at church. Did she also know the man's wife and children from church? Had she deliberately set out to split up a family, purely to get back at him for what he'd done more than a decade ago?

Massey wiped his hands down his face and blew out a big sigh. It would take a whole tribe of polka-dot pixies to knock him out now.

But he was wrong, for as soon as his head hit the pillow, he was dead to the world.

CHAPTER 46

Sunday, 20 October 2024

By morning, Massey felt as if a huge weight had been lifted from his shoulders. By rights, he should be devastated at Helen's betrayal. For weeks he'd drowned in grief and confusion, not knowing what he'd done wrong to push Helen into leaving. But never once had he *seriously* thought she'd be shagging someone else.

Did that make him conceited?

Scraping butter onto his toast, he huffed a laugh. Of course not. He'd always been conscious of how far above his weight he punched in having Helen by his side. If anyone had asked him if he thought she could ever be unfaithful, he'd have told them she was above all that. Yet now it seemed she wasn't.

But Flowers, for God's sake. Really? Jesus wept.

At least he couldn't run into the bastard at work now. Flowers had transferred to Cumbria Police a good few weeks ago, riding a wave of kudos in the wake of Operation Bryony's successful apprehension and prosecution of the serial rapist known as Musk Man, which had contributed to Operation Casper's solving of a forty-year-old cold case and the downfall of local drug lord Stevie Grant. Not that Flowers himself had contributed much. Operation Bryony had been on its knees with him as its SIO, until that one in a million DNA match with a cold case had cracked it all open. He'd been too busy sneaking away from work every chance he got.

Massey flung the butter knife into the sink, startling the birds on the feeder outside the window. There it was. The anger he knew must be inside him somewhere.

All that time Flowers had gone MIA had probably been spent shagging Helen, while muggins here had been doing all his work, leading his team, trying to save lives and prevent more women from being raped.

The fucking bastard. Just as well he was on the other side of the Pennines now.

And then another thought smacked him in the face. Had Helen brought Flowers here? Had she screwed him in *their* bed? Or in the spare room he'd moved into? Or up against this kitchen bench he was leaning against now? He stood up straight, threw his toast in the bin and tried to control a sudden urge to retch.

She wouldn't have, would she?

***

Sparks handed a piece of wholemeal toast to Dazz and slid the jar of chocolate spread along the bench towards him. He'd taken to calling on her early so they could go for a run together along the beach before work. This being Sunday morning, with him not working at all and her not having to start until late, he'd accepted her invitation to come in for breakfast after their run.

It felt weird having a man beside her in this tiny kitchen. Nice, weird though. In the living room there'd be less opportunity to accidentally on purpose brush up against each other, and she wanted him to brush up against her. It made her belly flutter.

They'd both worked up a bit of a sweat on their run. Normally, she'd have made straight for the shower when she got home, but this morning the breakfast invitation had just slipped out, and now here they were, two sweaty individuals, performing some sort of elaborate dance in a space so small that cupboard doors clashed together if opened at the same time.

She thought about announcing she was going to take a shower now. Leave it open for him to join her, if he wanted to. But was she ready for that yet? Getting naked with a man. She never had before, not fully naked. And of course being in the shower with him would inevitably mean having sex with him. It would be utterly wrong of her not to after having all but dragged him in there. And would she then allow him to carry her to bed to ravish her there too. She wasn't sure she was ready to take such a huge step. And besides – she glanced at her Fitbit – she didn't have the time.

And what if he hadn't joined her?

Then she'd be wondering whether not giving in to temptation made him too much of a gentleman to assume she wanted him to, or that maybe he wasn't bothered, while she ended up feeling like some sort of floozy for putting him into that position.

Good God, she had no idea how any of this courting game should go. If that was even what this was. She'd only ever slept with two men before, if you could call it that. Quick fumbles, both of them. Thank you and goodnight. Neither ever to be repeated. Dazz had never even kissed her yet, but already she knew he'd blow both previous experiences out of the water.

Just a moment. Why had he never kissed her? Didn't he think of her in that way?

Of course he did. She could feel the desire emanating from him now; she'd heard his intake of breath when she'd squeezed past him to the kettle. If she'd had the nerve to squeeze a little closer, she'd probably have felt his erection. He so wanted to do much more than just kiss her. So why didn't he try? Did he think she wouldn't want him to?

What if he was waiting for her to take the initiative and kiss him?

Maybe she should.

She looked up from the slice of toast she'd been studying so closely to find his hazel eyes on her. He licked his lips. His head moved closer to hers. She felt his untidy sun-bleached, cow-licked, dirty blond hair, which she desperately wanted to push her fingers through, brush the spiky magenta fringe of her own hair. She felt her lips part in response. This was it.

She tore her eyes from his. 'I should give James a call,' she said. 'Check he's alright.'

CHAPTER 47

Crowder had authorised overtime, although most of the team would have been in without it. Massey wouldn't get the preliminary pathologist report on Maureen Duffy until at least tomorrow and still awaited a fire investigation report on Stoneyriggs. But they did now have access to Durham's case, at least in theory, and permission to revisit anything relevant to the recent murders.

'That's what I want to concentrate on today,' Massey said. 'Including this list of local women alleged to have had affairs with Barron over the years, and a list of barbecue attendees on the day Kingsley died. There are three crossovers.'

One of which in particular would need careful handling.

'Did his wife know?' Jackson asked.

'We need to find out. Today, I want everyone at that barbecue reinterviewed. Maybe someone has reconsidered events from back then in a new light since these recent murders. Guy, can you organise that please? Christine and I will go and see Ursula Kyteler.' He looked towards Sparks. 'Do we know where she's staying?'

Donaldson rattled his keyboard. 'At Betsy Halliwell's. I'll send you the address.'

'She's another crossover. It makes sense for us to tackle both then.' He glanced at his phone as Donaldson's text came through, then looked at Sparks. 'By the way, Christine, how many more deaths are there in Macbeth?'

Sparks frowned and thought it through. 'Lady Macbeth goes doolally and dies. Possible suicide. Then Macduff chops off Macbeth's head in the last battle scene and presents it to the new King Malcolm.'

'So,' Keegan said. 'Verity Barron will top herself. No surprise there. She's already a whole sodding loaf short of a picnic. Duffy will miraculously recover and decapitate Barron, then everyone takes a bow, and we all get back to normal. Does that about cover it?'

Sparks laughed with everyone else. 'Just about.'

'Number three on this list is going to be a bugger,' Keegan said. 'How about asking DSU Portas to take that one on?'

'Good call.'

That was an understatement, given the sensitive nature of the questions that needed asking, and the respect due the widow of a retired Chief Superintendent of their own force. Elena Kingsley required someone of her own gender and as close in rank as possible to her dead husband. Durham should have pursued this line of enquiry further.

***

With so much on his own mind during the drive, Massey was happy with the silence, yet surprised Sparks ventured nothing about Helen's antics yesterday, even if only out of concern. It wasn't like her. Instead, she looked preoccupied. Not upset though. So, you know, sleeping dogs and all that.

Betsy Halliwell lived in the large double-fronted house Verity Barron had scuttled into yesterday.

It was Betsy who came to the door, looking professional. No longer the witch he'd seen spouting her lines at the tower, or the devil woman who – with the rest of her coven – had molested him at the after-match party. Like Ursula at the hospital after the fire, she had the grace to look abashed when she recognised him.

Today, a clinical emerald tunic made her olive skin glow, and prompted a memory of Ben Quinn telling him she was some sort of therapist who ran her business from home.

Was Verity a client?

'Ursula's through in the living room.' She indicated a door on the left of the huge modern entrance hall. 'I'll leave you to it.'

'Thank you. But actually, we'd like to have a chat with you too after we've spoken to Ursula, if that's possible.'

Betsy studied the Roman numerals of a huge, rusted metal skeleton clock on a wall between two doors and considered. 'I have a client due at half twelve.'

'We'll play it by ear then. We're happy to come back later.'

Betsy licked her lips. 'I'll call my client and try to change the time.'

He smiled. 'Thank you.'

CHAPTER 48

Ursula still looked haggard, but had pulled herself together a little since they'd last seen her and hid her devastation well.

It struck Massey that every woman they'd come across in this investigation had presented the team with multiple facets. Ursula Kyteler and Betsy Halliwell; brazen witches one moment, grief-stricken parent and efficient clinician the next. Verity Barron: devoted mother of a disabled boy the first time he'd met her all those years ago, seen variously now as a social-climbing snob, a terrified mouse, and a harridan determined to protect her abusive husband. And Trinny; seductive temptress one minute, busy single mother and brusque businesswoman the next, yet capable of morphing into a snarling vixen at the touch of a nerve.

And of course, Helen. Not part of the investigation, but overspilling into it. His beautiful religious wife of more than fourteen years, who'd lately mutated into a spiteful and unfaithful she-devil he'd had no idea existed.

'How is Fleur getting on?'

'Nothing has changed,' Ursula said in her Geordie/Scandinavian lilt. 'She is still in the coma. I don't know what to do for the best. I want to be there for her, but she does not know that I am. Talk to her, they say. She may hear you. But I do not think so. I try, of course I do. But it is hard not knowing if she hears me.'

'Has she been moved yet to the RVI?' Sparks asked.

'No. Still she is in NSEC. They do not want to move her just yet.' She waved her hands, dismissing her own problems. 'But that is not for you to worry about. Please sit. Tell me why you have come.'

Massey and Sparks sat on a squashy cream sofa. Ursula perched on the edge of a tan suede tub chair opposite.

'On the day Duncan Kingsley died,' Sparks said, 'you attended a barbecue at the home of Finn and Verity Barron. Tell us what you remember of that day.'

Ursula frowned. 'Why do you ask about that? What has that to do with what happened to my Ben and Fleur? You have the records of what we said then?'

'Did you go there on your own?'

'No. We all went together, the three of us. It was before Ben, and I... separated. We had argued... before we went. Some silly...' She looked as if she might burst into tears, but she sniffed and pushed back her shoulders. 'Ben and me, we were not friends that day. Fleur said we embarrassed her. So we stayed apart when we got there. But still everyone had a good time. Then those men came, they followed Duncan to the beach and killed him.'

'What makes you say that?'

Ursula threw up her arms. 'It says so on the news. But they did not know my Ben and Fleur. They had no reason to hurt them. Or Maureen. I am sorry. Betsy has told me what has happened. It is too tragic.'

'How well did you know Maureen Duffy?'

'Well, I think. She played one of the witches at the tower with Betsy and me last year. We spent a lot of time together.'

'Why did Maureen not take the part again this year?'

'Because she did not like...' Ursula put a hand to her mouth for a moment. 'She did not like being a witch. She preferred helping in the garden. So she... um...'

'Couldn't she have done both?' Sparks asked

'Yes, like me.' She gave her head a vehement shake. 'But she did not want to.'

Ursula was holding back, but they both instinctively left that thread dangling. There'd be another way into the subject.

'Who else was at the barbecue?' Massey asked.

'*Helvede!* Why do you need to know this now? What good will it do to... how do you say... rake over old coals?'

'Please, answer the question.'

Ursula pushed her fingers through her fringe. The sound of her bracelets jangling took Massey back to the lobby of the rugby club.

'Alright, alright,' she said eventually. 'I will tell you it all again. We were there, and Finn and Verity, of course. Duncan and Elena arrived before us with their two boys. Betsy too. The boys did not stay long. Then that man who plays Ross came, with his wife.'

'You mean Len Stafford?' Sparks asked.

'Yes. I never remember his name. It is like the rest of him; unremarkable. I have no idea of his wife's name. She too is unremarkable.'

'Anyone else?'

'Yes. Maureen and Michael, of course. And Trinity Moon with her son. Betsy says she has taken my place in the play. That is good. She will make a good witch. She is one already, I think.'

'Wow.' Sparks struggled to contain her scepticism. 'A real witch, playing a pretend witch. In Cresswell.'

'My name means cauldron. It is the name of a real Irish witch? Kyteler, I mean, not Ursula. Although Ursula is a witch's name too in a way because it is the name of a sea-witch in a children's movie. But Kyteler; Dame Alice Kyteler. The first woman in Ireland convicted of witchcraft. She was to be executed, but she escaped. Trinity told me all about it. Some people think Alice went to Flanders, but I think she went to Denmark, my home country. I believe she was my ancestor. Trinity says that Halliwell, Betsy's surname, is a witch's name too; a good witch, who helps people, and that is what Betsy does. And Scarlett too. Her last name is Crowley. It is the name of a great occultist, Trinity says.'

Sparks stared at Massey. 'Trinity says a lot, doesn't she?'

'About witches, yes. This is why I think she really is one. Her own name, Trinity, means three. Her surname is Moon and there is a moon goddess with three faces. Hecate, she is called, and she is in Macbeth, although we do not have her in our Cresswell Macbeth. So Trinity will make a good witch in my place, I think. She has even named her son with a warlock's name.'

What? 'Max is the name of a warlock?' Massey asked.

'No, I mean the boy's middle name. Christian. Trinity says it is the name of a famous warlock from Salem.'

Jesus. Max Christian Moon. His son was a junior warlock?

Sparks butted in. 'What about Maureen? Is her name a witch's name too?'

'Trinity says no, it is not.'

Sparks rolled her eyes. 'Oh well, if Trinity says so.'

'Is that why Maureen didn't want to play one of the witches this year?' Massey asked.

Ursula looked at him for a moment, recognising perhaps that she'd brought them back around to the point she'd been so reluctant to talk about before. 'No. It is because, um... She did not like making predictions for people. Like we, um... like we did for you, Chief Inspector. For Betsy and me, it is a game. But Maureen, she is – she was – superstitious about such things.'

Massey scratched his nose, wondering if she'd felt uncomfortable answering their earlier question simply because she felt embarrassed at what they'd done to him? Perhaps, but it can't have been the whole reason. 'I take it Scarlett doesn't have the same sensitivities.'

'No. For Scarlett it is different.'

'In what way?'

But Ursula refused to be drawn. They spent a further twenty minutes questioning her about the barbecue, particularly about when the landscapers arrived, but nothing stood out – apart from something she'd said at the beginning; that the Kingsley boys had left early, before most people had arrived. He'd only had a quick look through the Durham files so far, but could recall nothing about the boys being there at all.

'One other thing, Ursula,' Massey said, locking his eyes onto hers, 'Tell us about the affair you had with Finn.'

She drew in a sharp breath, then threw up her hands in frustration. 'That was long, long ago.' Then, suddenly, her face drained of colour. '*Ah, min Gud...*'

'What is it?'

'Ben is dead, and Duncan is dead. That is two...'

Her voice trailed off. Clearly, she knew about Elena's affair with Barron. And now both of their husbands were dead.

'Tell us about your affair.' Sparks said.

Ursula screwed her eyes closed and bit her lip. 'Fleur was a baby. It had been a difficult birth. We almost lost her. Ben, he adored her. He was so... thankful she survived. He gave her all his attention, for a very long time, and I felt, um... unloved I think. Neglected. Post-natal depression,

I think. Finn gave me back my confidence. In the early days, every day, he said I was beautiful. It was… exciting, I think, the secrecy. For a man to want me again, it… healed me.' She shook her head. 'This is not an excuse, you understand, for what I did, but it is a reason, I think. But then he stopped telling me I was beautiful. Our affair became a habit with him. And for me too, I think. And with no more excitement, there was only dread that Ben would find out. And although I knew the guilt of what I had been doing, I finally began to wonder what sort of man Finn must be that he could seduce his best friend's wife and yet always smile and joke to his face. And then it just stopped. With no words. One day, he just did not arrive at the place we used to meet. I waited for him, but I knew, and I was glad.'

'How long did it last?'

'A few months.'

'Did Verity ever find out?'

'I do not believe so. I hope not. That woman has had enough grief in her life. She has never said anything to me, so I think perhaps she does not know. Her son was still alive then, you understand. He was a child, disabled, and she was so busy with him. Perhaps Finn felt lonely, like me.' She gave a huge sigh. 'That is what I thought at the time. That is how I justified to myself what I did. Finn and me, we were just two lonely people clinging together.'

CHAPTER 49

'So Red's a witch now, is she?' Sparks demanded, when Ursula disappeared to find Betsy. 'And half the female population of Cresswell are witches too.'

'You're just upset about the Hecate bit.'

Sparks snorted. 'You know about the three faces of Hecate, don't you? The maiden, the mother and the crone. Red's version of a maiden looks more like a man-eating siren. We've seen the mother too now. I'm sure the crone will appear before long.'

Massey thought he'd possibly already seen that bit.

'You played the part of Hecate too.'

'Exactly. I just *played* the part, as a child. Red's claiming to actually *be* Hecate by the sound of things. Hecate's not only a witch in Macbeth, you know. She's a Greek goddess, if you please. Talk about ego. Red takes the biscuit.'

'Only according to Ursula who, quite apart from going through hell at the moment, is obviously more than a little gullible.'

Sparks would have responded, but they heard footsteps approaching.

Betsy poked her head round the door and glanced at another clock in the wall behind them. 'Can we get this over with now?'

Time was clearly important to Betsy.

'Of course,' Massey said. 'Thank you for sparing us the time.'

She flashed her eyes. 'I don't like messing my clients around. Establishing a structure they can depend on is part of the therapy, so disrupting their appointment times could risk destroying any progress we've made.'

'Noted. I'm sorry, but we'd still have needed to come back later if you hadn't changed the appointment.'

'*And* you've upset Ursula. I've just left her sobbing.'

'We're aware she's in a bad place right now, but we had questions for her. As we have for you.'

Betsy arranged herself in the tub chair. 'Then please, get on with it.'

'We understand you were one of the first people to arrive at the Barrons' house on the day Duncan Kingsley died.'

Betsy looked surprised, but recovered quickly. 'I was *the* first person to arrive, but only by moments. The Kingsleys arrived just as Finn poured me a drink. Their sons had given them a lift. Finn offered the boys a coke. I got the impression their plan in dropping their parents off was to have a few words with him. But they didn't hang around for long.'

'Did you hear what they were talking about?'

'I wasn't paying attention. Something to do with rugby. I felt obliged to act as peacemaker between Verity and Elena. They really don't like each other much. It was a relief when Ben and Ursula arrived with Fleur, and then the Staffords. I was more than happy to leave June Stafford mediating, while I went to join the fun gang. By that I mean Ursula and the Duffys, who'd arrived along the footpath through the fields at the back. And Trinny Moon of course, who arrived at the same time from along Beach Road.'

'With her son?'

'Yes, but he was picked up an hour or so later by that woman who runs the toddler group at the village hall. Anne someone or other. She has a son around the same age and was taking them to a birthday party somewhere.'

'Why didn't Trinny go with them?' Sparks asked.

'Probably because there'd be no free booze at a children's party.'

'She likes a drink, does she?'

'Oh yes. When she gets a bee in her bonnet.' Betsy laughed and raised her eyes towards Massey. 'Like when she saw you at the party last week. She sank a few that night, I can tell you.'

No-one broke the ensuing silence for an uncomfortably long time.

Allowing a silence to develop worked well with many interviewees, since it made people uncomfortable and forced them to fill the void. But Massey might have known a therapist would be just as practiced in the art as they were, and it was him who began to feel uncomfortable.

Eventually, he allowed Betsy her little victory and spoke first. 'You say Trinny had a bee in her bonnet at the barbecue. Do you know why?'

'No. She's not one to share, but she was in a strange mood from the moment she arrived and had words with Finn—'

'She argued with him?

'No shouting involved, and I didn't hear anything, but she was… brittle, I suppose you'd call it, for a while. Played with her phone to avoid getting involved in conversations. But then, typical Trinny, she became sweetness and light again later.'

'I thought you were all friends,' Sparks said. 'All witches together in your little coven.'

'Ah, I see. Ursula has been talking her nonsense, has she? She's taken what Trinny told her as gospel, I'm afraid.'

'She really believes she's a witch?'

'Who, Ursula or Trinny.'

'Either.'

Betsy blew out a sigh. 'Not sure if Trinny really believes it, or just likes winding people up. Ursula certainly believes everything Trinny told her about a witch called Kyteler. She looked it up online. There was supposedly an Irish woman convicted of witchcraft in the fourteenth century. She escaped and might have gone to the continent. But, well… People were superstitious then. Apparently, she'd mixed some remedies for a succession of sick husbands who subsequently died. All wealthy. All left her money. It was her fourth husband who accused her of witchcraft when he suspected he could be next on her list. So perhaps she was simply a murderess, or completely innocent.'

'And Halliwell is a witch's name too?'

'Ursula really has been chattering. Trinny laid it on a bit, and Ursula lapped it up. Apparently, Halliwell is the name of a *fictitious* magical family in some American TV series.'

'You like playing the part of a witch though.' Sparks said.

Betsy looked uncomfortable.

'Just a bit of fun.'

'Back to the day of the barbecue,' Massey said. 'You left June Stafford talking to Verity and Elena, while you talked to Ursula, the Duffys and Trinny. But what about Ben and Fleur, or Duncan and Len; where were they?'

'Oh, you know what men are like. Ben, Duncan and Len formed some sort of manly huddle around Finn and told each other tales of great barbecues of the past. Fleur, I'm not sure. Once the Kingsley lads left, she wandered around looking bored. Looking back, I have no idea why she stayed. There was no-one else her own age.'

'Why didn't Michael Duffy join the manly huddle?' Sparks asked.

'He and Finn tend to clash. Something to do with when Finn first moved here. I have no idea why he even went to the barbecue, unless Maureen insisted. He did whatever she asked. Not always with good grace. But she chivvied him along and joked about his grumpiness. How is he, by the way?'

'Was anyone else at the barbecue we haven't yet mentioned?'

'Not until the three men arrived. Since you're asking all these questions again, I take it there are doubts now about their guilt. Good. What reason could they have had?'

'Who do *you* think killed Duncan Kingsley?'

'No idea, but it's disconcerting to know they're going around killing people again now.'

'Can you think of anything anyone said or did back then that seems strange now in light of current events?'

'Nothing at all. The statement I made then still stands.'

Sparks smiled. 'Remind us.'

Betsy glanced at the wall clock again and sighed with impatience. 'Alright. No-one followed Duncan down to the beach. He went on his own, looking annoyed. Eventually, the three men left, and Finn came back to his guests in the back garden. No-one knew what had happened to Duncan until much later.'

'Was everyone within your sight the whole time?'

'No, of course not.'

'Then tell us who was where?'

'Must I? She rolled her eyes and sighed. 'While Finn was away, the men sat in a circle playing hunter gatherers who'd killed and cooked their catch over a fire to feed their tribe. Michael Duffy included, by the way. All the booze must have mellowed him. Duncan went off on his fateful walkabout, while us women fluttered in and out of the house, gathering up crockery and dirty glasses, loading the dishwasher,. You know, women's work. Because that's what—'

'You too?'

'What do you mean?'

'You helped with the "women's work" too? You don't seem the type.'

'Of course. I kowtowed to the pressure of fulfilling my allotted gender-stereotypical role. I didn't feel inclined to cause a scene by standing on my feminist principles in the presence of such a misogynistic host while enjoying the man's generous hospitality.'

'You think Finn Barron is a misogynist?'

'I *know* he is.' Betsy's lips had twisted.

'And yet you had an affair with him.'

She froze, her lips pressed into a hard line. Her eyes flicked to the clock, and she made a point of checking the time on her wrist. 'Did Ursula tell you that?'

'No. It's in the case files from last year.'

For a moment, Betsy looked confused, as if she'd been unaware Durham detectives had known about the affair, but then she rallied. 'I'm not sure "affair" is the right word. We rutted. That's all. We fucked each other. It was… basic, and it didn't last long.' She gave a swift bark of laughter. 'In both senses, I mean. The affair didn't last longer than a few weeks and Finn could never last longer than a minute or so. If that.'

'How long ago was this?'

'Last year.'

So recently? Massey was surprised. 'Was this before or after the barbecue and Duncan Kingsley's death?'

'Before.'

'Why did it end?'

'Finn moved on.'

'Onto another affair with someone else?'

'Why do you imagine that's something he'd have told me?'

'You didn't ask?'

'I have my pride, Chief Inspector.'

'Did anyone else know about your affair?'

'I didn't think so.'

'And now?'

'Ursula knows. It's something we have in common. I assume you've spoken to her about her own affair with Finn.'

'Is Finn seeing someone else now?'

Betsy pursed her lips for a moment. 'Finn is not the man he was a year ago. Some sort of health issue, I believe. So perhaps he can't even get it up anymore.'

'That doesn't answer my question.'

'It's all I have.' She stood quickly and brushed imagined creases from her emerald tunic, making a show of checking the time on her watch. 'That really is all the time I can spare. If you have more questions, you'll need to come back another time.'

***

Betsy closed her front door behind the detectives and sighed. Why had she said nothing? She'd had the perfect opportunity to unburden herself, but the ingrained principle of confidentiality had held her back. Her clients entrusted her with confidences they'd probably never told another living soul. Normally, she'd never contemplate breaching that trust. This was the first time in her entire career she'd had to weigh the ramifications of breaking confidentiality against the potential consequences of not doing so.

And really, the only thing holding her back was that what Verity had told her was not fact, but only her belief. If it had been just a small crime, she wouldn't be worrying about it. But murder, for goodness sake. That was not something she could ignore.

She'd tossed and turned through the night, fretting over what she should do.

Verity could be mistaken. Finn may not be the murderer his wife thought him to be.

Oh yes, she knew from her own experience he was a dick of the first order. And she could see the Barron's marriage was an abusive one, but not physically abusive. And that was the sticking point in the decision she had to make.

Verity had given no indication Finn had ever laid a finger on her in anger or malice.

But what if he really was the murderer, and had the opportunity to murder again simply because she'd decided that the debt of confidentiality she owed Verity was more important than the life of his next victim, or the next one? How could she ever live with herself?

Still standing behind the door, Betsy jumped when the bell rang. Her client had arrived. Struggling to replace the worry she knew must show in her expression with her usual professional serenity, she reopened the door.

'Come in Dom. I'm so sorry for having had to mess you—'

'What did they want? You didn't tell—'

'No, of course not. Everything you and I have discussed within our sessions is covered by the confidentiality policy we talked about at the start. The police are talking to anyone Maureen Duffy spoke to in the days before she was killed, and I happen to be one of them. Please, come on through.'

The last thing she needed was to upset Dom by telling him the detectives had asked about the day his father had been killed.

And now here was something else to worry about. She'd never considered the things Dom had confided to her in light of recent events, but now she'd have to. And that could open a whole new can of worms.

***

Sparks peered through the wing mirror at the figure disappearing through Betsy's front door. 'Did you see who that was?'

'Dominic Kingsley. He must be the client Betsy postponed for us.'

'Wonder what he's seeing her for.'

'Anger management sessions, probably.'

'Doesn't look like they're having much effect, the way he just stormed in there.' Sparks rubbed her hands together. 'So then, since we're here, are we going to call on Red too? If she had a bee in her bonnet, as Betsy put it, at that barbecue, then we need to know what that was about.'

'Keegan will have allocated that one to someone else.'

Seeing Trinny now was the last thing he needed. No way could he be the one to interview her. Given their previous relationship and the fact he'd fathered her child, he'd be mad to go within a mile of her until the murderer was behind bars. By rights, he should already have reported their relationship to Portas.

CHAPTER 50

The tap-tap-tapping of laptop keyboards gradually accumulated and rose to a crescendo as the rest of the team returned, until it sounded like a troupe of tap-dancing centipedes amid the background silence as the team concentrated on writing up their notes, each keen to claim back the last few hours of their Sunday.

Sparks wrote up their interviews with Ursula and Betsy, while Massey concentrated on his mounting pile of admin tasks. Fighting a losing battle, he was grateful when Keegan interrupted him with a rattle of knuckles on the open door of his cubicle office.

'Got a moment?'

'As many as you like, if it keeps me away from all this shit.'

Keegan closed the door behind him, his bulk shrinking the room's dimensions. 'You may regret saying that. I know you'll not want to discuss this.'

Massey raised his eyebrows and waited Keegan out.

'I know a good divorce solicitor, by the way, if you need one.'

'That's what you want to talk to me about?'

'No. Just saying. Alexandra Larkin. Here's her number. Extremely good, so I'm told.' Keegan slid a folded yellow Post-it note across the desk as he sat down, then laced his fingers across his belly and said nothing.

Massey unfolded the note and glanced at the surprisingly neat cursive script. 'Thank you, I think.'

Incapable of taking the direct route to making a point, still Keegan said nothing. But Massey had no patience today. 'Christ's sake, Guy. Out with it.'

'Lou will have spoken to Elena Kingsley by now. Doubt we'll find out what was said until the morning.'

Another detour.

'Very likely.' Massey tapped a finger on the desk.

Keegan shifted position.

'I'd prefer to adjourn to a pub somewhere to have this conversation, but I don't have time. Sarah has invited guests for dinner, and this can't wait.'

'The sooner you spit it out, the sooner you can be on your way.'

Keegan rubbed his hairy cheeks and grimaced. 'All right then, here it is. You need to be careful. That red-haired bint in Cresswell. I went to interview her myself today.'

'Trinny? Why?' He sighed and shook his head. 'I don't mean why was she interviewed. I meant, why you?'

'Because she's trouble, and she could bring you down if you're not careful. No way should you have gone, but I didn't want anyone else on the team there either. Not until I knew what sort of grenade she might be inclined to lob into the investigation, and into your life.'

'I don't know what you mean.'

'Yeah, you do. Remember a few weeks ago, just after Helen pissed off, when we went out for that drink? And then one drink led to ten and we both ended up legless, and I had to leave my car in the pub car park overnight.'

Massey knew the night he was on about but could recall few of the details. 'And?'

'Maybe you don't remember, but you told me all about what happened after that first charity match. About sneaking off to shag a woman who was on holiday in Cresswell at one of the caravan sites. You said Helen had found out and had never forgiven you, and you thought that must be the reason she'd left you now.'

Massey sighed. No, he didn't remember that.

Keegan scratched the back of his neck. 'I'd wanted to tell you then about her and Flowers, but it was just before he'd buggered off to Cumbria. Anyway, this *is* the same woman, is it not? That holidaymaker from back then is this Trinity Moon now. And lo and behold, she has a son just the right age to be a product of that night.'

Massey felt blood drain from his face. If Keegan had figured out Max was his son, then who else might? If this got out, it could finish him on the force.

With all the grief he felt over Helen's departure and the euphoria of realising he was a father after all, this was the first moment the stark reality of the situation and its potential repercussions had smacked him in the face. And one thing he knew immediately, without a doubt, was that he did not want to lose his job. Quite apart from the fact he loved doing what he did, he now also had to continue being able to financially support his son. He'd already missed out on ten years of the boy's life. He wasn't about to miss out on anymore.

'Does anyone else know?' he asked

'I'm sure Sparks has worked it out. But then she'd know if you all of a sudden had Weetabix for breakfast one morning instead of Frosties. No-one else, as far as I can tell. Yet. So you have two choices.'

'Only one, surely. I have to go to Lou and declare a conflict of interest, and hope she doesn't look too closely at why it's taken me so long to do so.'

'Or…' Keegan held up a forefinger. '… you can keep well out of the way of Cresswell until all this is over. Has the woman actually told you in as many words that you're the boy's father?'

He was about to say yes, but reconsidered. No she hadn't. She'd accused him of sneaking off into the night and leaving her with… something. But he'd cut her off in his haste to claim the child as his own. Then she'd said something about her being the only parent the boy had ever had and that he didn't need another.

'No. Not in so many words.'

In fact, in an effort to put him off the assumption that he could be Max's father, Trinny had taken pains to point out that he might not be the only man she'd slept with on that holiday. So, if she had no wish to acknowledge him or anyone else as the father of her son, why should he assume now that she would try to shove a knife in his back?

'At least the boy looks nothing like you,' Keegan said. 'That's a good thing.'

Massey's breath caught in his throat. Keegan had met his son. 'I still need to come clean with Portas.'

'Why would you do that? You know they'll take you off the investigation. Then they'll zoom in another DCI, who'll decide the

Macbeth theory is just too ridiculous to fly. It'll end up not being investigated properly, and those three landscapers will go to jail for life for something it's looking increasingly likely they didn't do. Fuck all that. You're the one we need to drive this.'

'They might ask you to act up. It's not like the DCI role is a stretch for you.'

Keegan snorted. 'Like that's going to happen. All this being back on the team now is just Lou winning me a temporary respite from my stint in Purgatory. I've a long wade through cold case shit to go yet before I'm forgiven. If I ever am. They're still busy trying to piss me off enough that I'll leave of my own accord to go and patrol a shopping centre.'

And yet, knowing full well his own punishment for breaking the rules, his friend was advocating he do the same. Although his issue with Trinny wasn't in the same league as the sins that had brought Keegan down.

'Look, just don't go off half-cocked before you've thought long and hard about all the possible repercussions. You just need to stay away from the woman and the kid. Christ, you can steer the ship just as well, if not better, from here.' Keegan glanced at his watch, then slapped his hands on his knees. 'Right, that's it. I've said my piece and now I'm off to play mine host. See you in the morning.'

He opened the door to leave, but another thought struck him, and he turned back.

'I found out what's up with Flint, by the way. He has cancer. He's been undergoing treatment for the last nine months, but has refused to go easy at work.'

***

Only once Keegan had gone did Massey wonder what Trinny might have said about the barbecue. He accessed Keegan's notes and began reading.

Trinny had gone with her son. The last guests to arrive. After a while, Max had been collected by his school friend's mother, who took both boys off to the birthday party of another school friend. That chimed with what Betsy had told them. Trinny had spent time talking to

Ursula, Betsy and Maureen, who told everyone they'd been asked to play the parts of witches at the gates of the tower at a Halloween event. Someone – Trinny couldn't remember who – had suggested they might raise extra money for the charity fund by making Macbethian prophesies for visitors, and they began making joke prophesies for people at the barbecue.

Massey had a sudden memory of Ben Quinn telling him about the women practicing prophesies on people last year. He hadn't known about the barbecue then though. Interesting that was when it started, but why the hell hadn't Ursula or Betsy mentioned any of that? Could it simply have been because it would draw attention again to what they'd done to him last week?

He turned his attention back to Keegan's report. Trinny had told him that Ursula and Betsy had gone too far when making predictions for Finn and things had turned a little nasty.

Keegan had asked what she meant.

Everyone, she'd told him, knew Finn was desperate to become club president when Duncan stood down, and so they told him that he would be, which was fine; he'd been pleased. He'd asked them for another prediction, and that's when things took a turn. They said he needed to watch his back, because the way he treated women was about to catch up with him. When he demanded to know what they meant, they said that although he'd become president, he'd quickly lose it if – and here Keegan had made a note saying Trinny claimed she was unable to remember the exact words used – he continued to mess a certain young woman around.

Originally, Trinny had claimed, she'd assumed they meant Fleur, and that it was a reference to Barron's antipathy towards women's rugby at the club, which Fleur was heavily into. But now she thought there was more to it, but couldn't be specific. Barron was angry, with Betsy especially, but then the three men had appeared from the front of the house.

The landscapers. The Blacklock brothers and their nephew, Wyatt.

Massey read on. Barron had begun boasting about the work he wanted done in the front garden: nothing but the best, and he was prepared to pay for it. Eventually, he took the men around to the front to measure up. By the time he came back, Trinny said, Duncan had already stomped off to the beach, never to be seen again, and Finn seemed to have forgotten all about the prophesies.

Massey counted the pages he had left to read. Too many for now. To be safe, on the off chance everything with Trinny came out in the wash, he accessed the reports of other interviews carried out that day and scanned through them so no-one could accuse him of being overly interested in this one. He didn't care if he was over-thinking. Better to err on the side of caution.

Through the door Keegan had left open, Massey saw Sparks take a call on her mobile. The look of delight on her face caught him by surprise. He'd never ever seen that look before. Whoever it was had better not be messing her around. They'd have him to answer to if they did, even if it was Dazz Albright. Sparks was overdue some happiness.

CHAPTER 51

Sparks raced from her rented garage to her flat, stripping off her jacket and shirt as she ran up the stairs. Five minutes to shower and slather herself in a body lotion her brother and sister-in-law had bought for her birthday. It took longer to decide what to wear. Not that she had much choice. Her wardrobe consisted of work clothes, running gear and a collection of jeans and casual tops. Nothing dressy. She wasn't the dressing-up type, which would never change. Dazz would have to take her as she was.

In less than half an hour of arriving home, she set out to walk to the Queen's Head.

With a big grin on his face and hands in the pockets of his jeans, Dazz watched her approach. They did an embarrassed dance, neither seeming to know what sort of greeting was appropriate on this, their first proper date.

'Hi,' he said eventually, opening the pub door for her.

'Hi, yourself.'

They sat at a table in a corner, squashed in on both sides by good natured punters who'd shuffled along to make room for them. Not so much room they could sit without touching each other though, so their thighs pressed together in a way she'd never have had the courage to initiate otherwise. Dazz rested his arm on the top of the seat behind her. Although not quite touching her shoulder, the gesture felt protective.

He'd spent the day with his children. Of course he had.

Apart from the bare essentials like, 'I see them as often as I can', or in one phone call, 'Sorry, can't run this morning, I have the kids,' it was a subject both had avoided so far. She because children were an alien species and he, she suspected, because he thought she wouldn't want to know. Until now, he'd have been right. But his children were an inescapable part of him. If she wanted to know Dazz, then she wanted to learn about that side of him too.

'Tell me about your kids,' she said.

He looked startled, but then his eyes crinkled and he grinned. 'Are you sure?'

'Yeah. What are they? I mean, apart from being little people. Are they boys or girls? I know they're only small. Are they at school yet?'

'I have two daughters. Mia and Grace. Mia is four. She's just started in reception class. Grace is three and attends a nursery four mornings a week. Angelica's mother has them other times when we're both at work.' He cast his eyes down to inspect his fingernails. 'Angelica is my wife.'

'Who left who?'

Dazz smiled ruefully. 'Neither. We came to a joint decision we were better apart.'

She felt compelled to ask her next question. 'Do you um… do you think that might change?'

He took hold of her hand in one of his meaty, rugby player paws – another first – and looked her in the eyes. 'No, I don't. But we'll always be friends, and we'll always jointly parent our two daughters. We've known each other since we were kids. We got together as a couple when we'd both just been dumped. You've met the woman I lived with before Angelica. Joanne Carr. She was involved in all that shit at Northumberlandia.'

She rolled her eyes. 'Oh, I remember her all right.'

He laughed. 'Yeah, well I learnt a lot with Joanne, most of it bad. Anyway, at the same time we split, Angelica's first husband left her too. We ran into each other one night in a pub, both drowning our sorrows, and we blurted out all the hurt. We clung to each other after that, and we healed each other. One thing led to another. We went on holiday to the US, and we came back married. It was as big a shock to us as it was to our families. Then the girls came, and the romance died, but the respect and friendship lived on, and it always will. I know, and Angelica does too, we've talked about it, that the fact we'll always be close might be difficult for future partners, but that's the way it has to be for our girls.'

She nodded slowly, appreciating his honesty. 'Are you getting divorced?'

'It'll happen eventually but, so far at least, it isn't a priority. We've done all the important stuff ourselves: separated our finances, sorted out the mortgage and maintenance arrangements, and whatever other practicalities were necessary. We've done everything, apart from starting divorce proceedings. Both of us think, why pay solicitors for stuff we're perfectly capable of doing ourselves, at least until it's absolutely necessary.'

'And what would make it necessary?'

He shrugged. 'When either one of us is ready to commit to someone else, I suppose.'

She could see in his eyes he was conscious of the risk he was taking in so truthfully laying out his situation, concerned she'd be put off by his ongoing entanglement with his wife. But she could see too how much it mattered to him to be honest, which spoke volumes not only about the man himself, but also about his intentions towards her. Because if he only wanted some casual fling, he'd be telling her whatever he thought she'd want to know in order to get her into bed, rather than all the things that might make her turn tail and run a mile. She felt a rush inside her of an emotion she didn't recognise. It almost brought tears to her eyes.

'We could go back to mine after this drink, if you like,' she said.

***

Everything fell into place after that. They wandered back towards her flat arm in arm, no hurry, stopping to lean against the railings and listen to the waves washing over the rocks in the darkness between Brown's Point and Table Rock Pool.

Dazz pulled her in closer and wrapped his arms around her.

She stood on tiptoes and kissed him on the lips, not caring about whether anyone might be watching from a window in the terraced redbrick houses opposite.

He brought one hand up to her face and they melted together for a long moment before he broke away, took her hand, and they ran the rest of the way home.

Once inside, Dazz slowed things down, as if afraid she'd take fright and back off if he came on too strong, too soon. And eventually, when they did finally get there, she realised she'd been right. Sex with Dazz was way, way better than anything she'd had before. For the first time in her life, she realised the difference between having sex and making love, and she knew she was falling hard for this man.

What a ridiculous expression, she thought. None of this felt like falling at all, not while they were flying together way above the clouds.

CHAPTER 52

Heading towards Cresswell, Massey mulled over his predicament. The only correct thing to do would be to tell Portas, but Keegan's words had made him pause. No other DCI in their right mind would give their Macbeth theory a fair crack. Yet he felt in his gut that it had not just something, but everything to do with the goings on in this small seaside village. He couldn't walk away from the investigation now, yet he'd have no choice if he admitted his relationship with Trinny and her son.

He turned right along Beach Road, drove past the village hall, and then left onto the narrow lane that led to the back of South Side, where Trinny's little cottage lay, parking as unobtrusively as possible, grateful his car was dark and its engine quiet.

No lights showed at the front of the cottage. He ignored the main door with its Ring Doorbell, and walked around to the courtyard. He could see a light in the kitchen.

He rapped gently on the door, not wanting to wake Max. No response. He let a whole minute go by before trying again, a little louder. About to give up, he spotted movement in a side window, then Trinny's face peered out. He stood back so she could see him better and reconsidered his wisdom in coming here.

Too late to worry now.

A security chain rattled. The door eased open a sliver. 'What are you doing here?' Trinny demanded, her expression anything but welcoming.

'I wanted to talk to you.'

'I assume this isn't official, since you're sneaking around in the dark on your own, and just this afternoon I had that big oaf round here asking me all sorts of questions. So what the hell could you have to say to me now?'

'Can I come in?'

Trinny thought about it for a moment, then spat out a sigh and flung the door wide, turning immediately and striding away, her shining copper mane bouncing behind her. She'd disappeared into the main part of the cottage before he could even close the door behind him.

He followed her, noticing as he passed through the spotless professional kitchen that two of her glass jars were out on the bench. He must have interrupted her in something. Checking stock perhaps.

Through a much smaller, homelier kitchen, he moved out into a short hallway. Trinny had disappeared, but two doors stood open. He paused at the first: toys lined up on a moonlit windowsill, a telescope aimed out to sea. Max's room. He didn't go in.

He found Trinny through the second door. A small lounge, lit by a couple of small incense burners and a string of fairy lights surrounding a large metal wall decoration: some sort of labyrinthian maze that, for some reason, reminded him of the hospital, where Fleur Quinn and Michael Duffy lay.

He reckoned this room would look out onto where he'd parked.

'Is Max in bed?'

Pointed chin raised, her chocolate eyes flashed. She gave him a long, measured look.

'I'm not here to argue, Trinny. I just want to talk.' Although now he was here, he couldn't think of a single word to say that she might believe.

He wanted to apologise for the deplorable way he'd left her all those years ago, because even if he didn't go to Portas, Keegan was right. He'd need to back away from Cresswell itself for the duration, and he didn't want her thinking he was running away. Again. He wanted to know too if, once this investigation was over and he was free to see her properly, she might like to go out with him. A date of sorts. To see if there could be a chance of something more between them. But most of all, he wanted confirmation he was Max's father. In her current mood, she could take any one of those questions the wrong way, and end up chucking an incense burner at his head.

And then, suddenly, her demeanour changed. Her aggressive stance relaxed. She stroked her hands down her thighs. Before his eyes, the spitting wildcat morphed into the sinuous feline he'd first known. She made a sound, almost like a purr, stepped into his personal space and rested a finger on his forearm.

'How about I pour us both a drink,' she said. 'And we can talk about anything you like? I have some wine already open.'

The scent of her filled his senses. Glancing down, he glimpsed that dusky mole in the valley between her breasts, right above her heart.

He already knew he'd ventured into deep water simply by coming here tonight, but now he felt the swell lift him off his feet. He should leave now, before it washed him so far out to sea he couldn't find his way back. But he couldn't go yet. Not until he knew for certain.

'That um… that would be nice,' he said. 'Just a small one though. I'm driving.'

***

She'd filled his glass almost to the brim. No way could he drink all that and drive. Perhaps that was her plan. If so, he was going to disappoint her. He was risking so much already simply being here.

He placed the glass on a side table without taking a sip. She disappeared again and returned with a plate of small square biscuits. Like some sort of mini cracker.

'I made these this afternoon with some leftover cheese,' she said. 'Parmesan and poppy seed crackers. Have some.'

The rich nutty aroma of the cheese made his stomach grumble, reminding him he'd only had a Mars Bar since breakfast. He took a couple. 'Thank you. They look delicious.'

They tasted delicious too. He took another couple and popped them into his mouth, then swilled them down with a slurp of wine.

She took the seat next to him on the small sofa, sitting so close he could feel the rise and fall of her breathing. 'What would you like to talk about?'

He hesitated, unsure how to start. 'Well, um… First, I'd like to apologise to you for how I behaved back then. More than a bit late, I know. Of course I don't expect you to forgive me. I mean, why should you? It was a cowardly thing to do. You see, I'd never intended to um… I'm not that sort of man. Usually. It's just that, um… well, you were just so beautiful. You still are.'

Her hand moved over to his knee, her fingernails tracing a pattern there that echoed the intricate design of her fairy-lit wall art.

He covered her fingers with his own and moved them back to her lap. 'That's not why I've come here.'

Something deep in her chocolate eyes flashed. She lowered her eyelids and held his gaze. Her lips parted.

He caught a groan in his throat before it could escape, disguising it as a cough and reaching for his glass, taking a big gulp of the wine. 'You know I'm investigating a series of murders here in this village. You'll have figured out we're looking again at Duncan Kingsley's death as part of that investigation, and um… well, you were a witness then. So…'

Her fingernails returned to his knee, lightly tracing the same pattern, moving to the inside of his thigh. He stilled her hand with his.

'… it wouldn't be ethical. You have to see that. We can't get involved with each other just now.'

Their faces were inches apart. She arched her back, deliberately pressing her right breast against his left arm. He could feel himself falling under her spell all over again. His own lips parted; their noses brushed together…

He jumped to his feet, upsetting the plate and scattering parmesan and poppy seed crackers across the carpet. 'I'm sorry. I can't do this. Not now. I have to go.'

***

Heart pounding, banging his head against his headrest, Massey raced his car up Cresswell Road in his hurry to escape his own stupidity. Keegan had warned him. His whole career could blow up in his face. Yet still he'd gone to see her. And for what? Because, despite her blatant efforts to seduce him, he knew his lame apology had fallen on stony ground. And he was no closer to confirming he was Max's biological father.

The wine on an empty stomach was getting to him. Sweat trickled down his back and under his arms. He ran a finger around the collar of his shirt. He was glad to reach dual carriageway at North Seaton that separated him from the over-bright headlights of oncoming vehicles.

Yet again, he'd failed to make time to eat properly, despite vowing to knock that bad habit on the head. He'd have to make himself something as soon as he got home.

But by the time he arrived, the last thing he felt like was eating. He lurched straight upstairs and flung himself down on the spare bed, his bed now, still fully dressed.

CHAPTER 53

Monday, 21 October 2024

Monday morning, seven-thirty. Massey woke, still feeling weird, with his quilt twisted into sweaty knots around him. He hung it over the banister rail on the landing to air and then stood under the shower for a full ten minutes, running the water as cold as he could bear it in an effort to pull himself round.

Perhaps he was coming down with something.

Before leaving, he downed a couple of cold and flu capsules with a large glass of ice cold water. No breakfast. He still didn't feel hungry, and yet he should be starving, since he'd eaten nothing substantial for more than twenty-four hours.

Despite the lack of traffic on the road at such an early hour, he debated the wisdom of being behind the wheel. A glittery aura surrounded his vision. He gave his head a shake, but failed to dispel it. He'd be fine once the medication kicked in, he told himself, and at least he'd had the foresight to push the packet of capsules into his jacket pocket.

Sparks arrived not long after him, an uncharacteristic radiance about her, until she looked at him closely. 'Are you alright? You look odd.'

'I'm fine. Just a touch of cold, I think.'

'I'll make the coffees. That'll sort you out.'

His mobile pinged. 'Portas. Better hold off on that.'

He pushed another couple of capsules out of the pack and slugged them down with the dregs from his mug first.

***

'James, take a seat.' Busy making coffee, Portas waved towards the table by the window.

The glare from the strip lights above her desk, such a contrast from the dim corridor outside, made Massey flinch.

'Are you alright? You don't look too good.'

He rubbed his eyes. 'Bit of a cold coming on. I'll be fine.'

'Light sensitivity? Could be measles. That's doing the rounds. My house guests left early. One of their kids came out in a rash. Turns out to be measles. Shame they had to leave early but Christ, the peace is lovely. Never fancied having kids myself. Doting auntie though. Make a fuss then hand them back.' She peered into his face, just as Sparks had done. 'Are you sure you're alright?'

'I'll be fine. Just a cold.' This conversation – the most personal they'd ever shared – felt weird. Every sodding thing felt weird this morning. Portas gave him another long look. But then, since Covid any unusual sign of illness tended to give people the heebie-jeebies. 'I've taken some cold and flu medication. That'll kick in soon.

Just get on with it, he wanted to shout, *and let me get back to work*.

Portas obliged. 'I've written up the conversation I had last night with Elena Kingsley. You should be able to access it now, but I wanted to give you a quick precis too. As you can imagine, she did not want to go there, but that wasn't an option.

'The affair started soon after Milo was born, and lasted for several months. Duncan was a DS at the time and involved in a big manhunt. You wouldn't have been in the job yet then, but you might remember the case. That big Westway Leisure Complex siege in London. Fifteen people gunned down: six dead. Three of the gang escaped and ended up in Northumberland. Huge manhunt. Went on for weeks. Duncan in the middle of it, leaving Elena on her own with a new baby, feeling abandoned. Barron called in one day while Duncan was at work, listened to all her woes, dried her tears, and so it started. Lasted almost a year. Only finished when Duncan nearly caught them at it. He'd called home for a change of clothes after some alky had spewed all over him. Barron hid in the loft while Duncan grabbed a conjugal quickie with Elena before heading back out to work.

'That was it for her. Too close a call. So she finished it, then spent years worrying over Duncan ever finding out.'

'And did he?'

Portas grinned. 'Yes he did. Someone told him at that barbecue, but Elena has no idea who.'

CHAPTER 54

Most of the team were in by the time he got back. Sparks pressed a mug of strong coffee into his hands and gradually he began to feel human again, although he probably still looked like shit.

'What's up with your mush this morning?' Keegan demanded, manoeuvring him into his office cubicle. 'It's like you and Sparks have changed places. She's all sweetness and light, and you look like…'

He leant in closer and stared him in the eyes.

'… Christ, are you on something?'

'Just a cold. I've taken some tablets. Or it could be measles, according to Lou.'

Keegan stepped away quick. 'Woah. Don't go passing measles around. It can shrink a man's bollocks. Or is that mumps? Yeah, probably. Mark my words though, measles will be just as bad, one way or another, for your average adult male and his wedding tackle.'

'What about your average adult female?'

Keegan shrugged. 'No idea. They might talk bollocks, but they don't have any.'

***

'Alright people,' Massey said. 'Let's get started. Quick recap, then we'll go through what we learnt yesterday.

'So then, Duncan Kingsley. Last year, Saturday fifteenth of July, a week before the original date for the charity match replay, the Barrons host a barbecue. At some point, Ryan and Justin Blacklock and Callum Wyatt arrive to quote for a landscaping job. They'd recently finished working at the Kingsley's home, and he'd given them an ongoing maintenance contract. Kingsley becomes upset and takes himself off for a walk on the beach across the road from Barron's house. 'He's eventually found stabbed to death on the beach, but because Northumbria is itself under investigation, and with Kingsley being one of our own retired officers, Durham Constabulary are asked to investigate.

'More than a year later, press reports claim they're about to arrest the three landscapers. Then we stick our oar in with our outlandish Macbeth theory, which links Kingsley's murder inextricably to those of Ben Quinn and Maureen Duffy.

'Reluctantly, Durham is beginning to get onboard with our theory because, in all honesty, their case against the landscapers is thin. Yes, all three have previous. Yes, they've found Kingsley's blood in the men's van and there's a fifteen minute deficit in their alibis. But could Kingsley's grumpiness over a garden makeover really be enough of a motive for such a vicious attack? And if they had the DNA more than a year ago, why haven't they charged the men yet? Because none of it stands up to close scrutiny, that's why.'

He grinned. 'And now we have an alternative explanation for Kingsley's bad mood that day, which could well blow Durham's whole case out of the water. But…' He held up his palms. '…we'll get to that later.'

It took several seconds for the murmurs to die down.

'Okay, so on Sunday the thirteenth of October – the day after the reorganised charity match – the home of Ben Quinn goes up in flames. Arson, we now know, to cover up the murder of Ben and the attempted murder of his daughter Fleur Quinn, who is unable to tell us any time soon what she may or may not have seen or heard. Ben's estranged wife Ursula Kyteler, who still lived at Stoneyriggs, stayed the night of the charity match and the day of the fire with a friend, Betsy Halliwell. Her alibi is sound.

'Like Kingsley's murder, we've found no motive anywhere near strong enough for such wanton destruction of life and property, although there's a link to Duncan Kingsley through the Ellington & Cresswell RFC. Kingsley was president. Finn Barron, as vice president, hoped to step into his shoes, but Ben Quinn, the club's head coach, was standing for election against him, along with another local man, Len Stafford.

'Less than a week later, on the evening of Friday, the eighteenth of October, Maureen Duffy is killed at home, while her husband is out.

Her dogs, who she thought of as her babies, are missing. Maureen's husband Michael Duffy is the club captain. He found her body when he returned home, managed to call it in, but had a heart attack before responders arrived and has been in intensive care since. We haven't yet been able to talk to him.

'Now, neither Duffy nor Quinn believed the landscapers killed Duncan Kingsley. In fact Duffy, due partly to the course of our investigation, decided Barron had murdered both Kingsley and Quinn because of his desperation to become the new club president. Duffy had been mouthing off about it in public. But if that were true, then surely Duffy himself would have been the target, not his wife, which would have made four victims with a close connection to the rugby club, and that's way too many for me, although once again we have no solid motive.

'But we do now have another link between the victims, in that their names are all similar to those of characters in Macbeth. And not only that, but their deaths happened in the same order as in the play. There are too many connections between the play and real events to ignore.

'So far, we've failed to locate the Duffys' dogs. We know they were out with a walker earlier that same day. So were they brought back home, and the killer later took them after having murdered Maureen? If so, why didn't the dogs attack them? We'd have found evidence if they had. Does the dogwalker still have them? If so, why not come forward? Their disappearance has been reported in the media. By all accounts, they're distinctive animals, and yet we have nothing. Are they even still alive?' He saw Donaldson raise his hand. 'Yes, Andrew?'

'Could Duffy be the killer? The dogs might not have attacked him. Maybe the blood on him didn't come from trying to help Maureen but from killing her.'

'We can't discount that yet. But surely the dogs wouldn't have allowed even him to hurt their mistress. They'd have become upset by the smell of blood, yet there was no evidence in or around the bungalow of that, and no-one heard them howling. I'm inclined to think they weren't there at all, although it could still have been Michael who took them away and then came back home to commit the murder.'

'But that wouldn't fit with Macbeth,' Sparks said.

'It would if it was Michael Duffy himself who came up with copying Macbeth, and he wanted to frame Finn Barron.'

'To the point he'd murder his own wife?'

'Unless,' Jackson said, 'the whole Macbeth thing has been an elaborate plot to hide his real motive for killing her.'

The discussion carried on for another ten minutes, every new suggestion even more outlandish than their Macbeth theory. And really, that's all it was. A theory on the execution of murder rather than a solid motive for it. As if the killer had invented a game for them all to play.

They took a break, during which time Keegan collared him. 'Did Lou get something from Elena Kingsley then?'

'Yes she did. A way more likely reason for Duncan's bad mood at the barbecue.'

'Come on then, give.'

Massey grinned, feeling much better now and enjoying the sensation of keeping Keegan dangling for a change. 'Later.'

'Bastard.'

***

Massey clapped his hands. 'Ready? Let's get through yesterday's interviews with the Barrons' barbecue guests on the day Duncan Kingsley died. Including the Barrons themselves, fourteen people attended that barbecue for some or all of the afternoon. Finn and Verity Barron; Duncan and Elena Kingsley, and their two sons Milo and Dominic Kingsley; Ben Quinn, his wife Ursula Kyteler with their daughter Fleur Quinn; Ursula's friend Betsy Halliwell; Michael and Maureen Duffy; Len and June Stafford; and Trinity Moon and her young son Max.' He glanced at Keegan, who raised his eyebrows and stroked his beard. 'We know that Milo and Dominic left early on, before most of the guests had arrived, and that Max Moon was picked up by the mother of a schoolfriend who took both boys off to a—'

'Jesus, what a name to saddle a kid with,' Phil Jackson said. 'Max Moon. Wasn't he some sort of crap wrestler?'

Massey bit his lip to stop himself from reacting. 'Okay, so Barron had been messing around with three of the women who attended that barbecue, but—'

'There'll be more than any three,' Keegan said. 'He's probably shagged his way around the whole of Cresswell and Ellington.'

His comment raised a few laughs.

'More than likely,' Massey said, 'but I want to go through the other guests first. Madge, you went to see Len and June Stafford.'

DI Madge Brown laid down the remains of a Penguin biscuit on its wrapper and dusted crumbs from her fingers. 'Lisa and I interviewed them at their home.'

She nodded towards a young blonde DC, drafted in to boost their ranks for the duration.

'Both were inclined to go off on tangents, but generally they stuck to what they'd originally told Durham. They arrived at the house at one thirty exactly, because the invitation had said from one o'clock, and apparently in June's book it's good etiquette, at a casual do, for guests to arrive thirty minutes late. On the dot. She was very particular about that.'

Keegan snorted. 'Which negates the word casual. Could Barron have shagged her too?'

'Only for a bet. Way too old maidish, I'd imagine. When they arrived, she sent Len into the kitchen with the container of salad they'd brought while she said hello to Verity, Elena and Betsy—'

'Which confirms what Betsy told us,' Sparks said.

'— then Len helped Finn with the barbecue, and all the men stayed together until the Duffys arrived, and Trinity Moon with her little boy. June thought it the epitome of rudeness that Michael and Maureen Duffy stayed together. Trinity and the boy sat with them and Ursula. Then Betsy left June with Verity and Elena to go and join them, which June wasn't happy about either.'

'Why was that?' Massey asked.

Madge snorted. 'I can't imagine many people would come up to June Stafford's exacting standards.'

'Not even her husband?'

'Particularly not him.'

'What about the Kingsley boys? Were they still there when the Staffords arrived?'

'No. June asked Elena why the boys weren't there, and Elena told her she'd just missed them.'

'Which means they left before half one. Do we have Durham's interview with them yet, Rob?'

Laidler shrugged his bony shoulders. 'Only as the sons of the deceased, from what I've seen so far.'

Massey cocked his head, thinking. 'Okay,' he said eventually. 'Guy, you talked to Trinny Moon.'

Phil Jackson gave a lascivious grin. 'Barron would definitely have tried his luck there. *Any* red-blooded bloke would be happy to shag *her*.'

Massey felt his fingers curl into fists and tried to relax them.

'Seriously, Phil?' Sparks demanded.

'I just mean...' Jackson looked sheepish. 'Well, she's more than just a bit fit, isn't she?'

'Now, now children. Are you going to let me get a word in?'

Keegan waited for the banter to calm down.

'Ms Moon confirmed that she and her son were last to arrive, and that the mother of the lad's best mate picked him up later and took both boys to the birthday party of another friend. She was hazy on timings though. She spent some time talking to Ursula, Betsy and Maureen, who announced they'd been asked to play witches at the gates of the pele tower for a Halloween event they were holding. Apparently Michael Duffy joked that they were hands down the best candidates for the job.' Keegan stroked his beard before continuing. 'Don't know about you lot, but if I suggested to *my* wife she'd be a shoo in for the part of a Halloween witch, I'd be sitting on a lily pad catching flies before I knew what had hit me.'

'Ribbit!' Jackson quipped.

'Anyway, someone – and the lady claimed not to remember who – suggested they dole out prophesies to help raise more for the charity, so they began making up joke ones there and then. All good natured at first, until Ursula and Betsy, although apparently not Maureen, got a bit too personal with the predictions they came up with for Barron. The first one, that he'd become club president when Duncan stood down, was fine, although I'm not sure Duncan himself would have been amused.

Barron's second and third prophesies were about the way he treated women, and one young woman in particular, and how it was all about to come catch up with him. Everyone assumed they meant Fleur, who then got upset by all the attention on her. Ms Moon says she now thinks there was more to it, but doesn't know what. So did Barron, who got angry. The situation might have blown up, if the landscapers hadn't arrived.'

Sparks looked unconvinced.

'Trinny Moon could have made up all that shit about prophesies. No-one else has mentioned it. Hers is one account against how many?' She started counting up on her fingers but gave up. 'Half a dozen or so. Can they all have lied by omission? Why would they? They'd all have had to conspire to keep their stories straight.'

Massey couldn't help himself. 'Why would Trinny lie about it?'

'Because she's a sodding nut-job. If what she's saying now is true, why didn't she say anything then?'

'And why did none of the others?' Ana said.

Keegan sucked in a big breath between bared teeth. 'A thought has just occurred. That barbecue is probably where this whole idea of imitating Macbeth began. Someone there that day looked around them, realised the likeness of certain people's names to those in Macbeth and thought, why not make murder imitate art? And that couldn't have been the landscapers. Apart from them being the most unlikely Shakespeare enthusiasts you'll ever find; they could never have known everyone's names.'

Madge Brown looked incredulous. 'You believe there's no motive at all for these murders,' she said. 'beyond imitating the play?'

'I wouldn't go that far. It would take a truly warped mind to murder just for the hell of it. And there's still a problem with Duncan, unless we can prove someone else *did* leave that party and follow him down to the beach, or that it was someone else entirely.'

'Here's something else to mull over then,' Massey said. 'Elena Kingsley has confirmed she had an affair with Finn Barron when Milo was just a baby. Duncan knew nothing about it until someone at that do told him. That's the reason he stormed off to the beach. Nothing to do with the landscapers.'

'Wouldn't have been Barron,' Keegan said. 'Why would he?'

'Who else could possibly have known?'

'Verity? Maybe she's always known about his affairs.'

'Or maybe he shot his mouth off to someone else.'

'Looks like Barron has a thing about new mothers too,' Sparks said. 'Ursula told us yesterday that her affair with him began when Fleur was just a baby. And Fleur was in the same school year as Milo. Maybe Barron was knocking off Ursula and Elena at the same time.

CHAPTER 55

Two messages awaited him when they emerged from their briefing. The first was from the hospital. Michael Duffy had insisted on seeing them and his consultant had deemed it potentially more harmful not to allow him to get whatever he had to say off his chest. Although there'd be a time limit imposed, and they could be kicked out at any point if Duffy became too distressed.

The second message intrigued him. Betsy Halliwell wanted to speak to him as soon as possible. Anywhere away from Cresswell. He thought about dragging her all the way to Middle Engine Lane and subjecting her to one of the intimidating interview rooms there. But while he wanted to challenge her about her account of what had happened at that barbecue in light of Trinny's statement, he didn't want to alienate her unless it became unavoidable. Instead, Sparks arranged the use of a small conference room at Hartington station. Closer to Cresswell but still far enough away. He was glad Sparks would be with him. After last night's events he was struggling to maintain any sort of objectivity when it came to Trinny.

They'd left Keegan making arrangements to interview the three landscapers as soon as possible and the rest of the team concentrating on examining all the records Durham had given access to so far. At least his vision had improved, and he didn't feel quite so spaced out behind the wheel. He had no time to be ill, and especially not with measles for goodness sake. Not with everything else going on, like all the strangeness surrounding this case, Trinny's sudden reappearance in his life, and having to deal with Helen's shenanigans too.

It wasn't that he thought Helen unreasonable wanting things from the house. Not if this truly was the end of their marriage. They'd both worked bloody hard for everything they owned and apart from personal possessions, they were both entitled to an equal share. It was just that he no longer trusted her to do the right thing. They'd been together for sixteen years and married for more than fourteen. Yes, he'd been the one to first put their marriage in jeopardy, but she'd forgiven him.

Or so he thought. Now he wasn't sure.

The fact she'd been messing around with Ray Flowers behind his back for at least the last nine months, and with who knows how many other men before then, would suggest not.

Did anyone at work other than Guy and Lou already know about her and Flowers? Had they been laughing behind his back?

There he goes, the cuckolded husband.

Jesus wept. He had no regrets now about changing the locks, despite being pelted with his precious vinyl albums in the street.

His laugh elicited a puzzled glance from Sparks. He shook his head to dismiss it as nothing.

He probably *should* make seeing a solicitor a priority now. The one Keegan had suggested. What was her name? Antonia or Alexandra? With a surname that reminded him of Bradley Walsh, for some reason? He'd slipped the Post-it note into his wallet. Maybe once they were finished at the hospital and in Hartington he could find a few moments to make an appointment. And then, once this case was over and done with, he could ask Trinny out. They could have a proper talk about their relationship, and about their son.

***

NSEC's labyrinthian maze of corridors reminded him now of Trinny's metal wall art, although they didn't need to venture quite so far into the maze this time, finding the Cardiology and Coronary Care ward without too much trouble.

Duffy looked like he'd aged at least ten years in the days since they'd last seen him. His cheeks had hollowed, and the natural furrows of his face had etched themselves into deep crevasses.

Desolate misery haunted the man's eyes.

Wired to bleeping monitors, he struggled to sit up until the nurse who'd shown them to the room rushed forward to quiet him, raising the head of the bed until he was almost upright.

A thin, compact man in crumpled green scrubs and black Crocs followed them into the room. 'DCI Massey? A moment please. I'm Steve Todd, Mr Duffy's consultant. I spoke to you on the phone. I must remind you that Mr Duffy is very ill and needs to stay as calm as possible. I appreciate the nature of the conversation you need to have with him will make that difficult, but please try not to get him worked up.' He turned towards the patient. 'And you, Mr Duffy. Ten minutes and no more.'

'Have you arrested him yet,' Duffy demanded, once they were alone, his voice much weaker than before.

'Who?'

Duffy gave an exhausted sigh. 'Let's not play games. Finn bloody Barron, of course.'

'Tell us why you believe we should.'

'Why?' Duffy's face crumpled in his effort to spit the words out. 'Because that man murdered my wife.'

'Did you see him there, at your bungalow?'

'Of course not. He'd gone by the time I came home and found… oh God, Maureen…'

'We have no evidence to arrest—'

'What the hell have you been doing all this time? He murdered Ben, and Duncan. Of course it was him who killed Maureen. You must have something on him.'

'Why did you go out that evening, Michael?' Massey could see the effort it took Duffy to control his frustration. 'Where did you go?'

'To see… Milo.'

Like Macduff travelling to find Malcolm, leaving Lady Macduff behind. Sparks was right. It *did* all come back to Macbeth. 'Why did you do that?'

Duffy's legs began to tremble. Had his lips turned more blue?

'Because he… asked me to meet him.'

'Was that before or after we saw you that afternoon?'

'Just after you'd gone. Maureen was annoyed because it meant we'd be eating late. She doesn't like that. Never has.' Duffy's eyes reflected the moment his brain caught up with his words. It no longer mattered how late he chose to eat in the day.

Massey felt a pang of sorrow for the man. 'Why did Milo want to see you?'

'I never found out. Not properly. We chatted and played darts. Then a couple of his mates distracted him, so we never actually talked about why he'd called.'

'Where did you meet?'

'The Benton Ale House. And don't worry. I had the car, so I drank coke.'

'Milo drives, doesn't he? Why did he not go up to Cresswell to see you?'

'The lad wrote his car off last year.'

Sparks shifted forward in the slippy blue armchair next to the bed. 'How did he manage that?'

'No idea. Wrapped it around a tree. Lucky to walk away unscathed, from what I heard. Uses his mother's car now, when she allows it. What has any of this got to do with anything?'

'Was that before or after Duncan's murder?'

'After. The grief, probably. Look what is— *Aagh!*'

He pressed both hands to his chest and grimaced.

A machine next to him bleeped faster.

'I'll get a nurse,' Sparks said.

Duffy shook his head violently. 'No you bloody won't. I just need a… minute.'

Massey and Sparks exchanged a look. They should go. They were putting his life at risk. They could speak to Milo if they needed to know more.

'Had the dogwalker brought the huskies back before you left to go and see Milo?' Sparks asked.

'No. I… said I'd pick them up on my way home, but then I didn't need to when he told me he'd already dropped them off there.'

'Who is the dogwalker?'

Duffy waved the hand with the cannula, pulling the tubing tight. 'I don't want to get the lad into trouble. He doesn't… do it as a proper job.'

'We're not interested in that. But if he'd taken them back, where are they now?'

Duffy looked at Massey, and then at Sparks. Teeth gritting in pain, he processed what they *hadn't* said – that the two big huskies can't have been taken home after all.

Eyes scrunched now, knee jumping up and down in the bed, Duffy's fingers clutched the front of his surgical robe. An alarm screeched out from the machines beside him.

His lips really had turned blue now.

Massey had already flung open the door. 'Nurse!' he shouted.

***

They waited in line at the car park exit, it's electronic arm on a go slow.

'We still have no idea who the dogwalker is,' Sparks said.

'You saw the state of him. Jesus Christ, we could have killed him.' They'd hung around outside the ward until they knew Duffy had been stabilised, Massey's own heart pounding in his chest at the thought they could have caused irreversible damage to Duffy's. They should never have gone to see the man; he could have died because of the pressure they'd put him under.

'I know what you're thinking,' Sparks said. 'But it wasn't our fault. You heard what the doctor said this morning; it could have made him worse if he *hadn't* been able to tell us what he needed to say.'

'But he didn't tell us anything, did he? Other than having another rant about Barron.'

'He did, in a way though. We now know it was Milo who got him out of the house that night, at the last minute. We can speak to him to find out what it was all about. We also know the dogwalker is male and probably young. He doesn't declare the income, so probably doesn't advertise beyond word of mouth. Therefore he's unlikely to be one of the small businesses we've been looking at. We also know that he lied. He can't have taken the dogs home at all that night. So he is definitely on top of *my* list of people for an urgent talking to.'

'Mine too, if only we knew who the hell he is.'

'Here's a thought, if Milo and Duffy are such bosom pals, the lad might know who the dogwalker is.'

CHAPTER 56

By the time they'd cleared security at Hartington station and exchanged some small talk with Desk Sergeant Bob Fossey, Flossie to all and sundry, a small meeting room had been vacated for their use.

Betsy looked more flustered than they'd seen her before. 'I thought I was going to be late,' she said. 'I got stuck behind a tractor for ages.'

'You're here now,' Massey said. 'So tell us what this is all about.'

Betsy puffed out her cheeks. 'This is difficult. I'm not comfortable at all with breaching confidentiality. It's something I'd never, ever do normally. This is the first time in my whole career I've ever found myself in this position, so I'm not going to lie, this is tough for me.'

'We appreciate that. We—'

She held up a hand to silence him. 'You see, if it wasn't for the small matter of safeguarding, I wouldn't be here at all.' She laughed, with not a trace of humour. 'Small. Hell, this could be huge, or it could be nothing at all you need to know about. I don't know. But I can't take the risk.'

This time, both Massey and Sparks allowed her the time to gather her thoughts, which involved another couple of deep calming breaths before she was ready to continue.

'I'm a psychotherapist, specialising in hypnotherapy. As a matter of course, I inform all my new clients of the high level of confidentiality they can expect. You'll appreciate, I'm sure, that clients sometimes tell me things they would never divulge to their family or friends, and they need to know that their secrets are safe with me. However – and this is important, although I don't suppose many clients take much notice – I do also cover the limited situations in which I may be obliged to breach that confidentiality, which I've never had to do before. But in this particular instance…'

Betsy scrunched up her face.

'You mustn't get the wrong impression…'

'How could we do that?'

'Because I know exactly what you're going to think. That I'm just blabbing to you out of some warped sense of jealousy or revenge. Which is not true at all.'

'How about you just tell us?' Sparks said, looking pensive.

Betsy exhaled one final big breath, as if preparing herself for an ordeal. 'During a recent hypnotherapy session,' she said, 'Verity Barron told me she believes her husband is the murderer you're looking for.'

Whoa.

'She said that in so many words?' Sparks asked.

'Several times over the course of an hour. But here's where this is all so difficult for me. You see, this is only what Verity believes, not what I know to be fact. And I don't want you thinking that I've come running to you just because Finn threw me over last year. For a start, he is not the man he used to be.' Betsy twisted her mouth. 'He used to be such an attractive man, but not anymore. If you ask me, he's ill. He looks spaced out most of the time. Verity too, now I think about it, although she insisted to me twice when I registered her that she's on no medication but a hydrocortisone cream for her eczema. But anyway, this is murder we're talking about. I can't just sit and hope that Verity could be wrong. What if someone else dies and I could have done something to prevent it?'

***

They spent another half an hour with Betsy, probing her professional opinions on the things Verity Barron had told her, hitting a brick wall whenever they attempted to push her beyond the line in the sand she'd drawn to protect any other confidences Verity had entrusted to her. If she herself had judged them to have no bearing on whether or not Finn was their murderer, then that should be sufficient, she told them. It wasn't, but they couldn't force her to expand without a court order.

Given Betsy's intimate knowledge of Finn, they asked whether she herself believed he could be guilty of the murders. She thought about it for a full minute before coming back with a highly qualified negative. The Finn she'd known then could never have done those things, but he *had* changed a lot recently.

Having got the issue off her chest, Betsy began to gather up her coat and bag in preparation for leaving.

'Something else you might be able to help us with,' Sparks said. 'Seeing as you're already here.'

Betsy looked at her in surprise. 'What's that?'

'The day Duncan Kingsley died. Finn and Verity's barbecue. We've spoken to everyone who was there now – or at least all those still alive – and we want to revisit some of the points you made yesterday.'

Betsy's smile became fixed. 'Of course. Whatever you need.' Slowly, she sank back down into her chair.

'You didn't tell us the whole story. Things happened at that barbecue that you conveniently left out.'

'Well, it was more than a year ago. You'll forgive me for not remembering all the ins and outs.'

'You and your coven spun some prophesies that day, didn't you? You and Ursula. And Maureen of course, but she's no longer with us to talk to.'

'What point are you trying to make here?'

'Things became a little heated, we've heard.'

'That was nothing. Just a stupid joke.'

She conjured up an apologetic look and turned it on Massey.

'Exactly as we did to you at the Rugby club. We do tend to get a bit boisterous when we've had a drink, I'm afraid. Finn shouldn't have been so generous with the booze.'

Sparks snorted. 'You told DCI Massey he was going to *die* when the moon wanes, or some such crap.'

'Yes well, I'd had a few. I had to go one better than the others. Is that really what I said?'

'You don't remember?'

Betsy put her head to one side. 'Um…'

'Jesus. So which one of you told Finn Barron at the barbecue that the way he treated a certain young woman was about to catch up to him?'

'Someone has been telling tales, haven't they? Alright, look, I'll come clean. It was me. I may not be bothered about Finn now, but back then he'd just dumped me for a much younger model. Someone far *too* young for him, if you get my drift. It was disgusting. She was still almost a child. So yes, I was jealous, but I was also determined to protect that girl.'

'Are you talking about Fleur Quinn?'

'What? No, of course not. Fleur was there at the house, with her parents. I wouldn't have put her into such a position. And I wouldn't have done that to Ursula. She's my friend. Is that what you've been told?'

Neither Massey, nor Sparks responded.

'Well you've got it wrong. It definitely was not Fleur.'

'We'll need the name of the girl,' Massey said.

'Oh no. No, no, no. I'm not giving you that. I've broken one confidence today. I'm not breaking another.'

'Really?' Sparks looked at her in disgust. 'I find it more than a little ironic that you don't appear to have questioned the ethics of taking Verity on as a client after you'd been screwing her husband.'

Betsy huffed and straightened the collar of her blouse. 'That,' she said, 'was more than a year ago. It was over and done with long before she asked me to see her.'

'Perhaps not for Verity, if she were ever to find out.'

'Is that a threat?'

'An observation. On the off chance there is a genuine conscience lurking in there somewhere.'

'Right. I see.' Betsy lifted her chin and sniffed. 'Am I free to go?'

***

'You were a little harsh there.' Massey said, after they'd seen Betsy out and collected their things.

'She deserved it.'

'She did. So tell me what's up. I know something is. I'll take a guess. Something to do with Macbeth. I caught the bit about Duffy going off to see Milo and leaving Maureen at home, just like Macduff went off to see Malcolm, leaving Lady Macduff at home. Exactly as you'd said. But there's something else now, isn't there?'

'There is.' Sparks shook her head. 'And it's got me baffled. You see, in the play, Lady Macbeth's gentlewoman tells the doctor about her lady's strange behaviour. Lady Macbeth had started wringing her hands and muttering about the murders while sleepwalking. And now we've got her real world equivalent with eczema of her hands, telling a hypnotherapist stuff about our current murders. Verity was hypnotised. So, in a way, she was sleepwalking. And Betsy is a sort of doctor, isn't she?'

'What's so baffling? Surely this reinforces the Macbeth theory. And what does the doctor in the play do about it?'

'He tells Macbeth.'

'Well there's a plus. Betsy came to us instead. So how is it bothering you? Beyond the whole ridiculousness of a murderer imitating the plot of a Shakespeare tragedy, I mean,'

'It's just that I can't see how the killer could have engineered this situation. I mean Kingsley's murder, yeah, at a push. It fits with the play, and it's probably what started the whole thing off and got the killer thinking about Macbeth in the first place, rather than it being their first set piece of an entire murder plot masterplan.

'Ben Quinn and Maureen Duffy though, their murders had to have been planned to fit with the play, although the fact Michael Duffy had a heart attack doesn't fit and can't possibly have been planned. But all this with Lady Macbeth and the doctor, or Verity Barron and the hypnotherapist, does still fit with the play, and yet I can't see how it could have been part of the plan. The killer might want to point us in the direction of Finn Barron, but they couldn't have known Verity would go running to Betsy. It's like the play is developing a new life of its own.'

'Unless the real killer is Verity or Betsy, Massey said. 'They both have a motive for wanting Finn out of the way.'

'As we've said before though, would they kill innocent people just to point the finger at him?'

'Okay, so you think Kingsley's murder is what sparked the Macbeth idea in the killer's mind. That means Kingsley may not have been killed by the same person.'

'Possibly. And are we really to believe that the tower staging Cresswell Macbeth at Halloween is a coincidence?'

'You have a point. Maybe we need to look at the people of the tower again. We might have to upset your mate Tom Kirk while we're at it.'

'Bog off, James. He is not…'

She gripped her hands into fists.

'Just winding you up, Christine. But we do need to go back up there.'

As he spoke the words, he remembered Keegan's warning. Nothing he could do about that if he wanted to speak to Kirk face to face as soon as possible.

CHAPTER 57

Tuesday, 22 October 2024

Another stupidly early morning in the office after yet another wakeful night. But at least he'd woken with no rash, no cold-like symptoms, and his eyes were fine now, so he couldn't have measles. Therefore, while he still felt more tired than any dog had a right to be, he wasn't about to die. His fatigue surely had more to do with all the other shit going on in his life.

Jesus Christ, why the hell had he thought about dying? Immediately, it brought Betsy Halliwell's prophesy to mind. He'd managed to forget about it until Sparks mentioned it yesterday. Betsy had told him he'd be facing death before the moon wanes. And what else? Ah yes. That only he could decide if he wanted to live or die.

Of course he'd choose to live. Why the hell should he not?

Complete load of codswallop anyway.

Yet the memory hooked itself into his conscious mind like a burr into an animal's coat, and he couldn't resist googling the phases of the moon to find out how much time he potentially had left to live. Which was utterly ridiculous and something he blamed on his lack of sleep.

But still...

Betsy had made the prophesy on the twelfth of October; the day before Ben Quinn was murdered. Then, on the evening he'd almost run Trinny over, he remembered looking up at the moon as he'd locked up the village hall. That was the night Maureen Duffy was killed, so the eighteenth. A super full moon, the Hunter's Moon had already begun to wane, and the new moon, he now knew, began on the first of November.

According to Betsy then, at some point between now and the thirty-first of October, he could expect to find himself facing death.

Which, of course, was rubbish. Complete twaddle.

And yet the other two prophesies had come true.

Ursula's, for instance. She'd told him that before midnight on the night of the party he was going to come face-to-face with something from his past that he'd far rather forget. And then, lo and behold, right in front of him had been Trinny, the woman he'd spent more than a decade trying to forget.

But not only that. Scarlett's prophesy had come true too. She'd told him he'd be presented with a fabulous opportunity, which would have difficult conditions attached.

And then, wonder of wonders, he'd discovered he had a son. He'd fathered a child with Trinny on that fateful night all those years ago. Was it a fabulous new opportunity? Absolutely yes. A fresh chance to become a father after all the years he and Helen had tried and failed to become parents again.

But much as he wanted to, he couldn't claim the boy as his own without risking his entire career. At least not until they'd solved these murders and put a killer behind bars. And perhaps not even then, if he failed to convince Trinny to allow him to be part of Max's life. So, 'difficult conditions', to say the least.

Maybe not such complete twaddle after all. Perhaps he should start being a little more careful with his personal safety.

In his tiny office, he unwrapped the Gregg's sausage, bacon and omelette baguette he'd picked up on his way in and began eating while contemplating his fate. A knock at the door made him jump.

***

It was another unseasonably clear day, although a bit nippy outside now, even in the sun. Massey walked Greg Ferguson from Fire & Rescue out to the car park, thanking him again for calling in so early with some information they'd be receiving later anyway as part of an interim report; something odd enough Ferguson had thought an explanation in person was in order.

It had certainly been that, and now Massey had to explain it to the team.

'Just a quick catch up this morning. I know DI Keegan needs to be off in ten minutes. Greg couldn't hang around to chat, but he did bring us something important. He believes they've identified the weapon used to kill Ben Quinn and injure Fleur. They found remains of animal bones on the kitchen floor tiles, next to where Fleur lay.'

Everyone looked puzzled. The Quinn's had no pets. Why on earth would there be animal bones in the kitchen?

'Ah, I get it,' Jackson said, grinning. 'It was the Sunday roast. Fleur had her head bashed in just as she was taking the meat out of the oven.'

'You may laugh,' Massey said. 'But you're not that far from the truth. Greg believes the murder weapon *was* a joint of meat. A leg of lamb to be precise; likely frozen and wielded as a club. Remember, there was a big freezer in the cellar. Both Ben and Ursula worked at a wholesale butchery place, so it was likely jam-packed with meat. It looks as if Ben was killed first. Bashed in the head by his own leg of lamb. It fits with the wounds sustained by both of them.'

'A spur of the moment thing then,' Sparks said. 'The killer didn't go there with the intention of committing murder and just seized something they could use as a weapon.'

'But that,' Keegan said, 'would likely blow your Macbeth theory out of the water. Something that detailed is not going to just spring fully formed to a person's mind at the drop of a hat.'

'Or else it was someone who knew perfectly well there'd be the ideal weapon in that freezer,' Brown said. 'And who could that be but Ursula?'

'She might have a beef against her husband. Get it?' Keegan's beard bristled around a huge grin. 'But she's not going to brain her own daughter too, is she?'

'She might,' Jackson said, 'to save her own bacon.'

'God, that's offal.' Massey said, and waited for the groans to die down.

'Alright, back to business. Forensics found a partial shoe print in the bungalow. Someone other than Michael trod in Maureen's blood. We now know it wasn't one of the paramedics, so the print may belong to our murderer. Just the edge of a sole, but with two unique markings that will allow us to put the owner at the scene if we find the shoes. They're searching the database for a potential brand match now. They've also discovered traces of a fine black dust on the nightdress Maureen was wearing. Nothing else similar in the bungalow. So this too may have come from our killer, unless Maureen was in the habit of wandering around outside in her nightie. Or it could be something the dogs picked up on their coats at some point and transferred to Maureen. Although, if that were the case, we'd likely have found the dust scattered elsewhere in the property too.'

'No news on the dogs yet? Ana asked.

'None. Michael Duffy told us that the walker they used is young and male, and doesn't declare his dog-walking income, so he probably hasn't set up and advertised as a business. Michael's too ill for us to push him any further on the lad's identity, but someone must know, and we need to find out quick. The fact he hasn't come forward may mean he's implicated in Maureen's murder at least. Does he still have the dogs? They're distinctive. Assuming they're still alive, they'll still need to be fed, watered and exercised and, trust me, they are going to be vocal. So why haven't we found them yet? Andrew, Lisa, I want you to drop whatever you're working on this morning and concentrate on finding that dogwalker and those dogs.'

He spotted Keegan taking a look at his watch. Flint had called first thing. The three landscapers had been brought in and were awaiting his pleasure in Durham. Keegan would be permitted to interview each of them in turn, although not without Flint in attendance.

'Okay then, that's it for now. Madge, I'd like you to work with Phil and chase up Brian Truman and Jodie O'Neill. Ray and Ana, I know you still have your hands full going through the Durham case files. Guy's off to interview the landscapers. Christine and I are off to Cresswell Pele Tower to see Tom Kirk and Colin Chirnside. We'll take it from there and I'll keep you all updated.'

Keegan paused just outside the door, where only Massey could see him, and shot him a warning look, but he already had every intention of staying as far from Trinny Moon as possible.

CHAPTER 58

Over the last couple of days, Sparks had found it difficult to know what to say to Massey unless it was something with direct relevance to work. He was her best friend, but she suddenly felt tongue-tied in his presence. Dazz had become such a massive part of her life within such a short space of time. What was it now? Just ten days since the charity night party. Nine since she'd forced him to accompany her to Cresswell to help discover the identities of Red and her coven. Not nearly long enough to reconcile everything else in her life around this new relationship. It felt like trying to fit an extra piece into one of those 3-D shape puzzles.

She had two big issues. Firstly, how might her growing relationship with Dazz impact her relationship with Massey, which was too precious to mess up? Over the past two or three years, Massey had been there for her throughout the dark days following the death of her father, and then her mother's worsening dementia. As a mentor, he'd protected her, shown her how to manage all the anger she had inside, and generally helped her feel human again. She owed him her career, certainly. But it felt like so much more than that.

In January, when Portas and HR had ended the mentoring arrangement, she'd panicked, terrified it would mean the loss of her friendship with Massey too. But instead, it had blossomed to the point she'd even been welcomed into his family. Not by Helen, of course, whose opinion no longer mattered. But by his mother Ellie, who she'd come to know in the midst of a reopened forty-year-old cold case that had almost got Ellie killed.

So now 'friendship' felt like too small a word.

'Love' might be more fitting, although not in any romantic sense; that would be weird. Not in a paternal sense either. She hadn't latched onto him as a replacement parent after her father's untimely death. She couldn't even say she loved him like a brother – probably because her relationship with her actual brother had been dysfunctional for most of their lives, although it had gradually begun to improve now their mother was in a care home.

So, 'friend' he remained, as well as work colleague, and she'd been happy with that, until Dazz had questioned her motivation when she'd persuaded him to accompany her on her little witch hunt. He'd asked if she was jealous. Of Red, of all people. She'd told him then she was just concerned about Massey being targeted by such a predatory woman in the midst of his marriage break-up. Perfectly true at the time, and it still was now. Yet, as Dazz's role in her life grew to be so much more than just the co-conspirator she'd originally cast him as, the need to label the pigeonhole Massey occupied in her life had begun to rankle.

Her second big issue lay in why she should even feel the need to justify what Massey meant to her; she never had before. Eventually, she'd concluded it was because Dazz had brought it up in the first place, therefore it must matter to him – although, to be fair, he hadn't mentioned it since – and she was discovering that what mattered to Dazz mattered to her too, which was completely out of her comfort zone. So, in case he ever asked again what her feelings were for Massey, she wanted to have the right words available so he could see that Massey posed no threat to their own new… whatever it was. And that led to a third big issue: the need to define her relationship with Dazz too.

She'd never experienced romantic love before, and it frightened her to define this thing she had with Dazz in those terms. But it was happening so fast it was scary, and led to a compulsion to wrap a protective layer around her inexperienced heart. Safer by far to think of it as just an infatuation. A short-term affair that could end at any moment. Not that the word 'affair', with its connotations of something illicit, sat right with her. Partly because, with every day that passed, her need to keep Dazz in her life deepened. So short-term 'affair' it was not. Not for her.

At least the whole girlfriend/boyfriend thing hadn't yet been mentioned. The thought of introducing Dazz to *anyone* as her boyfriend horrified her. It sounded so… naff. At their ages, for goodness sake. There should be an age limit, somewhere in the early twenties, when it became illegal to call the person you were seeing your boyfriend or girlfriend.

Or person-friend even? Jesus, was that a thing now, or had she just coined a new, politically correct, gender neutral term?

But what did that leave? Lover? Doubly naff. Partner? Significant other? Nope. Not yet, at least.

Christ, did everyone go through this shit with a new relationship, or was it just her?

They were driving through Lynemouth before it occurred to her that Massey hadn't even attempted to engage her in conversation either. In Ellington, he turned right onto Cresswell Lane, and she wondered what was on his mind.

He glanced towards her and smiled. 'Is it too soon to tell you how pleased I am about you and Dazz?'

'What? I don't know what you mean.'

'Come off it. It's written all over your face. And you don't have to worry. Dazz is a good man.' He turned a mischievous grin in her direction. '*He's* the one who needs to worry about what he's letting himself in for.'

She laughed and punched his arm. 'Bastard.'

***

A Luton box van had been backed up to the open gates, its rear doors open, and an electric platform lift in the down position. A battered old Volvo estate had pulled up to the kerb below it.

'That's Colin Chirnside's car,' Sparks said. 'Tom Kirk must walk here, or cycle.'

'Probably walks. He lives up at the top of the village, I think. Not far from the Duffy's bungalow.'

Kirk appeared at the gate with a couple of men in work gear. He waved. 'Just go up. Colin's inside. I need to deal with this, then I'll be with you.'

After the bright sunlight outside, it took them a moment for their eyes to adjust to the gloom inside the tower. They heard Chirnside's muffled voice before they saw him. 'Come on in, my darlings. You're blocking the light, standing over there. If it wasn't so cold and breezy, I'd sit out in the sun to do this.'

As their eyes adjusted, they spotted Chirnside perched on a folding chair, spectacles on the end of his nose, and what looked like old rags draped across his lap. He spat a mouthful of dressmaking pins into his hand. 'That's better. I never imagined when I took on this gig, that my sewing expertise would become just as vital to this godforsaken play as my skills as a director. And if it's the production you're here to talk about, then I'm going to have to insist on something.'

Eyebrows raised; Massey looked at Sparks.

She shrugged.

'I may be in theatre, darlings,' Chirnside continued, 'but I'm not naturally superstitious. But with everything that's been going on around here lately, we need all the sodding help we can get. So I'm asking you, please do not, under any circumstances, state the actual name of The Scottish Play while you are anywhere within the tower, the grounds, or the garden.'

Massey stifled a bark of laughter.

'I'm serious. Terrible things have been known to happen. People connected to The Scottish Play have died in mysterious circumstances. And you can't say that hasn't already happened in Cresswell, can you? Ben and Maureen were both connected to this place. So we've had quite enough tragedy from the curse already, thank you very much.'

He raised a hand to run it through his untidy thatch of hair before remembering the pins he held. He groped around on the stone floor, hampered by the draped skirts of the garment he'd been working on.

Sparks bent to retrieve a ladybird pin cushion and handed it to him, along with his copy of Macbeth in its tatty folded brown envelope..

'Thank you, dear. I do hope you found it useful.' He gave her a wry grin and pushed the pins en masse into the cushion and deposited it back on the floor before shaking out the garment and carefully folding it. 'The curse goes right back to the first ever production. The Bard himself had to stand in as the Lady when the actor playing her dropped down dead. And in the eighteen hundreds in New York, two theatres staging the play at the same time sparked a riot. Dozens of people killed or injured. People have fallen off stage, or been hit by falling scenery. Real daggers have been mistaken for imitations.

'Even the great Larry Olivier almost died eighty years or so ago, when a stage weight fell and just missed him. So I've decided The Scottish Play truly is cursed, and you'll excuse me for being a little concerned after everything that's already happened. I'm not prepared to take any more chances. I've even banned the witches from rehearsing their lines here. They're word perfect anyway, so I want no more spells flying around until the day its—'

A shuffling of feet at the door heralded the arrival of Tom Kirk.

'Isn't that right, Tommy dear?' Colin raised his now empty hands in a flourish. 'No-one is to say the dreaded name or cast the witches spells anywhere near this blessed tower until the first performance on Saturday.'

'If you say so, Colin. Sorry about the interruption, folks. That was a couple of pop-up stages and some outdoor lights arriving. They weren't due until Friday, but I persuaded the board we should get them delivered early. It's costing a bit more to rent them for additional days, but it's worth it just for the reassurance. One thing less to go wrong, eh? I just have to remember how to put the bloody things up.'

'How can we help you today?' Chirnside asked. 'Tommy dear, a couple more chairs over here will make this ordeal a lot cosier.'

'Certainly, Colin. Whatever you say, Colin.' Kirk rolled his eyes but passed over two folded chairs from a stack against the wall, and grabbed another for himself.

Chirnside chuckled. 'Now, now dear boy. You know you love it.'

'We need to check a few names with you,' Massey said, 'to find out what involvement they have with the tower's activities, if any.'

'That's Tommy's department,' Chirnside said. 'I only really know about those who're involved in the play.'

It was the play they were particularly interested in, but Massey didn't want to specify that just yet. 'We have the names of your trustees from the Charity Commission website. We know that Finn Barron is Chair and Len Stafford Vice Chair. We know Ben Quinn was a trustee too, and that Michael Duffy resigned from your board some time ago.'

Kirk nodded. 'That's right. And there are three others. Edna McCord is our Treasurer. She's playing Lady—'

'Tommy!' Chirnside waggled a forefinger.

Kirk sighed. 'Sorry. Edna is our leading lady. Then we have Gurjas Singh and Angela Barnes-Brown. Angela probably isn't listed with the Charity Commission yet. She just joined the board a couple of months ago.'

Massey couldn't recall seeing that name. He'd get Donaldson to check her out. 'Was Duncan Kingsley ever involved?'

'Not that I know of. Maybe, before my time, although I think something would have been said last year if he had. Elena though, yes. Not as a trustee, but as a volunteer. Particularly at the beginning. She was into all the archaeological stuff going on then, but she left when she moved away from the village.'

'Were her sons involved here too?' Sparks asked.

'Not beyond dropping Elena off and picking her up now and then if they wanted to borrow her car, but then the eldest... What's his name again? Milo, that's right. He got himself an old banger eventually, although it looks like he's back borrowing his mother's car again now—'

'You've seen him recently?'

'Once or twice, going in and out of Ben's house. He and Fleur were close. I think Ben entertained ideas of them getting together eventually, but I don't think either of them saw it that way. Just good friends.'

Chirnside nodded sagely. 'As the bishop said.'

'When was the last time you saw Milo or Dominic there?'

Kirk puffed out his cheeks. 'Now you're asking. I saw Milo a week or so before Ben died, probably. Maybe a bit longer.'

And yet, apart from the day of the charity match, Dominic had claimed neither had set foot in Ellington or Cresswell since the family had moved to Forest Hall, and Milo hadn't contradicted him.

Massey smiled. 'Back to the people actually involved here at the tower. How many paid staff do you have?'

'Not I,' Chirnside said with another flamboyant wave of his hands, which knocked the garment he'd been working on to the floor. 'I do all this for love.'

'Only me.' Kirk said. 'Part time.'

'Other volunteers then. We've seen Verity Barron here with her husband. Is she a volunteer?'

Chirnside barked out a laugh. 'She's our own White Lady, isn't she Tommy?'

Kirk looked embarrassed. 'Verity doesn't volunteer here as such, but she's supportive of her husband. She accompanies him whenever he calls in.'

'Even for trustee meetings?'

'They usually take place at the hall, not here. Or the club.'

'Have you heard about our White Lady?' Chirnside asked. 'I mean the ghost, not Verity. Although she looks more like a ghost every time I see her these days. That white coat does her no favours, not with her skin tone. She won't be upstaging our *real* White Lady any time soon. Legend has it she was the daughter of the Cresswell family, the local bigwigs who owned everything around here. She fell in love with a drop-dead gorgeous Danish prince and watched out to sea from the top of the tower for him coming to claim her. But, when his ship did land, her brothers ambushed and murdered him. She saw it all and died of grief, and now she haunts the tower, still waiting for him.' Eyes wide, he sat forward. 'Actually, now I think about it, there have been an inordinate number of White Lady sightings recently. She'll be concerned about all these violent deaths, I shouldn't wonder. I hope that bodes no ill for the weekend.'

Massey hoped so too. They didn't need any other unnecessary deaths.

'Talking about our volunteers,' Kirk said eventually. 'Do you mean just those who live locally? We have volunteers who travel from all over.'

'A list of them all would be good,' Massey said, 'but let's talk about the locals first. I know Maureen Duffy was one of your garden volunteers—'

'Very much so. She loved the garden. It's so sad.'

'We understand she played one of the witches last year, but didn't want to reprise that role this year. Any idea why?'

Kirk shrugged. 'I think she preferred gardening, and didn't want to over-extend herself trying to do both.'

'I heard from my wife,' Chirnside said from the corner of his mouth, 'that she had a bit of a falling out with Betsy and Ursula.'

'In what way?'

'Oh, don't ask me. Completely different personalities. I think the other two together could be a bit much for Maureen at close quarters.'

Massey and Sparks waited for either man to expand on that. They didn't.

'What about June Stafford,' Massey asked. 'Is she involved in any way.'

'God, no!' Kirk said. 'Luckily.'

'Nor in theatre,' Chirnside said. 'Thank heavens.'

'What makes you say that?'

'This place is Len's escape, I think,' Kirk said.

'How did Scarlett Crowley get involved,' Sparks asked. 'We know both Betsy and Ursula played witches last year. Did you advertise the role of third witch after Maureen refused?'

'We didn't need to,' Chirnside said. 'Betsy and Ursula suggested her. Told me how perfect she'd be for the role and brought her in to meet me one day. They were right.'

'Not so much the old hag you'd expect of a witch though, is she?'

Chirnside laughed out loud. 'Are you casting aspersions towards the other two, dear? Suggesting they are old hags? I'll have to be careful not to drop you in it. But seriously dear, a bit of beauty can't go amiss in the unremitting darkness of a play like M—'

Chirnside clamped his hands over his mouth.

'Good grief, I almost brought the curse back down on us myself.'

'And we have Trinny now too,' Kirk said. 'A double whammy.'

Massey bit his tongue. Sparks looked like she wanted to puke.

They talked for more than another hour, going through all the people involved in any way with the Cresswell Pele Tower charity, before touching on the upcoming performance.

'Is there anyone else you can think of, Colin,' Massey asked, 'who has as good a grasp of Shakespeare, and of… The Scottish Play as you have?'

'I don't believe so, no. Not around here.'

'Has anyone asked any detailed questions about it, or said things beyond their engagement in the play that might indicate they'd been taking more interest than you'd expect?'

Head on one side, Chirnside thought about that one for a few moments, then nodded slowly. 'Ah,' he said. 'I see. No, sorry.'

Before they left, Sparks had one last question. 'Can you confirm for me please Colin, whose idea it was originally to do the Cresswell... um, Scottish Play?'

'Certainly, dear. It was Trinity who suggested it to me originally. Clever girl. I chewed it over. Wasn't sure if I could devote the time to such a big project, at first. But the seed had been sown. I'd watched this place develop, and I could see the possibilities for a truly immersive theatre experience on a shoestring. And the rest, as they say, is history. Apart from anything else dear, I expect it to do wonders for my CV – if we can just keep Hecate and the White Lady onside.'

As they left, it occurred to Massey that Sparks had asked that last question for his benefit. She'd known already it had been Trinny who'd first suggested putting on a Cresswell Macbeth.

He'd think that one through later.

In the meantime, the fact that Milo had been in the village so recently was interesting. And it exposed both brothers as liars. They would need to be brought in.

CHAPTER 59

DCI Flint greeted Keegan at Durham Constabulary's Aykley Heads HQ, on the outskirts of the ancient city centre. They shook hands and exchanged small talk until they were in the lift.

'Come to blast what's left of our case out of the water?' Flint said.

Keegan laughed. 'You still don't like our Macbeth theory then?'

'It's pants. You have no decent motive and bugger all suspects.'

'We know it wasn't these three jokers I'm about to meet though. Any problems bringing them in?'

Flint shook his head as the lift doors opened. 'Not so you'd notice. We'd released them under investigation, so they knew we'd be back. I can't figure out why, if they're innocent of Kingsley's murder, they're not shouting about what they *were* doing so we can clear them.'

'Still up to no good, I'll bet.'

'Without doubt, but it can't have been worse than murder.'

'I think it's more to do with the shit they could bring down on their own heads and their families' heads if they do cop for what they were really up to. They can't have failed to have heard about what's been going on recently up in Cresswell. They'll be hoping we find the killer before you get to the point of charging them for murder.'

They picked up some coffees and snacks and spent some time closeted in an empty office working out an interview strategy for all three men that they hoped would become redundant before they finished with the first one.

'Right then,' Keegan said. 'We're agreed. Wyatt first.'

***

Handsome in a young Cillian Murphy way, twenty-two-year-old Callum Wyatt – being the only son of their only sister – was the nephew of the brothers Blacklock, who waited in the wings for their turn to be interviewed under caution. Physical labour had given Callum the sinewy build of an older man, and a weathered tan he could never have achieved through a fortnight sunning himself between hangovers in Ibiza. The cowed look he gave Keegan when the interview room door opened however, gave him away as a scared young boy who'd been dragged into a pile of someone else's excrement that reached way above his head.

Keegan wondered what his uncles had threatened him with to keep him silent. Whatever it was, he felt pretty confident he could trump it. He started the recording, stated the purpose and context of the interview and asked everyone present to identify themselves.

Flint took up a position against the wall, arms folded, one foot propped up behind him.

Keegan bared his teeth in a grin he intended to look non-threatening. 'Fancy a coffee or a drink of water before we get started, Callum? No? Okay then. If you're sure. But let me know if you change your mind.' He offered nothing to the sour-faced, middle-aged woman in a yellow-grey suit sitting beside the boy.

Wyatt grunted. His head didn't move, but wary eyes swivelled rapidly between the two detectives, unsure which was the biggest threat.

'Sorry to be dragging you away from work, Callum. Good weather like this; it's got to be the best time for you lot, isn't it? Landscapers, I mean. You need to fit the work in when the weather allows, don't you? It could be chucking it down tomorrow, yet here I am, pulling you back in here, stopping you from making your money while the going's good. I'm sure your uncles can do without all this shit too. Especially when none of you actually did it.'

Wyatt's eyes stopped swivelling and fixed on a spot on the wall between Flint and Keegan, but he said nothing.

'Come on, Callum. You didn't kill Duncan Kingsley. Your Uncle Ryan and Uncle Justin didn't either. I know that, but DCI Flint here and his team disagree with me. As you know, they've found Kingsley's blood in your uncles' van and there's a fifteen minute hole in your alibis that none of you are keen to address. So they think they've got it all tied up with a nice big bow, and if I didn't know different, I'd probably be cheering them on.

'It doesn't even matter to them which one of you they think actually stuck the knife in because, in law, Joint Enterprise will say you're all guilty anyway. So make no mistake Callum, the way things are looking now, you're all going to be spending a lot of years behind bars, and I won't be able to do anything to prevent that if none of you will say where you really were during those missing minutes, even though I've actually got a pretty good idea. But, you see, I'm not interested in the drugs.'

Wyatt began picking at a scab on one of his knuckles.

Grey Suit said nothing.

Keegan let a few seconds tick by, then gave a low laugh. 'It doesn't matter what I think anyway. DCI Flint doesn't give a toss. Not when he has the blood, and the fifteen minute hole. So, me knowing for a fact that you didn't do it, that none of you did it, means nothing at all unless one of you takes the lead here.'

Wyatt continued picking at his knuckle.

'You're a nice looking lad, Callum. I bet you get the pick of all the girls, don't you? Or boys. I'm not here to judge.' Keegan grinned. 'You're a bit too handsome for your own good though, if you don't mind me saying. For where you're going to be going, anyway.

'Do you know what happens to pretty boys in prison? No? Well, I'm sure you've got a good imagination. It's not nice, Callum. Not nice at all for pretty boys like you. And do you know what? Your uncles won't be able to protect you whenever some big hairy-arsed con gets a hard-on for you and invites his mates to get their rocks off with the new pretty boy too. They'll be elsewhere, you see. They'll split you up, being family. Oh, don't get me wrong, they may incarcerate you all in the same institution, but in different units. So Ryan and Justin aren't going to be able to come running when they hear you scream. They won't even be able to protect each other.'

Grey Suit stirred herself. 'Harsh, detective,' was all she said.

Keegan imagined she'd be pleased too if he managed to persuade Wyatt to tell the truth, since he'd effectively be doing her job for her.

'Incarceration,' he said. 'Lovely word, isn't it Callum? It means locked up, imprisoned. Which in practical terms means no going out with your mates whenever you fancy and coming home pissed at stupid o'clock in the morning. No hot dinners and warm cuddles from your mam. No being able to watch whatever you want on the box or see your favourite bands. No chasing bits of skirt and getting your leg over. And that tan you're so proud of, and the ripped physique? They'll fade in no time. Not that the lags in there will care; all they'll see is fresh meat.'

Wyatt sniffed and wiped his nose on his bare forearm. He looked close to tears.

The detectives waited.

Thirty seconds ticked by.

A minute.

Wyatt broke. Clenched fists on his forehead, he sobbed. 'I can't do this.'

'You know what has to happen then, Callum? And it'll not be just yourself you'll be saving; it'll be Ryan and Justin too. None of you committed that murder, so why the hell should any of you have to go down for it?'

'They were supposed to have said something by now. Ryan said they'd come forward; that everything would come out alright. We just had to keep quiet.'

Keegan held his breath and waited, but Flint levered himself away from the wall. Planting both hands on the table, he loomed over the young man. 'Who, Callum? Who should have said something by now?'

'They know we didn't go down to the beach because they saw us driving away. Why would they not come forward?'

'Who, Callum?'

'Mr Kingsley's sons. We couldn't tell your lot what we were really doing, but Ryan said all we had to do was to say nothing and wait. Milo and Dom are honest lads, he said. They'd tell your lot they saw us leaving the village without going down to the beach, and then everything would be cool. We'd be in the... clear.'

Hot, snot-filled tears rolled down Callum Wyatt's cheeks and left slimy streaks on his bare forearm when he tried to swipe them away. He lifted the hem of his tee-shirt and blew his nose on it.

Disgusted, Keegan turned away. 'Jesus, Callum!'

CHAPTER 60

'Sir.' Phone receiver to her ear, Lisa waved Massey over as soon as he and Sparks entered the MIT room. She hung up and grinned.

'We've found the dogs. That was the owner of a boarding kennel near Backworth. Julie Willans. Calls herself the Fairy Dog-mother, would you believe? Someone brought in both dogs on Friday. New customer, and a bit weird. He told them a family emergency meant he had to be away from home for a while. Said he'd already tried a couple of other kennels, but they had no availability at such short notice. She'd just had a cancellation, so she agreed to take them if he paid for two weeks' board up front in cash. £225 per animal; £450 in total. He agreed, had the cash on him there and then, and left the dogs there. Two pure white Siberian huskies.'

'What made her call it in before the two weeks was up?'

'She saw something on the news about the Duffy's huskies going missing. Decided to ask her veterinary friend to check them for microchips. The ID numbers came up as belonging to Maureen Duffy, with a completely different address to the one the man gave the kennels.

Massey hoped to God it wasn't Michael Duffy. He'd believed him yesterday. He'd looked into the man's eyes and seen someone incapable of murdering the woman he loved.

'If he lied about the address then he's unlikely to have given his real name. Could she describe him? Do they have CCTV?'

'Cameras only on the kennels themselves unfortunately, and he went nowhere near them, so nothing there we can use. That in itself was unusual, Julie reckons. Most owners want a tour of the place before they leave their dogs. He told her his name was Jason Fletcher, gave an address in Morpeth and a mobile number where she could reach him, but said he was in too much of a rush to hang around and inspect the place there and then. Some relative on their death bed, he told her.'

'Don't keep us in suspense,' Sparks said. 'What did he look like?'

'Tallish. Young. Hood pulled up, with a beanie pulled down beneath it, so she couldn't see his hair, but his eyes were brown or hazel, his skin looked like the sort that would tan easily, and he had a north east accent.'

Massey and Sparks looked at each other. 'One of the Kingsley lads?' he asked. 'That could fit either of them.'

'We need to get someone over there with photos.'

'Shouldn't we try the phone number he gave Julie?' Lisa said. 'You never know.'

'I want the Kingsley brothers brought in anyway. Best if we don't warn them first.' Massey pulled his ringing phone from his pocket. 'Guy. How's it going down there? Okay… Right… He said what?'

CHAPTER 61

Wednesday, 23 October 2024

Milo and Dominic Kingsley had disappeared, which only compounded their guilt in the minds of the investigation teams.

Flint insisted the collar should be Durham's, since his team had been investigating Kingsley's murder for more than a year. But that took no account of the more recent murders, nor of the geography – Cresswell being smack in the middle of Northumbria Police's coastal territory. And with Dominic now confirmed as the dogwalker and the person who left the Duffy's two huskies at the boarding kennel, Milo having lured Michael Duffy out of the house on the night his wife was murdered, and both lying about not going near Cresswell for months, Northumbria had an equally, if not more valid claim to lead. Not only was Massey's team on the cusp of catching the murderer of Ben Quinn and Maureen Duffy, but they'd also be solving a case that should have been theirs in the first place.

Negotiations late last night between Chief Superintendent Crowder and his Durham counterpart had resulted in a compromise. Two members of Flint's team would arrive at Middle Engine Lane HQ first thing this morning and work alongside Massey's MIT for the duration. Flint and the rest of his team would assist with online investigations from their own headquarters.

***

Minutes before seven, Flint's colleagues arrived. A stocky man, mid-thirties, with Mediterranean looks. And a forty something woman with poker-straight, bleached-blonde hair and fake tan. They took the last two chairs from a stack of spares wheeled in from a storeroom earlier at the back of the packed out MIT room.

Along with Massey's core team, additional personnel had joined them over the past ten days or been roped in at short notice for the hunt, every one of them oozing the reined-in impatience of racehorses at the starting gate, despite most having already been working for hours. Inspector Brian Truman, several members of his Neighbourhood Policing Team, and Jodie O'Neill were also in attendance. Media and Comms Manager Nicola Pendleton sat at the back of the room, looking fresh and business-like.

He'd been closeted with Nicola in his office for a good half hour earlier. Given her naturally haughty expression and immaculate tailored suit, he'd expected her to turn her nose up at the crumpled state of his jacket and the dark smudges under his eyes after the twenty-four hour shift he'd put in so far. He'd been preparing to tell her she could like it or lump it. That he only had one fresh suit and change of shirt left with him and needed to keep those for the press conference she'd arranged for midday. But she was made of sterner stuff. 'My dad's a long distance haulage driver,' she told him. 'You want to see the state of him when he gets home sometimes, stinking of diesel after two nights sleeping in his cab.'

She'd done a sterling job in keeping a lid on press speculation over the recent murders, but now they wanted to harness the press in helping them to apprehend the two Kingsley brothers. And given it looked like the boys had murdered their own father, a retired Chief Superintendent of Northumbria Police, that would require a truly delicate touch.

He made his way to the front, every eye in the room following him. 'First of all,' he said, 'massive thanks to all those who have worked through the night, and welcome to those who are joining the team this morning. I don't know all your names yet, so please forgive me if I get yours wrong.' He gazed around at the sea of faces. 'No time for a round of introductions; we'd be here until tomorrow. I do need to introduce two newcomers though. We have with us two officers from Durham Constabulary: DS Emma Tweddle, and DC Marco Shadforth. Welcome.'

Tweddle and Shadforth each held up a hand in acknowledgement.

'Right,' Massey continued, 'let's get to it. We have two new suspects in the murders not only of Ben Quinn and Maureen Duffy, but also that of retired Chief Inspector Duncan Kingsley in July last year, which Durham Constabulary have been investigating. Our new suspects are

Duncan Kingsley's two sons, Milo and Dominic Kingsley. It appears they had information that could have cleared the three previous suspects. The fact they failed to come forward raises questions about their own activities around the time their father was murdered.

'We now also have a witness who contradicts what both boys have said about them not having visited Ellington or Cresswell at all since the family moved to Forest Hall, other than to watch the charity match and attend the after-match party on the twelfth of October. That witness claims to have seen Milo Kingsley more than once over recent months calling at Stoneyriggs, the home burned down in an act of arson to conceal the murder of Ben Quinn and serious assault on his daughter Fleur.

'As of yesterday, we also know that both boys were involved in events surrounding the murder of Maureen Duffy on Friday the eighteenth of October. Dominic acted as a paid dogwalker, employed by Maureen. He collected the animals sometime during the afternoon. Milo then called Michael Duffy and invited him to a pub. We believe Milo's motive was to lure Michael away from home so that his wife would be alone when her murderer arrived. We now believe that murderer to be Dominic, who had by then checked the dogs into a boarding kennel under a false name for two weeks, paying in cash for the last minute booking.

'So,' he continued, 'we have both Milo and Dominic Kingsley's likely involvement in all three murders, but there are huge gaps we need to fill if we are to stand any chance of proving their guilt. So our work for the foreseeable is to fill those gaps and to find Milo and Dominic Kingsley.

CHAPTER 62

Sparks peered into Keegan's car, which wasn't as untidy as she'd feared given she remembered the state he'd kept his office when he'd been DCI, before his demotion. The office Massey now occupied.

'For God's sake,' Keegan said. 'just get in. You're not going to catch anything.'

Before she did, Sparks plucked a long pale hair from the passenger seat headrest, flicked it with disgust out of the car door and watched the breeze carry it off.

'That'll be from my eldest. I gave her a lift to her boyfriend's house last night.'

Sparks tried to imagine some tremulous, love-struck teenage swain coming face-to-face in the dark with big, barrel-chested, shaggy bear Keegan and realising that this was the father of his beloved. The thought made her snort a laugh out loud.

'What's so funny?'

She buckled her seatbelt and gave him an innocent look. 'Nothing.'

The road going north was quiet and their progress good. With two prime suspects in their sights, the briefing this morning had been a lot briefer than most. No need to touch upon the whole Macbeth thing; that could take a back seat now they had solid leads to chase up. It had taken longer to dish out the actions and, with Massey stuck at HQ for the press conference, she'd drawn the short straw getting stuck with Keegan.

Actually, that wasn't fair. Keegan was a good bloke when you got to know him, which she had done over the course of this past year, and a bloody good detective.

'You've met Betsy,' he said. 'Do you think she'll cooperate without a fuss?'

They'd tried contacting the therapist by phone earlier. Ursula had answered and told them Betsy had one hour appointments all day, except for a gap from ten.

'She came in off her own bat the last time, but then we managed to upset her, so—'

Keegan shot her a look.

'Okay,' she said. 'Hands up. It was me who upset her. Either way, she's not going to give up Dominic Kingsley easily.'

'She'll be just finishing her nine o' clock by the time we get there. We'll have a quick word. Tell her what we need, then she can consult her rule book while we talk to Ursula. It shouldn't be difficult. Disclosure necessary in preventing or detecting a crime, and it's in the public interest, so she has no grounds to refuse.'

But Betsy wasn't going to be chomping at the bit to help them either, Sparks thought. Not after their last exchange.

***

Ursula answered Sparks' enquiring look with a tight smile while brushing her hands down the smart skirt suit she wore. 'I want to go back to work. It is not good for me to sit around here and get under Betsy's feet. She is very good to me. She says I should not worry so much about it, but I need to be doing something, or I will go mad, and I will be no use to my Fleur when they wake her up.'

She led them through to the room with the cream sofa and suede tub chair.

'Has there been any change in Fleur's condition?' Sparks asked.

'They confuse me. The doctors and the consultant and the nurses all say things I do not understand. Not the English. I don't mean that. My English is excellent. It is not even the medical terms, although that is a small part of it. It is all just so overwhelming. They tell me she will be like this for another four weeks, and then they say eight weeks, and then that it depends on... something else this time. I think they do not know, so how can they tell me. I worry that perhaps she will never recover, and I cannot sit there and watch her day in and day out. But I cannot be here getting in Betsy's way all day either. I cannot even arrange a funeral for my Ben until his body is released. Yet I need to be doing something to keep me busy or I will go mad. That is why I want to go back to work. So ask me your questions and then I can go and see my new boss.'

'We had hoped to have a quick word with Betsy first,' Sparks said. 'If that's possible.'

Ursula glanced at the big clock on the wall and sighed. 'Please sit, and I will see.'

She returned quickly. Betsy had agreed.

Keegan went through to the kitchen on his own to have a word, leaving Sparks perfectly well aware he didn't want her alienating Betsy any more than she already had.

'Have you got sorted with a car, Ursula?'

'I have. The insurance company have given me a courtesy car until the claim is sorted. It is fine for what I need.' She gave a short laugh. 'Already it is beginning to know its own way to and from the hospital.'

Keegan returned. 'Sorry to keep you waiting. We'd like to talk to you about how often Milo and Dominic Kingsley might have visited Stoneyriggs since they moved away from Cresswell with their mother.'

Ursula pouted. 'I cannot remember Dominic there since he was little. Milo is Fleur's friend. Girlfriend and boyfriend, I thought, for a little while, but friends always. They were in the same class at school and took the same subjects. They did homework together, and…'

'And in the past year?'

'Milo continued to study but Fleur got a job in sport with Northumberland council, so they have not seen each other every day in the same way. I think it hit Milo harder than Fleur.'

'When's the last time you remember him calling?'

Ursula pouted again. 'I am not sure. Perhaps a week before the fire?'

'He didn't call on the day of the fire?'

'I do not know. I was out with Betsy. Wait, are you saying you believe Milo hurt Fleur and killed my Ben? And burnt down our house?' She raised her hands, pushing the thought away. 'No, I cannot believe that.'

'What about Dominic?'

'As I said, I cannot remember Dom coming to our house for many years. When he was little, yes. I used to look after both boys sometimes for Elena. We had only one child and we were happy for Fleur to have friends here to play with. The cellar was her playroom. There is a door straight out into the garden, so they could go in and—'

Startled, Sparks looked up from her notes. 'You're saying both Milo and Dominic have used that cellar door into the garden?'

'Oh yes, when they were children, but not for a long time. Milo comes – *came* to the front door. Dominic has no time now for Fleur. Which is fine. He is not such a nice boy as Milo.

'I will tell you something I could not even tell Ben. When Fleur left school, she told me what Dom used to do when they were little. He used to kick her and punch her, always when Milo was not looking. He told her never to say anything to anyone about what he did, or he would sneak into the house through that cellar door one night and find her in her bedroom, and he would cut off her lips and her nose and her fingers while she slept. Can you believe that? Children can be so wicked. This was finally an explanation for the nightmares she suffered in those days. And of course, if I had known this at the time, I would never have…'

Ursula's eyes grew wide. She raised both hands to her cheeks.

'Oh, my goodness. It is him. Dominic. He did it. He killed my Ben. He hurt Fleur.'

Horrified, every muscle in her body began to tremble. Huge tears sprang to her eyes and quivered for a moment before rolling between her fingers and down into the sleeves of her smart, return-to-work jacket. After a moment, she raised her head. Eyes bulging, she dry heaved, then released a huge, heart-wrenching wail into the air.

Betsy flung open the door and hurried to Ursula's side. She glared at them both. 'What have you done to her?' she demanded. 'What have you said?'

***

A patrol car passed them as Sparks climbed back into the passenger side of Keegan's car. Both occupants held up a hand in acknowledgement. Another couple of marked vehicles were parked outside the village hall. Cresswell residents would be pig sick of seeing police on their streets before today was over.

'You think Betsy would have obliged if Ursula hadn't been in such a state?'

'I do not. You played a blinder there by the way, DS Sparks. The right question in just the right place. Well done. Ursula nearly burst my eardrums mind.' Keegan bared his teeth in a grin. 'But I'll survive.'

It wasn't like she'd had any specific strategic objective in asking the question that had set Ursula off. But the fact Milo and Dominic had both known about that cellar door long before the fire might well end up being the one piece of the puzzle from which all else flows.

And if Ursula hadn't realised what that could mean herself and started wailing, Betsy probably wouldn't have provided them with details of Dominic Kingsley's therapy sessions, which Keegan now held in front of him on the steering wheel.

The speed at which Betsy had arrived – empty-handed – in response to the commotion suggested she'd already been on the way through to tell them exactly where they could shove their request. Yet, once Ursula had calmed down enough to explain, Betsy had led them into her office, brought up Dominic's file onscreen, copied and pasted some of the details into a new headed document that she printed out for them and shoved into a large envelope. 'If you want anything more than that,' she'd told them, 'you're going to have to come back with a court order.'

'Bloody hell' Keegan said, looking through the papers. 'The little prick could be Chucky in human form, according to the good doctor in there.'

'She's not a doctor. She's a therapist.'

'Metaphorically, I meant. And according to your Macbeth theory, she is.'

'Maybe, but it wasn't King Duncan's sons who were the killers. What else is in there?'

'Looks like she's been treating him since May 2019. More than five years. Hypnotherapy for sodding anger management.'

'Shows what a crap therapist she is then, if she hasn't succeeded in all that time.'

Keegan shrugged. 'If he, or his parents are daft enough to continue paying, why turn him away? She's actually given us quite a bit. It'll take some going through, and here is not the place. We'll take it back to HQ as soon as we've made another call.'

'On who?'

'Finn Barron. I want to know what he argued with the Kingsley boys about at that barbecue. From what I've seen, the Durham lot don't seem to have even been aware they were there. If we're lucky, Finn will be as accommodating today as...'

Sparks grimaced and sucked in a breath through her teeth.

'What? Don't tell me you've alienated him too.'

'To be fair,' she said. 'That's hardly difficult, if you happen to be a woman and ask him questions he doesn't like.'

CHAPTER 63

Barron looked ill and spaced out when he came to the door. Hiding behind him, Verity looked almost as bad.

'Guy Keegan. What the hell do you want?'

'Are you alright?' Keegan asked. 'You don't look well at all.'

'More bloody questions from your lot aren't going to help me feel any better? When is this whole debacle going to be over and done with?'

Keegan flicked on his bared teeth grin. 'When we catch the killer, or killers.'

'You can come in.' Barron pointed to Sparks. 'But I don't want her—'

'Non-negotiable.' Keegan stepped over the threshold and into Barron's personal space, forcing the man to take a step back. 'DS Sparks is with me.'

With a defeated shrug of his shoulders, the man led them into the washed out whiteness of the lounge, where a tray piled high with used breakfast dishes still sat on a chalk-painted side table, a few crumbs and poppy seeds having overflowed onto the table.

After an annoyed look from her husband, Verity stepped forward and picked up the tray. 'I'll just... um...'

Sparks wondered if she should follow her, but a miniscule shake of the head from Keegan made her stay. He probably thought her ability to rile Barron might come in useful.

Barron dashed sweat from his brow. 'Are you going to tell me why you're hounding me? Do *you* think I'm a murderer too?'

'Are you?' Sparks asked.

'What? No, of course I'm bloody not.'

She'd expected the man's face to flush with anger, but instead it blanched, and he looked for a moment as if he would fall. He sat down heavily on the armchair next to the window instead.

'Are you sure you're alright?' Keegan asked.

Barron waved away his concern. 'Just get on with it.'

Sparks remembered the man's collapse at the club just a few days ago. Verity had insisted then that whatever it was would pass, but what if it didn't this time? However much she disliked the man, she didn't want to make him worse now. For a start, if it became necessary to caution him, anything he said in this state would be useless in court.

'We can come back, when you're more up to it,' she said.

Barron slammed his fist onto the arm of the chair. 'You'll ask your questions now and then leave me in peace.'

She looked at Keegan, who shrugged and held out a hand, inviting her to take the lead.

'Okay. We have some questions about what happened at the barbecue you held here on the day Duncan Kingsley—'

'For God's sake. I have gone through all of that far too many times to repeat myself in detail now. I did not follow him to the beach and stab him to death. That's all you need to know.'

'That's not what we're interested in. We'd like to know about the conversation you had with Milo and Dominic Kingsley when they dropped their parents off.'

Barron's brows came together over his nose. 'What? Why does that matter. They left ages before Duncan went down to the beach.'

'Humour us. What do you remember of the conversation you had with them that day.'

'It was just more of the same crap I got from them all the time. Or from the younger one anyway. Dominic.'

'What about?'

'Being on the first team. Look, Milo's a great player. We got RFU approval to play him as an adult on the first team as soon as he turned seventeen. On talent, mind you. Not because of who his father is, or was. In all fairness, he should have moved to one of the bigger clubs to give him better opportunities. He has what it takes to go far, and I told him that. But he wouldn't leave because of his brother, who is mediocre at best.'

'And?'

'Dominic believed that he had the right to play on the first team as soon as he turned seventeen, because Milo did. But Ben, as Head Coach, told him he wasn't ready. In my opinion, he never would be. That's what we talked about. I told them what I thought, and that was that. They left.'

'What did Duncan have to say?' Keegan asked.

'He refused to get involved, which I respected him for.' Barron huffed a short laugh. 'And, of course, it also suited him to have me put the kid in his place rather than have to do it himself. But look, this was early on in the afternoon. Before the party had even really started. Milo and Dominic had already gone by the time most of the guests arrived, so what has any of that got to do with what happened to their father later on?'

'What was it that made Duncan angry enough to leave the party and go down to the beach?' Sparks said.

'Those three landscapers, who are about to be charged with his murder. That has nothing to do with me.'

As he spoke, Sparks walked to the open door and checked for signs of his wife returning. She heard dishes clinking together. Verity must still be washing up.

She closed the door. 'That's not what I mean,' she said. 'Duncan had another good reason for getting angry that day.'

Barron looked genuinely puzzled. 'Did he?'

'Someone at that barbecue told him about the affair you had with his wife when Milo was just a baby.'

Barron's eyes popped. His mouth fell open. 'Who told him that?'

Sparks could swear his complexion had turned a couple of shades whiter. 'Is it true?'

'I have no idea. I knew nothing about that. I was talking to the landscapers, so—'

'I meant is it true you had an affair with Elena?'

'Um... Alright then. Yes, we did have a fling.' He curled his lip and nodded towards the closed door. 'Can you blame me?'

'Who else at that barbecue knew about it?'

'Elena, obviously. But that all happened years ago.'

'Perhaps the prophesies you were given that day brought it to someone's mind. Remember those? How did the last one go? Something about the way you treated women being about to catch up with you?

Oh wait. They didn't say women, did they? They mentioned a specific young girl. Who was she?'

Barron stammered, but failed to form any coherent words.

Yet, with the image of witches at the tower in mind, in conjunction with the barbecue a year ago, Sparks suddenly realised who Betsy must have meant. The youngest of this year's coven. The girl she and Dazz had seen working in the Plough on the day of the Stoneyriggs fire. And who also, she recalled, did the odd shift behind the bar at the rugby club.

She stared at Barron in disgust. 'Betsy was warning you off Scarlett Crowley, wasn't she? A girl less than half your age.' Although not exactly underage, but still... 'And Betsy's another of your old flames, isn't she?'

The colour that had drained so recently from Barron's face came flooding back. 'I did nothing to that girl. Nothing at all.'

'Not for the want of trying though, eh?' Keegan said.

***

'Did you see Verity's face when she realised we weren't arresting him?' Sparks said. 'She probably already had the flags ready to hang out.'

Keegan did a U-turn on Beach Road, then turned left onto Cresswell Road, driving past the ruined Stoneyriggs on the right and the pele tower on the left. Further up, the gateway of the Duffys' bungalow was still festooned with police tape. 'At the charity do,' he said, 'Michael Duffy described Verity as having ideas of grandeur, but I can't believe that. She's more like a terrified little mouse.'

'I think that's a man thing? It's Finn who has all the grand ideas, but he thinks it's more socially acceptable to blame Verity for pushing him into things. Lots of men do it. I bet you do too.'

'Bloody cheek.' Keegan fell quiet for a few minutes after that. 'Hm, maybe,' he said eventually, 'but not to that extent.'

'At least we now have a potential motive for the boys to have killed their father. Or for Dominic at least. He wanted what Milo had, and he didn't like anyone saying no.'

'It wasn't Duncan who said no though. It was Finn, after Ben had said the same thing.'

'Dominic probably thought his father should have overruled them. He was the club president, after all.'

'What on earth possessed the kid to think he should be in the first team. It's exceptional enough for anyone just turning seventeen to make the grade.'

'Didn't Ursula say he was jealous of his older brother even as a little kid? Always wanted what Milo had, and turned nasty if he didn't get it. She said he threatened to cut Fleur, so maybe he has a thing about knives. And—'

'And Duncan was stabbed to death. I know. I thought the same thing. But whether Milo had a hand in the deed or not, all three landscapers now say they saw both Milo and Dominic in Cresswell that afternoon. At the very least, Milo has colluded after the fact in his father's murder, and we know he's up to his neck in the murder of Maureen Duffy.'

'If Durham had done their job properly, they'd have got them for their dad's murder a year ago. How did they not?'

'I'd say it's down to Flint's illness. It's common knowledge over there, so I'll tell you. He has cancer. He's been undergoing chemo and radiotherapy, and refusing to take any more time away from work than he absolutely has to, and I think it's affected the performance of his team. He's a good bloke, and a well-respected detective, under normal circumstances. But he should have done the right thing and allowed someone else to lead the team.'

It didn't come as a surprise. You only had to look at the bloke. But that still didn't excuse the probability that two more people had died, and two others now barely clung to life because that idiot decided to soldier on. And because his bosses allowed him to.

'Talking about illness,' she said. 'What do you reckon is up with those two? They have to be on something.'

'You're right. They're taking something. Finn's on the sick from work. Maybe it's something prescribed.'

Sparks snorted. 'What, and Verity does her wifely duties and takes it with him? Yeah, right.'

CHAPTER 64

The press conference went well, or as well as one could ever go. Portas led, with Massey on her right. On her left sat Flint's boss and then Flint himself. All facing the baying hordes and flashing lights. Portas confirmed the murders of Maureen Duffy and Ben Quinn, the assault on Fleur Quinn and the arson at Stoneyriggs, had all now been officially linked to the murder of Duncan Kingsley the previous summer.

Even though news outlets had already come to the same conclusion and filled screen time and column inches with rabid speculation for more than a week, this sparked a storm of questions that Portas fielded admirably.

Crowder's concerns over the press regurgitating the traumatic events that had led to Duncan Kingsley's murder inquiry being handed to Durham Constabulary had proved justified, although Nicola Pendleton had done her utmost to keep a lid on the worst excesses. But now, Crowder welcomed the connection as a distraction, since not one news hack had latched onto their Macbeth theory. And long may that continue. At least until they had the killers in custody and had gained some sort of understanding of why they'd chosen to imitate Shakespeare's Scottish tragedy.

At the last minute, Crowder had changed his mind on involving the press in the hunt for the Kingsley brothers. He'd decided not even to give away the fact they were persons of interest in all three murders. He'd wanted no false leads from the public to hamper the team. However, in the time since then, all efforts to find the brothers had failed

Milo had not attended university this week, and Dominic had missed his Jobcentre interview this morning. Their mother claimed they hadn't been home, and that she had no idea where they were. The boys' passports, she told them, were still in her wall safe along with her own, and their mobile phones and smart watches – which they'd never normally be separated from – had been left in their rooms. She couldn't tell if any other electronic devices were missing, having little idea of what gadgetry her sons even owned.

An all-points bulletin had been issued. DS Emma Tweddle and DC Marco Shadforth had spent the day chasing up the Kingsleys' family and friends locally. From their own HQ in Durham City, the rest of Flint's team tracked accounts for electronic transactions, and monitored transport networks: road, rail, air and sea – although, without passports, the boys' options were limited.

So far, nothing. Milo and Dominic Kingsley had disappeared.

Massey's own team had concentrated on filling blanks to strengthen their case. This morning, a forensic report had confirmed that a knife used to kill Maureen was the same one used on Duncan Kingsley.

The boys had most probably disposed of the knife or taken it with them, but Massey immediately requested a search warrant for the Forest Hall address, where they both still lived with their mother..

However, the fact the householder was the widow of a retired and well-respected Chief Superintendent, who was himself one of the murder victims had muddied the waters. So Massey had spent the afternoon dotting more 'i's and crossing more 't's than there could possibly be in the English translation of War and Peace.

But eventually, he did get the warrant and planned to execute it first thing tomorrow morning.

It was now after six thirty in the evening and his core MIT, including Tweddle and Shadforth, had gathered for a quick debrief on the day's activities.

'Alright folks. Let's get through this quickly so we can all go home and grab some sleep. As you know, we've failed to find the Kingsley brothers so far. To our knowledge, they have no passports or electronic devices with them and have not accessed their bank accounts. But we do have some forward motion in tying them into our murders, assault and arson.

'Brian's NPT have confirmation from two Cresswell residents, both close neighbours of the Quinns, that Milo has indeed been a regular visitor to Stoneyriggs over the summer, although no-one saw him there on the day of the fire. He's been observed on one occasion taking Fleur out in a vehicle we know belongs to his mother, and he's also been spotted by a next door neighbour sitting out in the back garden with Fleur.' He nodded towards Sparks and Keegan. 'You've spoken to Ursula today. Do you want to jump in here?'

'We have,' Keegan said. 'She told us she looked after both boys when they were children. The cellar then was a playroom then, so both boys have always known about the door to the garden. She also said that Dominic is a nasty little shit, always jealous of his brother, and in recent years Fleur has told her mother that, as children, Dominic used to get off on hitting her and threatening that if she told anyone he'd sneak into the house at night through that same cellar door to cut her up. Ursula lost it a bit when she realised the implications of what she'd said, which ended up working to our benefit, since it was her distress that persuaded Halliwell to hand over records of Dominic's therapy sessions with her.'

'Which,' Massey said, 'are now being analysed, but the headlines so far are that Betsy Halliwell registered Dominic as a client in 2019, when he was only thirteen years old and has been treating him – in their most recent sessions at least, and possibly for the whole five years – for anger management issues. We'll keep you all up to date on that. But hear this everyone, we have at least one angry young man here who may also be in possession of a knife that has already been used in two murders. So, whenever you're out there, until this is over, I want you all wearing your stab vests. And I do not want anyone to tackle either one of the Kingsley's alone. If you get a sniff, call it in.'

Madge Brown cleared her throat and looked at DS Tweddle. 'Talking about knives. Sorry, just occurred to me, and I should know this already. Could the knife used on Duncan Kingsley have been stolen from the barbecue?'

'We checked that.' Tweddle looked as if she were chewing a wasp. 'Of course we did. All accounted for, according to both Finn and Verity Barron. We did several bloody sweeps of the beach and the rocks at low tide for it too, thinking the killer might have thrown it into the sea. But now we know he sodding kept it, don't we?'

'And the report states it was likely an old-fashioned folding knife with an Imperial-shaped blade of illegal length,' Massey said. 'So doubtful it would be used in cooking, I'd have thought.'

He imagined how difficult this must be for both Durham officers, feeling as if they had to justify their own team's performance at every turn, knowing that the recent murders may not have happened if they'd caught the killers sooner.

He looked at Sparks and Keegan. 'Anything else either of you?'

Keegan nodded. 'Just that we also paid a visit to Finn and Verity Barron, who both looked like death warmed up, by the way. Definitely something up with them. But anyway, Finn told us about the conversation he'd had with Milo and Dominic on the day of the barbecue. It seems Dominic thought he should be on the first team, just because Milo had been given that honour as soon as he'd turned seventeen. So, once his own seventeenth came around, Dominic began haranguing the head coach, and this is Ben Quinn we're talking about, remember. Ben refused. Had to break it to Dominic he wasn't good enough for the first team whereas Milo, Dominic can't have failed to have known, is way too good still to be playing for a lowly club like Ellington & Cresswell.

'So it's likely the lads gave their parents a lift to that barbecue deliberately to give Dominic the opportunity to collar Finn about that, but Finn, like Ben, knocked him back, and Duncan failed to jump in on his son's behalf. So, in effect, even his own father knocked him back. Imagine how that would have felt to a young man like Dominic, so full of his own self-importance and jealousy. A kid we know has anger issues and even had a thing about cutting up little girls when he was knee-high.'

'That,' Marco Shadforth said, 'gives the kid a motive for all three. Kingsley, Quinn and Barron—'

'And yet, the killer has never gone after Barron. And it doesn't explain Maureen Duffy.'

'They *have* tried to frame him though,' Sparks said.

'So where does all the Macbeth crap come in?' Tweddle demanded.

No-one felt like getting into that rigmarole right now. Not if they wanted to get any sleep tonight. Tweddle could access the information on her own later. But then Donaldson raised a finger.

'I've had a thought about that. It turns out that Milo is doing a BA in English Literature and History at Newcastle University. He can't have failed to study Shakespeare to some extent in school since he's been the only compulsory author on the English National Curriculum for the last thirty five years. And, since Milo's chosen to study English Lit *and* History, there has to be a good chance he's pretty knowledgeable in Shakespeare's works.'

Massey nodded slowly. 'Good point, Andrew. Thank you.'

'Another couple of things we got from Barron,' Sparks said. 'He says he did not know before we told him that someone at that barbecue had informed Duncan Kingsley about his affair with Elena all those years ago, and has no idea who could have done that. He did also admit that Betsy's prophesy that same day referred to advances he'd been making to Scarlett Crowley, who took Maureen's place as a witch this year, and not to Fleur Quinn. Scarlett is the same age as Fleur and Milo. So a good bit less than half of Barron's age.'

'Pervert,' Laidler said.

Tweddle sat up straight and flicked her yellow-blonde hair back from her bronzed face. 'So if Barron was shagging around with Elena Kingsley when Milo was just a baby, and given there's just over a year between the boys ages, isn't it possible it's him who is the biological father of Dominic, and not Duncan Kingsley.'

The silence was broken by DSU Lou Portas, who'd entered the room unobserved. 'Perhaps', she said, 'that thought hit Duncan right between the eyes just before he was murdered.'

'And perhaps,' Massey said, 'that's precisely *why* he died.'

CHAPTER 65

Massey picked up his post from the doormat. A couple of circulars he dismissed immediately, a letter from his dentist, and another bearing a Law Court stamp. He ripped it open, knowing straight away what it would be, and he was right; it was a divorce petition and acknowledgment of service form, giving him fourteen days to respond. Helen wasn't waiting around, but he didn't have time to look at the documents properly now.

Oh, he was all for divorce, now that he knew his marriage had been a farce for the past year at least. Jesus, how she and Flowers must have been laughing behind his back when he'd found himself transferred to Flowers' team during the hunt for Musk Man back in January. All those flirty phone calls Flowers took in his presence. All the times the man went AWOL from work, when he must have been meeting with Helen. So yes, he wanted the divorce. But it would be him calling the shots from now on, not saint bloody Helen. Starting from when he had the sodding time to deal with it.

He threw the divorce papers down on the coffee table with the rest of the letters and went to the fridge to get himself a beer. Just one and then straight to bed. Despite having worked solidly through the previous night and all of today without a decent break, he didn't feel so exhausted he could be assured of sleep as soon as his head hit the pillow.

Taking a long swig of his beer, he put a whole platoon of polka-dot pixies on notice that their services would likely be required at any moment. He needed to be up and out of the house early in the morning, and preferably feeling fully refreshed. Tomorrow could well be the day they brought in two killers. For that, he needed to be on top form.

Milo and Dominic Kingsley. Two young men, both still only in their teens, who looked to be guilty of multiple murders, grievous bodily harm and arson with intent.

If Flint's team had managed to apprehend them a year ago for their father's murder, Ben Quinn and Maureen Duffy would still be alive, Fleur

Quinn would not be lying comatose in her bariatric chamber, and Stoneyriggs would still be standing as a family home.

He'd organised the search of Elena Kingsley's whole property, including outbuildings and vehicles, for six o'clock in the morning. Nothing out of bounds, not even Elena's personal space, since her sons had always had easy access. She'd already allowed officers inside to search for Milo and Dominic, but they hadn't had the power or the resources at the time to conduct a proper search of the property.

He'd nominated Keegan to lead the search, and arranged the services of a PolSA - although not Jodie O'Neill this time, a full Police Search Team, and a CSI. His own and Sparks' roles would be to more closely question Elena on what she knew of her sons' whereabouts during the most relevant times.

As well as signs of where the brothers might have gone, they'd be looking for bladed weapons that might have been used in the murders; fine traces of a black dust; and a mass-produced, non-designer sandshoe of unknown size bearing traces of Maureen Duffy's blood on the outside edge of the sole. Some sign of an obsession with Macbeth would be good too, so they'd be seizing digital devices, note pads, and anything else relevant, including Elena's own personal devices in order to check for any communications she might have had with her sons recently. That had been another sticking point for the warrant, but he'd held his position. There'd have been no questions asked on that point if she hadn't been Duncan Kingsley's widow.

He yawned, drained his beer bottle and made for the stairs.

Polka-dot pixies, stand by for action.

***

Sparks turned the corner onto her own street at a jog and spotted Dazz sitting on her doorstep cradling a white carrier bag. Her heart leapt, but then immediately she regretted having texted to let him know she was finally finished for the day. Much as she wanted to be with him, she needed sleep tonight above all else. He couldn't have failed to know her team had something big going on. Not the details. They never talked to each other about the details of their respective work, but he'd know that a few hours shut eye grabbed in the midst of a big murder inquiry were precious. He should have respected that.

He must have seen the change in her expression for his own face fell. He held up both hands, almost dropping the carrier. 'No pressure. I know you need to get your head down, but you should eat first, and I remembered your fridge is just about empty. I can leave yours here and go now, if you want. I got you beef and mushrooms with noodles.'

She caught the aroma as he held out the bag towards her. Her favourite. He'd remembered. And she couldn't argue. He was right; she needed to eat. 'It's okay,' she said, unable to prevent a smile as she turned her key in the lock. 'Don't go. I'm starving.'

They sat cross-legged on the floor in the lounge with their meals. She finished eating first. Then, belly full, she watched him until he felt her scrutiny and became self-conscious, which made her laugh.

'What?' he mumbled, around a mouthful of Char Siu Chow Mein and prawn cracker. 'You've seen me eat before.'

She giggled. 'I know.' Then she giggled more at the thought of how out of character her colleagues would consider it if they saw her laughing like this. But being with Dazz allowed her to leave the horrors at work, where they belonged. She'd never had that luxury with anyone else. Man or woman. Not even Massey. Well no, of course not Massey. Much as she loved him as a friend as well as her boss, her contact with him was ninety percent confined to work.

Dazz laid his plate aside, jumped to his feet and pulled her up with him. 'Bed time for you, young lady. I'll clear this lot up and let myself out.'

'You don't have to go. Come to bed with me.' She laced her fingers around his neck and cocked her head. 'After you've sorted this lot out, of course.'

'Nope. You're on your own tonight. You know that neither of us would get much sleep if I stayed. So...' He kissed her on the forehead, turned her around and gave her a gentle push towards the door. '... off you go. Get some sleep.'

CHAPTER 66

Thursday, 24 October 2024

Park Drive, Forest Hall. 5.55 am. Only the ominous presence of half a dozen police and forensic vehicles to disturb the sleepy peace on the narrow pot-holed road. Through the skeleton branches of tall deciduous trees, a half-moon glimmered behind wispy clouds. Massey remembered Betsy's prophesy; that he would face death before the moon waned, and it was halfway there already. Hopefully, they'd have the killers in custody long before it disappeared entirely.

He took a sip of coffee from his insulated mug. Beside him, in the passenger seat, Sparks twisted and untwisted her fingers. Feeling the tension. This was the worst part of any operation. The waiting. They'd had a whispered conversation with Keegan a few minutes ago. Everything was set. As soon as Elena answered the door, Keegan would send her off with Lisa to get dressed, while he and the PolSA got the search underway. They'd clear the hallway and the lounge first, leaving the room free for himself and Sparks to question Elena.

He knew the woman would be devastated already that her sons were now suspects in her husband's murder and had seemingly run away rather than face what they'd done, so having her house invaded by a police search team might well send her over the edge. And, even though she herself was under no suspicion, as the widow of a senior police officer, all this would surely feel horrifically shameful.

Even the strongest person in the world, under those circumstances, couldn't fail to be distraught. Yet surely, given the fact she *had* been married to a senior police officer, some small part of her must be expecting what was about to happen.

Either way, better to play safe. So, as a precaution, he'd put a doctor on standby, although he hoped they wouldn't need to make the call.

They watched the white-suited figures of the search team move forward and heard the wrought iron gate squeal on its hinges. Would the noise have immediately alerted Elena to their presence? Was she watching them now as they made their way up the winding garden path? She'd been waiting at the door for him and Sparks that first time they'd come here. But perhaps, this early in the morning, she would still be asleep. If she'd managed to find sleep at all, while her world was falling apart around her.

***

They stepped through the door onto the black and white floor tiles and Massey took a moment to examine the stark black ink figure drawings on the caramel walls, wondering if they'd been bought new after her move here, or something she and her husband had chosen together years ago.

The sound of their footsteps changed as they stepped onto the oak flooring of the lounge, where Elena sat in the same comfortable armchair, dressed in a hurry in matching claret leisure pants and tee-shirt, her head laid back and her face devoid of make-up.

She couldn't have failed to hear them enter the room, but she kept her eyes closed.

Lisa jumped up from the unyielding black Chesterfield and attempted to surreptitiously dislodge the seam of her white forensic suit from between her buttocks. 'Sir. Sarge.'

'Thanks Lisa,' Sparks said. 'We'll take over here now and we'll give you a call when we're about to leave.'

Lisa smiled acceptance and backed out of the room.

'Elena,' Massey said. 'I understand that this will be difficult, but we do need to talk to you about your sons.'

Still with her eyes closed; her tone flat, Elena spoke. 'They didn't do any of this. You have this all wrong. My boys did not do this.'

'Then talk to us. If they're innocent, help us to prove that.'

Elena's sigh shook her whole body. She turned heavy-lidded, red-rimmed eyes on them. 'I have no idea where they are. I'm not sure I'd tell you if I did.'

'You must realise that their disappearance makes them look guilty.'

She clamped her lips together to stop them from trembling and screwed her eyes closed again to prevent the tears from falling.

'Let's see if you can help us put them elsewhere at the relevant times then, shall we?

Elena nodded, as if her head were way too heavy for her shoulders to bear.

'How about Friday gone. The eighteenth. Let's start there, shall we? Can you take us through what happened that day. What were you all doing?'

Massey suspected that this was going to be more an exercise in helping Elena to accept that her sons really could have committed these crimes in terms of opportunity, although it would take much longer for her to realise that the boys she'd brought into this world could have turned out so evil?

CHAPTER 67

Friday, 25 October 2024

The search of Elena Kingsley's home in Forest Hall had taken most of the previous day, and they'd have to wait for forensic results on many of the items seized. Particularly the digital devices. They already had access to Milo's and Dominic's phone records, but they'd found nothing that could help locate them. The smart phones themselves, which the boys had left in their rooms along with smart watches, may well be more informative, although it was doubtful they'd have been left behind if they held anything relevant.

Elena had had no idea where Dominic had been in the late afternoon and early evening of the day of Maureen's murder, although she did know Milo had met Michael for a drink that evening.

Contrary to what she'd told them originally, she'd confessed that on the day of the Stoneyriggs fire there'd been a two hour interval between them all visiting the cemetery in the morning and going to the Holystone for a meal in the afternoon, and she could not recall where her sons were during those hours or what they'd said they were doing.

She'd broken down when they asked about the day of her husband's murder, admitting she had no idea where the boys had gone after Dominic's argument with Finn Barron. They'd said something vague about going to meet friends, and she'd assumed Flint's team had followed that up and discounted them.

Massey had checked Durham's case notes again when they returned to HQ, and found that Flint's team *had* known the boys had taken their parents to the Barron's house and then left. There was nothing about an argument with Finn, although they had confirmed Milo and Dominic's presence at a friend's house less than half an hour later. The brothers and the friend had then gone to meet others at a local park for a kick around. However, no specific time had been logged for them leaving the park.

Still no sign of the brothers at bus depots, train stations, ferry terminals or airports. No record of any card payments or cash withdrawals.

No communications, as far as they could tell, with any friends or family members. Milo and Dominic Kingsley had effectively disappeared off the face of the earth.

At around 8 am, Massey received a call from Steve Todd, the hospital consultant to inform them that Michael Duffy had suffered a fatal heart attack and stroke in the middle of the night.

Madge Brown – a dog lover – wondered what would happen with the two huskies, more concerned it seemed with their fate than with the tragic deaths of their owners.

'Maybe Maureen's mother will take them,' Massey said. 'I think she's next of kin and will get the bungalow too.'

All this talking about the dogs reminds me of when I was a teenager,' Donaldson said. 'I used to earn extra pocket money by taking our neighbours' dog out for walks during school holidays, while they were at work.'

'You mean they'd drop the dog off in the morning and you were stuck with it until they came back?' Jackson looked aghast.

'Of course not. They gave me a key to the house.'

The simplicity of it struck Massey and Keegan simultaneously.

'They gave Dominic a key,' Massey said.

'They're at the Duffy's bungalow,' Keegan agreed.

CHAPTER 68

The bungalow was still an active crime scene. All external doors and windows had been locked. Both gates had been secured with new padlocks. Unbroken police tape still surrounded the perimeter, and patrol cars carried out regular checks.

Ideally, Massey would have had officers still posted 24/7, but his resources didn't allow that. Two fit young men with a key could have gained access to the property without too much effort.

But would they have risked coming back here?

Why would they not, Massey thought. They'd be off the streets. There were cupboards full of tinned and packet provisions, and likely food still in the fridge and freezer. The utilities were all still turned on, as far as he knew, so everything would be running. The curtains were closed already, so they wouldn't need to worry about being spotted through a window. He'd seen to that himself as an added precaution against dauntless reporters. The boys would need to keep the lights and TV off, but that was a small price to pay for somewhere warm and comfortable to stay while the police ran themselves ragged searching for them.

An armed response officer silently turned the key in the padlock on the back gate and withdrew the PVC-sheathed security chain. They'd already drowned the hinges with WD40 to minimise creaking.

Entering through this gate gave them the best chance of approaching the bungalow itself undetected, since it faced the back right hand corner of the building, where the only window that could have had a view of the gate was the frosted bathroom one, close to which was a solid external door leading into the kitchen.

They'd debated using the keys they'd found in the house and had used to lock up the property, which had presumably belonged to Maureen, but fumbling for the right key might well be heard from inside. They'd lose the element of surprise, increasing the chances one or both of the boys could be armed when officers entered.

If they were in there.

Three armed officers ran across the grass towards the corner of the building. Without them blocking his view now, Massey got his first look at the place since it had been locked up. Everything still looked secure.

Reaching the door, the lead officer drew back the big red enforcer and rammed it into the wood next to the lock. The door flew open.

'*Armed police! On the floor!*' The officers moved inside, their shouts becoming muffled as they moved towards the front of the building. '*Armed police! Get down. On the floor. On the floor.*'

Massey had expected to see the place in a mess; dirty plates and discarded food containers everywhere, yet apart from blood-spattered walls and a dark stain on the carpet where Maureen's blood had pooled, at least one of the boys must have been keeping the place clean and tidy, and had even washed their dishes.

He followed the sound of shouting, through the kitchen and into the hallway, where two bin bags filled with what must be empty tins and packets had been stacked against the front door to delay entry if anyone came to check on the house. They'd have given the brothers a few extra seconds to escape through the back door and over the gate into the woods.

In the lounge, armed officers loomed over Milo and Dominic, who lay prone on the floor, legs outstretched, hands cuffed behind them. Massey was surprised to see the ceiling light and the television were on. Then he noticed a thick blanket taped across the curtained window to help block out any light from within.

A large kitchen knife lay against the skirting board, probably kicked out of reach by one of the armed officers. All three officers held their weapons pointed up, away from their prisoners.

Defeated, Milo kept his head down, facing away. Not so his younger brother. Dominic glared in fury. Hawking, with blood streaming from a wound in the middle of his forehead, he hawked and spat a huge gobbit as far as he could manage towards Massey's shoes. Not quite far enough.

'What happened to his head?' Massey asked

The nearest officer laughed. 'The idiot tried to head-butt my helmet.'

CHAPTER 69

It didn't take long for Milo to crack. At least not as far as the death of his father was concerned. Watching via the live camera in the next room, with Christine Sparks and Guy Keegan interviewing, it felt to Massey as if the boy had been waiting desperately for an opportunity to unburden himself; for someone, anyone, to stick a pin into just the right spot to release the pressure that had built up inside him over the past year at least.

He and Dominic *had* gone to the friend's house, he told them, and to the park, just as they'd told Flint's team. But then one of their friends had begun talking about his father buying him a car for his eighteenth birthday, which had incensed Dominic and started him ranting about how their own father wouldn't even stick up for him in an argument. He'd left Milo, saying he was going to walk back to Finn's house for a showdown with his father.

At first, Milo hadn't taken him seriously. It was quite a walk. He'd assumed Dominic just needed time to calm down, but when after a while he hadn't reappeared, Milo had got into his car and gone looking for him, catching up with him in Ellington at the top of Cresswell Road. He'd persuaded Dominic to get into the car and had tried to calm him down, eventually agreeing to go back to the barbecue with him.

'Why?' they'd asked.

Because whenever Dominic got like that, nothing could hold him back until he got what he wanted. Not completely. All Milo could do was the same he'd had to do for as far back as he could remember. Be a calming voice in the black hole of Dominic's fury.

He'd reasoned that, at the barbecue, his mother could help him calm Dominic down.

'If he was that angry, wouldn't it have been best to take him home?'

'Probably. Looking back.'

'So what happened?'

As he'd turned the car onto Beach Road, he told them, and driven past the holiday park, Dominic had pointed out their father, oblivious to their presence and looking furious, striding away from Finn's house and down the grassy slope to the beach. Dominic had demanded Milo stop the car, but instead Milo had engaged the central locking system to stop Dominic from jumping out. He'd kept driving, past Finn's and all the way along the back road to Lynemouth, refusing to stop, with Dominic yelling at him, punching him in the arm, and almost causing him to crash into the bollards that restricted traffic to single file over the old bridge by the power station.

But then, like the sun coming out from behind black clouds, Dominic's anger had switched off. He'd calmed down and said he was fine, that he'd got it out of his system, but he would still feel happier if he could have a few words with his father. And Milo had fallen for it. Again.

'Or maybe,' he said, 'I was just so pig sick of being Dom's keeper.'

He'd driven back towards Ellington and down to Cresswell, completing one big circle. At the bottom of Cresswell Road, as they turned right onto Beach Road again, Dominic had decided he didn't want to go straight back to Finn's. Instead, he wanted to go down to the beach to see if their father was still down there. Better to have it out with him there, away from the party. No point airing their dirty laundry in public, he'd said. Which Milo had agreed with whole-heartedly. His father could deal with Dominic easily enough, he'd told himself. He could explain why he wasn't able to override a club's selection decision to get his own son on the team. That would be nepotism.

As Massey watched onscreen, Milo began sobbing. Wiping his forearm across his eyes, he turned devastated eyes on them. 'If I hadn't... Oh God, if I hadn't taken Dom back...'

Keegan and Sparks allowed him a moment to pull himself together.

'So you went down to the beach,' Sparks said. 'Both of you?'

'No, no, just Dom. He wouldn't let...'

'Where did you park?'

'Behind South Side. The old cottages. There's a couple of holiday lets there. And a space that ... I dunno, maybe it was a boatyard once...'

Shit, Massey thought. He meant next to Trinny's place.

'You mean next to Blue Moon Bakery?' Sparks asked, as if she'd heard his thoughts through the wall.

Milo lowered his head. His fists clenched on the table. He couldn't find the words, but he nodded.

'For the tape please Milo. Where did you park?'

Milo panted a couple of rapid breaths before squeezing out a reluctant assent. 'I parked right in front of the bakery. Next to Trinny's.'

'And you went down to the beach.'

'No, I told you. Dom went. I stayed by the car. He said… he said he wanted to go alone, see. So I let him. He climbed down to the rocks from there and ran around.'

'The sea must come right in close there. Why didn't he run along the road until he was closer to where you'd seen your dad?'

'The tide was out. Dom thought Dad would stay on the beach and he'd catch him if he was walking along.'

Why hadn't Flint's team discovered this? They must have spoken to people who were on the beach that day below the holiday park. Dominic would have had to run past them to find his father. It had been a hot summer day. A lone teenager running across the rocks and striding along the beach would have stood out among the families who'd still have been down on that part of the sands late in the afternoon.

Again, Sparks echoed his thoughts. 'What were you both wearing?'

Milo looked up. His brow creased. 'Um, shorts and vests. Why?'

Not so out of place on a beach then. Dominic would have looked like any other young man enjoying the sun at the seaside.

'And on your feet? Both of you.'

'Trainers. No, wait. Dom took his off. Left them in the car.'

'Why would he do that.'

'Um, easier to walk on sand probably.'

'He'd have had rocks to clamber over too though. First to climb down from where you parked. It's not exactly sandy beach there, is it? Then he'd have had to negotiate that rocky headland at the end of… what's that bit called?' Sparks glanced down at her notes. 'Ah yes, Broadsands Beach, leading to the cliffs at Snab Point. Quite a climb round there before he found your father. Not so comfortable in bare feet.'

Milo shrugged. 'That's nothing. We grew up in Cresswell. Ran barefoot around there most of our childhoods.'

'So Dominic knows that shoreline well.'

'Hell yes. We both do.'

'What did you do while Dominic was running along the beach?'

Milo snorted. 'What do you think? Enjoying the peace. It's hard work, dealing with Dom when he goes off on one.'

'But he'd calmed down by then, you said.'

'Yeah, but for how long? I was sick to the back teeth of him wanting to go wherever I went, like we were still little kids, and having to deal with all his shit. So I sat on the sea wall, watching the sea, dreaming.'

'About what?'

'What do you mean?'

'What were you dreaming about? Simple question.'

'About getting away. Wishing I'd got a place at a different uni, so I could leave home. Leave Dom…'

'How long did you stay there, dreaming?'

'I dunno. Until Dom came back. A while, I suppose.'

'And how did he look when he got back?'

'Wet.'

Both detectives gave Milo an enquiring look and allowed the silence to develop.

'He swam back,' Milo said.

'Why would he do that?' Sparks asked. 'You said the tide was out.'

'It was. I have no idea why. Or I didn't then. Not until later, when I realised what he'd done.'

'You're saying Dominic killed your father.'

'He says he didn't, but he must have.'

'How did he kill him?'

'He used a knife.' Fat tears rolled down Milo's cheeks. 'My knife, from my grandad. He must have taken it out of the door pocket; killed Dad with it. Why else would he have gone down to the sea and swum back if not to wash off the… to wash off Dad's… blood?'

'Where's that knife now?'

'I got rid of it. I… I had to. Don't you see?'

CHAPTER 70

'Dominic is still saying nothing then?' DSU Portas said.

'Hasn't cracked yet.' Massey told her. 'Stubborn bugger. Hasn't stopped yelling and shouting since we brought him in either. Took two officers to restrain him while a medic took care of the wound on his forehead. It'll take a while to get him to say anything intelligible, but that's okay. We've got him anyway on B&E, and assaulting an officer.'

'Nasty little shit,' Keegan said. 'Pleased I just have daughters.'

It was late. The Kingsleys' legal representative had insisted on a long uninterrupted break, which was fine with everyone involved. Dominic would talk, eventually. The clock was not an issue. Both boys had been arrested for actual breaking and entering and for suspected involvement in the three murders, grievous bodily harm and arson. Dominic had also been arrested for actual assault on a police officer.

Milo and Dominic were going nowhere.

It was almost over. He'd be free to sort things out with Trinny. Starting, hopefully, tomorrow evening.

His tickets for Cresswell Macbeth were in his wallet. He'd bought them to support the charity, with no real intention of going, but now he was determined to be there. Surely he'd be able to grab a few words with Trinny at some point during the performance. This whole immersive theatre thing still had him baffled, but he imagined groups of people would be guided around from one scene to another, which would leave Trinny and her coven at a loose end for at least some of the time. He'd get his opportunity then to hopefully persuade her to meet up sometime soon. Maybe they could even rekindle their mutual attraction into an ongoing relationship. They could build on that. If he played things right.

By the time he got home, he was so exhausted he knew he'd need no polka-dot pixies to lull him to sleep. Sure enough, the minute his head hit the pillow, he slept the sleep of the dead.

CHAPTER 71

Saturday, 26 October 2024

Up in a dark and fretful sky, a crescent moon shone. Related to fertility, and to life and death, or so Massey had discovered when his newly developed interest in the phases of the moon had led him to carry out a bit of online research one sleepless night. Waning, as this one was, it might symbolise surrendering to the inevitable and preparing for the next stage in life. Except that his life could be over before this particular crescent moon faded away to nothing.

If he believed all that shit. Which, of course, he didn't.

The gates to Cresswell Pele Tower stood open. Sinuous fingers of thick mist from a fog machine whipped and wove themselves together in the stiffening breeze through beams of orange and blue lights aimed upwards from the ground, disguised by groups of carved pumpkin lanterns arranged at either side of the gate, each of them lit by what had to be flickering LED candles, since real candles would surely have blown out quickly. However they were lit, the pumpkins enhanced the spooky Halloween theme.

At the head of the queue, Massey heard the voices of cackling witches – one recognisably Trinny's – casting Macbethian spells and spinning prophesies for visitors as they passed through the gate. He thought about the curse Chirnside had mentioned and that Sparks had later expanded on, laid upon the play by real witches back in Shakespeare's day because they didn't appreciate their incantations being stolen and used for people's amusement.

If one believed that real witches did exist, of course. Which he did not. Although he might be persuaded to believe in ghosts.

It had taken a while to realise that the wraith-like being he'd glimpsed drifting between trees inside the gate was actually Verity in her distinctive white coat, and not the tower's ghostly white lady. He wondered where Finn was. And where the hell was Sparks? She and Dazz had tickets for this evening's performance too. Maybe they were already inside.

He felt a hand on his shoulder and turned.

'Alright, mate?' Dazz said.

Sparks's face glowed. Somehow, Dazz had managed to get through all her defences, and Massey couldn't be more pleased for them. They looked so right together. Perhaps tonight could be the start of him and Trinny reaching a similar happy unity. He hoped so. That was why he'd come tonight.

A man wearing a dark medieval costume, came down the queue to collect their tickets, making a count as he went. 'Won't be long folks. You're the last lot to go through.' His focus changed as he looked beyond them. 'Here they are. Last ones. Just in time.

All three turned, to find Keegan approaching, with a curvaceous woman at his side. Keegan gave them a wink. 'Sarah, meet Flash, Dazz and Christine. Team, this is my wife, Sarah.'

Possessing an hourglass figure, sun-streaked fair hair and amused blue eyes, Sarah Keegan stood almost as tall as her husband. Massey wondered what the hell she saw in the big, bearded brute at her side, other than his obvious adoration of her. Whatever it was, they looked well together too.

'How did you get tickets?' Sparks demanded, 'I thought they were all sold out.'

Keegan tapped the side of his nose. 'I have my sources.' Then he laughed at their expressions. 'Actually, I bought them early, at the party after the charity match. Sarah loves a bit of culture. Don't you, pet?'

***

Standing at the back with Dazz and Keegan, so others didn't have their view blocked by their height and bulk as they all gathered around to watch this first scene, Massey watched the witches sway, waving long black fingernails in dramatic flourishes. Trinny, Scarlett and Betsy, in their ragged black robes; their warty faces lit by a purple light emanating from inside their smoke-filled cauldron. Some sort of miniature fog machine, he imagined.

It looked effective.

Weaving her head from side to side, holding Massey's gaze from beneath her white feathered lashes, Trinny spoke first in a loud cackle.

'When shall we three meet again, in thunder, lightning, or in rain?'

Betsy's own cackle sounded a touch too menacing in the next line.

'When the hurlyburly's done, when the battle's lost and won.'

Scarlett's turn.

'That... will be ere the set of sun.'

She'd spotted him in the crowd and almost messed up her line, probably remembering her wanton forwardness the first time they'd met in the lobby of the rugby club. One hand cupped to her ear, she rallied for her next line, as two male actors approached from through the trees.

'A drum, a drum!' she cried, *'Macbeth doth come.'*

Sparks looked puzzled, and then more so as one of the men came to a dramatic stop in front of the witches.

'What are these, so wither'd and so wild in their attire,' he demanded, *'that look not like the inhabitants o' the earth, and yet are on't? Live you? Or are you aught that man may question?'*

Beside him, Massey heard Sparks' disapproving whisper. 'That's Banquo's line. They've missed loads out. We should have met King Duncan at a campsite before Macbeth and Banquo come across the witches.'

Hands on hips, looking more like a swashbuckling pirate than a Scottish thane, the man playing Macbeth planted his feet in front of the witches.

'Speak, if you can,' he demanded. *'What are you?'*

'Didn't you say this would be an abridged version?' Dazz whispered.

Sparks huffed. 'Yes, but I still thought we'd see King Duncan at the beginning.'

Dazz put an arm around her shoulder and laughed. 'They can't exactly leave him out altogether, can they? Doesn't the whole play pivot around what happens to Duncan?'

That was exactly what it came down to in their actual scenario too, Massey thought. Everything pivoted around the murder of Duncan Kingsley more than a year ago, for which they'd now arrested the man's two sons, which in itself was a huge departure from the plot of the

Shakespearean tragedy. So maybe their whole theory of their murderers imitating Macbeth was a load of old tosh after all.

They'd yet to hear Dominic's side of the story, but – so far, at least – Milo's account was compelling. Dominic might have committed the actual murder, but Milo couldn't have failed to know that in choosing not to report the crime and in helping to get rid of the weapon, he would be judged equally guilty. Lots of sticking points, of course, which a second day of questioning had failed to clarify. Not least Milo's claim he'd got rid of the weapon, because the same knife had been used on Maureen Duffy. So had they later retrieved it?

Milo had claimed that neither he nor his brother had had anything to do with what happened to Maureen, or to Ben and Fleur Quinn. And yes, while he *had* studied Shakespeare, since the author had been a required element of his academic choices to date, he wasn't particularly enamoured of his works, he'd insisted. Absolutely not. He preferred the romantic poets, Keats and Byron in particular. Completely opposite, he'd told them. Lord Byron, so flamboyant and defiant and melancholic in style; Keats finding astounding beauty in the everyday.

Massey had no idea if all that were true, but Milo's academic record could be easily checked, if necessary. And the lad *had* come across as sincere; thankful, at long last, to have been relieved of a millstone of responsibility for his brother.

A third man had approached unseen. With a bow and a flourish, Len Stafford introduced himself as Ross, a messenger sent to guide them to the next scene, inside the tower. The group followed him, listening to him recount what they needed to know – the bits in between Chirnside's next chosen scene, presumably – before they got there.

Massey hung back, hoping for a word with Trinny. She must have had the same thought for, as her fellow witches stood and moved away, easing cricks out of their backs, Trinny grabbed hold of his sleeve.

'Wait.' She moved in close to him, making his heart jump. 'Can we meet later, James? Once we're all cleared up here?'

A grin spread across his face. That was exactly what he'd wanted to ask her.

She laughed. 'Good. I'm glad. We have lots to sort out.'

Halfway up the path, Sparks and Dazz waited for him, Guy and Sarah Keegan had followed the rest of the group.

'What time do you think you'll be finished?' he asked her.

'Around nine-ish. I could probably get away a little earlier, but I'd be leaving everyone else with the clear-up. I wouldn't be very popular.'

'That's absolutely fine. Nine-ish is good.'

The play itself was due to end at around seven thirty, with an option for guests to stay for a witch's brew and Halloween-themed finger buffet in the garden afterwards. If he stayed for that, he wouldn't have to wait around for very long.

He could see Sparks growing impatient.

He smiled. 'I'll um… I'll see you then.'

'Absolutely. Oh, wait a moment.' She grinned through her thick stage make-up and black-painted teeth, held up one claw finger and ducked down to grab something stowed behind the cauldron. 'Here. Something to munch on during the rest of the performance. I know how much you liked them.'

She thrust a paper bag into his hands. Puzzled, he opened the top and inhaled the delicious aroma of cheese.

'Just some of those Parmesan and poppy seed crackers you liked so much,' she said. 'I brought them to share with Betsy and Scarlett between scenes, but they brought snacks too, so we've got loads hidden down there. Take them. Please.'

He clasped her fingers, not wanting to let go, wishing he could kiss her, but he'd ruin all that scary witch's make-up and get it all over himself.

Rejoining his friends, he offered the little mini crackers around. Only Sarah and Dazz accepted one, each agreeing they were indeed delicious.

***

Moving with the group, having forgotten to make time for dinner, again, Massey tried to make his Parmesan and poppy seed crackers last.

For all he was enjoying the rest of the performance, he had only one thing on his mind now; the moment when he and Trinny could get together and talk about the future. He'd be seeing her as a witch in the performance again first, he assumed, in the scene where Macbeth is given the second set of prophesies. They'd all be guided back down to the gate for that. And then the procession would work its way through the wooded grounds again and there'd be the final battle somewhere, and then refreshments in the garden.

Behind the tower, on the stage he and Sparks had seen being built, they'd already watched Lady Macbeth persuade her husband to kill King Duncan. Then, inside the tower again, their group had taken part as guests at a banquet to witness Macbeth's descent into madness when he sees Banquo's ghost.

It was during the banqueting scene that he'd caught sight of Verity again, flitting in and out of the tower, as if distracted by something, holding herself apart from the groups that passed each other now and then as they moved between scenes.

Seeing Macbeth's descent into madness alongside Verity's strange preoccupation had brought to mind her husband Finn, their modern day version of Macbeth, and how he'd appeared to be going mad too at the celebration event in the upstairs room in the rugby club.

Yet, unlike Macbeth, it had always been a stretch to think of Finn as the murderer, despite likenesses to the plot and what his wife had told Betsy.

Oh yes, the man might be a serial Casanova and a shit of a husband, and both he and Verity clearly had some sort of substance abuse issue and other health problems going on. But none of that made him a murderer. Or mad. And, now that Milo had confessed, it was looking more likely that the whole Macbethian thing had been nothing more than an over-elaborate, and yet clumsy attempt to frame Finn. But why?

As revenge perhaps, for not giving a nasty, spoilt little scrote a place on the first team? Really? All this: four people dead, one at death's door, and a family home in ruins because a teenage kid couldn't accept the fact he didn't have the chops to play with the big boys? In a minor league rugby union team for Christ's sake. Extreme, or what?

Yet so far, it all appeared to fit. Perhaps a little *too* well.

Why wait over a year after killing their father before striking again, for a start? Had it taken that long to figure out the links with the play?

And, if Milo had told the truth about getting rid of the knife after Dominic had killed their father, how had it later been used to kill Maureen?

They were back inside the tower. Lady Macbeth, now queen, dismissed Len Stafford, i.e. Ross, and another character named Lennox from her presence. The two men took their leave and wandered together through the door, inviting the group along with them. At the top of the path, an older man – greeted as a lord – joined them in discussing Macduff *'living in disgrace'* because he hadn't attended the Macbeth's banquet.

'Sent he to Macduff?' Lennox demanded.

The old man gave a dramatic nod. *'He did: and with an absolute "Sir, not I,"…'*

Massey blinked and shrugged his shoulders a couple of times, feeling all of a sudden light-headed.

***

'Some holy angel fly to the court of England and unfold his message ere he come,' Lennox said, *'that a swift blessing may soon return to this our suffering country under a hand accursed!'*

'I'll send my prayers with him,' the older lord said.

At the top of the path, looking down towards the gates, Massey threw the last Parmesan and poppy seed thin into the air and caught it in his mouth. He upturned the paper bag and shook out the crumbs, then scrunched it up and stuck it in his pocket, noticing how strange his fingers looked in the ghostly white light of the crescent moon through the skeleton branches.

Sparks nudged him. 'What the hell are you doing?'

He lowered his arms, wiping his hands down his face to straighten his expression. 'Nothing.'

'Are you alright?'

'Of course.' He couldn't prevent himself from laughing at her concern, realising in that moment just how deeply he loved her. Detective Sergeant Christine Sparks. He loved her as a colleague and as a friend.

She had his back. Always. Yet, had it not been for all the problems she'd had to fight through in her own life, he might never ever have had the opportunity to discover how wonderful it could be to have such a deep abiding relationship with a woman without even a jot of lust or romance in the mix to screw things up. Just pure, uncomplicated friendship.

He felt her eyes on him, still watching, and grinned.

'What?' she demanded.

'Nothing. Really, I'm fine. More than fine.'

'You don't look it.'

He smiled again, thinking that if everything went the way he wanted it to tonight, Sparks might develop a more favourable attitude towards Trinny, especially now that she had such a positive relationship going on in her own life.

With sweeping bows and a flourish of arms, Ross and Lennox directed the group back down towards the cauldron, where all three witches danced and chanted.

'Double, double toil and trouble; Fire burn and cauldron bubble.'

Then Betsy continued alone.

'Cool it with a baboon's blood; then the charm is firm and good.'

They all heard a rustling in the undergrowth as Betsy raised a clawed hand to her ear.

'By the pricking of my thumbs, something wicked this way comes. Open, locks, whoever knocks!'

Macbeth stepped out in front of them. *'How now, you secret, black, and midnight hags! What is't you do?'*

'A deed without a name,' the witches chanted.

Massey felt Trinny's eyes fixed on his. Every weave of her arms and crook of a finger felt like a provocative invitation he had to fight to resist. It wouldn't do for him to go charging through the group and seize her in his arms here, now, in front of everyone. Not exactly a part of the script. Even Colin Chirnside's version. He laughed, then covered his mouth.

Oblivious, Macbeth, his feet planted wide, puffed out his chest and placed his hands on his hips.

'I conjure you, by that which you profess, howe'er you come to know it, answer me...'

Massey's companions were not so oblivious. He noticed Sarah nudge Keegan and incline her head in his direction. Sparks elbowed him and Dazz put a hand on his shoulder.

'I'm okay,' he said. 'Really.' Feeling feverish, he closed his eyes, then opened them again, trying to banish a gathering shimmer that had developed around the edges of his vision. Maybe he really did have measles.

CHAPTER 72

'Macbeth! Macbeth! Macbeth! beware Macduff; beware the thane of Fife.'

Trinny's line sparked a vision of Michael Duffy lying so ill in his hospital bed, so angry and so convinced that Finn Baron had murdered Duncan Kingsley.

Had the man realised before his own death that he'd been lured out of the house that night so that Maureen would be alone when her killer came calling?

Macbeth responded. *'Whate'er thou art, for thy good caution, thanks; thou hast harp'd my fear aright.'*

'Macbeth! Macbeth! Macbeth!' Betsy cackled.

'Had I three ears, I'd hear thee,' Macbeth replied.

Betsy waved her arms in a frenzy, as if calling down her next words from the heavens. *'Be bloody, bold, and resolute; laugh to scorn the power of man, for none of woman born shall harm Macbeth.'*

He remembered Sparks telling him and Lou Portas that Macduff *did* slay Macbeth at the end. But since Macduff had been delivered through caesarean section rather than by natural birth, in a way, the prophesy had been proved right after all.

He recalled too the way Betsy had delivered her mock prophesy to him in the lobby of the rugby club two weeks ago tonight. Bewitching in a different way, dressed in black, dramatically made-up, like tonight but glamorous rather than scary.

She'd been determined to go one better than Ursula and Scarlett with the prophesy she'd spun for him, she'd admitted, telling him he'd face death before the moon waned. He looked up now at the crescent moon that remained, which seemed to pulse in the sky, mocking him, telling him there was still time yet for that prophesy to come true too.

A sudden wind rattled through the branches, setting drifts of fallen leaves rustling, whipping the witches' black robes until the material snapped like a ship's mainsail.

For the first time, he noticed ominous clouds creeping their way across the sky from the east and wondered whether the rain would hold off until the event ended.

He felt himself sway, then staggered to right himself.

'C'mon, mate.' Dazz said. 'Let's go find somewhere to sit down.'

Yep. Exactly what he needed. Somewhere to sit until Trinny could get away. He remembered some bench seats he'd seen around the walls of the tower.

'Thanks Dazz, but you stay here with the others. I'll be fine on my own.'

Sparks pressed her water bottle into his hands. 'Drink it all. Maybe you're just dehydrated.'

'Yep, that's all it is. Thanks Christine'

A lack of fluids. Not measles at all. He wasn't so far gone though that he missed the calculated look Sparks shot towards Trinny. Maybe she wasn't quite ready to put aside her reservations yet after all.

The walk back up the path, with the strengthening wind swaying the skeleton branches above him, seemed longer than before, and yet at the same time, the tower loomed towards him.

What was it he'd told himself only a couple of weeks ago? That he was a grown man, for Christ's sake, responsible for his own health and wellbeing, and perfectly capable of looking after himself.

So why did he keep on forgetting to do so?

His mouth felt so parched. He probably shouldn't have eaten all of Trinny's Parmesan and poppy seed crackers in one go. Delicious, but salty as hell. By the time he reached the top, he'd almost drained Sparks' water bottle and wished he'd brought his own.

From the long stone mounting block, he clambered up onto the boundary wall and stared out to sea, conscious of the speed of the clouds moving inland.

He leant into the wind, feeling as if he were flying high atop the wing of an old-fashioned biplane, with no harness to keep him safe, and hoping it might help to clear his head.

Reality hit him at the same time as a griping pain in his stomach.

Shit!

He climbed down as the stomach spasm eased. Puzzled by his own foolhardiness, he dropped onto a bench seat, taking a sip from Sparks' water bottle, then stretched out his legs and leant his head back against the ancient tower.

***

After a while, he heard Trinny, Betsy and Scarlett as they entered the tower, their own performance over, his friends and the rest of the group presumably having been moved along to the next scene.

The cast must be using the upper floor as a changing room again.

Unbidden, his mind conjured up Trinny slipping out of the black robes, her naked body just as he remembered it all those years ago; those sinuous feline movements, arms reaching out to him, drawing him towards her, his eyes transfixed by that irresistible mole in the valley between wondrous breasts. 'Look at me,' she said. So he raised his head and opened his eyes to the warty face of an ugly old crone, with straggling grey hair and long white—

'James, look at me.'

Jesus. 'Christine.'

'Were you asleep?'

He laughed. 'I think I probably was.'

'Are you okay? You don't look it.'

Conscious of another stab of pain in his belly, he thought about it. 'Yeah, I think so. Just an upset stomach. I'm fine here for a little while, then I'll just get myself away. You go back and watch the rest. Enjoy yourselves.'

As she walked unwillingly away, he congratulated himself on having come up with a solution to how he could hang about for Trinny without having to have an argument with Sparks about it. He'd just stay out of her sight. She'd think he'd already gone.

CHAPTER 73

The crescent moon looked increasingly like a giant's toenail the more he stared at it. He had no idea how many minutes had passed since Sparks had left him, when he heard voices again. Women's voices, leaving the tower. He couldn't see the door from where he sat, but he thought he recognised Betsy's and Scarlett's tones, laughing about a child who'd cried in terror at the sight of them earlier.

Trinny must be with them, but she didn't speak.

Not long now.

He tried to see the time on his watch, but the storm clouds chose that moment to cover the moon. He shook his head and squinted in an effort to clear the sparkling aura, worse now than before. Then he remembered his smart phone and pulled it out of his pocket. That would tell him the time, wouldn't it? He tapped the screen to wake it, just as the device rang in his hand. Automatically, he swiped the green icon.

'James. Oh, thank God you answered. I need some help up—'

'Trinny?'

'Verity's gone up onto the roof. I think she's going to do something stupid.'

'Where? In the tower?'

He looked up towards the battlements, but he was too close to see. He moved away, towards the boundary wall, and looked again. He could see a white mass up there. Verity's coat?

'What do you mean, she's going to do something stupid?'

'I think she's going to jump. James, you have to help me.'

Something clicked in his befuddled mind. Didn't Lady Macbeth kill herself too? And Verity was Lady Macbeth, wasn't she?

He ran towards the tower door, dizziness making him clumsy.

Bloody hell, Massey. Sort yourself out.

He flung open the heavy door. Everything inside in darkness. But why, if there were people still inside? No time to look for switches. He turned left, making for the north east corner behind the door, where he knew the narrow winding stone staircase lay making for the north east corner behind the door, where he knew the narrow winding stone staircase lay.

'Up here,' Trinny cried. *'Hurry.'*

The stone wall closed in on him. The tight right-turn spiral made him want to puke. Every steep step felt like climbing a mountain.

'Hurry, James!'

At the top, on the next floor, another pain ripped through his stomach. He leant on the metal safety rail until it passed, swallowing down a feeling of nausea. Where to now?

He heard Trinny above him somewhere. Shouting to Verity. Trying to sound calm. Every third or fourth word whipped away by the wind. 'Come down from— Verity. We can talk about— Please— No, stop. Nothing can be that— No, Verity—'

'Trinny!' he yelled, as huge raindrops splattered onto the skylights above. Heavier by the moment. Becoming a thunderous roar.

'Up here,' she cried. *'On the roof. She's going to—'*

CHAPTER 74

On a small temporary stage, halfway down the tower garden, its awning snapping and cracking in the heightening wind, Macbeth raised his sword in the air.

'Hang out our banners on the outward walls; the cry is still "They come" …'

Sparks hurried towards their group, all now armed with a collection of wooden swords and broomstick spears – props for their roles as part of the immersive battle scene coming up – and slipped her hand through Dazz's elbow. 'We need to leave.'

'Is he alright?'

'No. Something's off. He looks like he's been spiked. We need to—'

'What's that?' Keegan demanded. 'Who's been spiked.'

'James, I think. We need to make sure he's okay. He might need to go to hospital.'

'Are you sure he's been spiked?'

'No, but he's acting weird. Someone needs to be with him.'

'…were they not forced with those that should be ours, we might have met them dareful, beard to beard, and beat them backward home.'

They moved aside to allow two women to creep past them on tiptoe. Betsy and Scarlett, heads down, making for a gazebo, where earlier groups were already making subdued merry on the refreshments provided, keeping a wary eye on the marching clouds, wondering whether to flee a possible onslaught of rain now, rather than risk getting wet when they had to bunk over to give the last group a turn at the table.

No sign of Trinny.

Finn Barron walked towards them, looking worried, stopping people to ask if they'd seen his wife. He caught sight of them and swerved away, cutting across the grass, making for a group of people on the other side of the garden to ask.

'Who on earth would have spiked a police detective?' Sarah asked, her face full of concern.

'Red.' Sparks spat, struggling to contain her anger. All her instincts about the woman, from the first moment she'd set eyes on her, were being proven true. 'That bitch did it. She put something in those bloody cheese crackers.'

Sarah looked at her husband. 'Red?'

'Trinity Moon. One of the witches tonight. She and James have history.'

'Not the crackers though. I ate one and I feel fine.'

'Me too,' Dazz said.

'But James scoffed the rest of the sodding bag, didn't he?' Sparks began to panic. She needed to get back to him. 'Don't be fooled. That woman is poison. We need to find her. Find out what she put in them, but first we need to make sure James is safe.'

'Let's go and find the daft sod then,' Keegan said. 'Where is he?'

'Sitting by the tower, when I left him.'

From the direction of the tower, they heard shouting.

Onstage, intent on his lines, Macbeth put his hand to his ear.

'Wherefore was that cry?'

'The queen, my lord, is dead.'

CHAPTER 75

Fumbling in the dark, with Trinny's desperate plea ringing in his ear, Massey found the door out onto the roof open and stepped through onto a planked walkway. Unsteady on his feet, stinging rain pelting into his face and smacking into the stone by his head like gunshot, he grabbed a railing on his right – a continuous metal fence guarding the tower's replacement roof. On his left, ancient battlements faced out to sea, each embrasure barred by stout wire safety panels, all connected to another railing above stone merlons. New replacement stone, some of it, he saw now. Not all the original fourteenth century stone.

At the end, against the pole of a beacon fire basket, a bundle of white hung from the rails. He couldn't make it out. Was that Verity?

'Trinny?' he yelled. *'Where are you?'*

'Up here, James.'

Her voice, by his right ear, no longer sounded panicked. He turned his head and saw her crouched like Gollum on some sort of a platform. The remains of the ancient lookout turret. Her copper hair coiling in the wind and rain like Medusa's head of serpents, her face cleansed of her witch's prosthetics and stage make-up, yet still contorted in demonic madness.

'What are you doing?' he demanded, struggling to make sense of what he could see. 'What's wrong with Verity?'

As quick and agile as a cat, Trinny jumped down to the walkway and locked the door behind him. Her eyes bored into his as she rattled a bunch of keys in his face. 'Verity's,' she told him. 'Well, Finn's really. She steals them at night and comes up here to play the White Lady. Pathetic. But she doesn't need them anymore. None of us—'

'What the hell have you done?' He turned back towards the white bundle, blinking to clear his vision. He saw movement. Saw something fastened to the railing.

Verity had been tied with twisted wire to the rail by her wrist.

'*Jesus* Trinny, what the hell have you *done*?'

Still disoriented, he tried to run towards Verity, but the deluge felt like a water cannon against him. He bounced off a metal panel on his left, then against the railings on his right, struggling to stay upright.

Christ's sake, Massey, get a grip.

'High up here, isn't it James? Just like you. High as a kite.'

'Jesus Trinny!'

Now it made sense. She'd spiked him. That's why he felt so weird.

'Those cheesy crackers… Shit, Trinny. Why?'

'You're a big bloke, and I need to be able to manage you.'

'Manage me? Why?' His mind began filling in the blanks. The odd looks she'd given him over the past couple of weeks. Blowing hot and cold. Off-hand one minute, captivating the next. He'd chosen to ignore the bad, focus on the good.

'You have the *gall* to ask me why,' she screeched. 'After what you did to me? *Leaving* me like that—"

'I didn't mean any of that to happen.' He couldn't believe he'd allowed her to string him along. Letting him believe there might be a future for them together, with their son. 'I was a married man. I shouldn't have—'

'No, you *fucking* shouldn't. And yet you did.'

'Would it have made any difference? Really Trinny? I don't recall you holding anything back.'

'Shut up. *Shut the fuck up!*

She clenched the keys in her right hand.

For the first time he saw what she carried in her left.

A knife.

She marched a couple of steps towards him. He shifted his feet, hoping he was capable of catching her, grabbing the knife and the keys from her.

But then she turned and skipped out of his reach, knowing he couldn't move quickly without falling. Whatever she'd doped him with pounded in his veins.

Blinking back tears, or rain – he couldn't tell which – her face crumpled, yet she laughed. A nasty bitter laugh.

'Should I tell you what happened to me, because of you?'

Clinging to railings on both sides, he looked behind him. Verity, conscious now, quivered in wide-eyed terror, a gag pulled tight between her teeth, slicing into her cheeks.

'Are you alright?' he asked, or at least he tried to, but the wind whipped away his words. He couldn't swear to it, but he thought she gave a slight nod. Maybe she had heard. He hoped so. Somehow, he had to get them both down from here. Alive.

He turned back to Trinny. 'What has Verity to do with any of this? Why do this to her?'

Fuck her!' Trinny snarled, a trail of saliva in the corner of her mouth whipped away on the wind. *'She's nothing. Nothing. At. All.'*

'Then why is she here? Let her go. Open that door and let her go. You'll still have me.'

Vehemently, Trinny shook her head. 'James fucking Massey. Everyone's knight in shining armour. Well, not this time. Now I think about it, she could be the cause of the whole sodding thing. Everything – and I mean *everything* – is probably her fault. She was going over the top anyway tonight, but now we'll be going with her.'

Bloody hell, the woman's nuts. From nowhere, his brain conjured up the clinical term for committing suicide by jumping from a height. Autokabalesis. Something his pathologist friend Lorraine had told him when she still worked in A&E, back when he was in uniform. He'd accompanied a casualty there while Lorraine was on duty. Someone who'd survived, which apparently lots of jumpers do, although not without severe consequences, like paralysis.

'Shall I tell you, James? Eh? Do you want to know what happened to me after you left?'

CHAPTER 76

'He's not here.' Sparks raced around the tower. She couldn't tell where the scream had come from. Why the hell hadn't he stayed where he was? She tapped his number on her phone, ducking her head away from the rain, seeking shelter in the lee of the tower. 'He's not answering.'

'It's chucking it down,' Dazz shouted. 'Maybe he went inside.'

Of course. Stupid, stupid, not to think of that herself. She raced round to the door, Dazz at her heels.

'Perhaps he's gone home?' Sarah called, shivering under the trees at the top of the path, bracing an umbrella against diagonal rain.

'He'd better not be behind the wheel,' Sparks shouted back. 'Not in that state. Stay here. Wait for Guy.'

Inside, the darkness swallowed them. Sparks groped for a light switch, but found none. She didn't like this. Even in the state Massey was in, he'd have found the lights, or he'd have stayed by the door. He'd know they were here. He'd have called out.

If he could.

'James,' she called in an urgent whisper, then felt stupid. *'James!'* she shouted.

She tried to recall the layout. A stone flagged floor. A winding stone staircase to the left. Vaulted stone ceiling – low in places.

'Watch your head,' she told Dazz. Hadn't there been display cabinets and the odd chair lying around? 'And your feet.'

Squinting in what little light came from the door, she pressed redial and glanced at Dazz. 'Do you have a torch on your phone?'

Dazz fumbled in his pocket. She waited for her call to connect to Massey's mobile, hoping to hear his ringtone somewhere inside. Nothing.

Suddenly, she was blinded. *'Shit, Dazz!'*

'Sorry.'

He moved the torchlight away from her face and around the cavernous space, it's bright white ray like a spotlight, illuminating everything directly in front of it, casting the surroundings into deeper shadow. He probed every corner, swept the beam across the Macbethian staging. Nothing.

Sparks grabbed his sleeve, and he aimed the beam to the side of her. She pointed up towards the vaulted ceiling, then nodded over her shoulder. 'This way.'

Dazz led. He wouldn't have it any other way, and she'd be having words with him about that later. No time now.

He was a big man, not quite as tall as James, but broader. Aiming the beam in front of him, his body blocked the light, so she had to follow blindly, left hand on the stair rope, right hand clinging onto his belt.

At the top, he almost stumbled, then turned and helped her up, the light darting about while he juggled his phone.

He steadied it, and ran it around the wall. More display cabinets, a couple of ornate wooden chairs against a wall, several deep stone recesses.

Fireplaces probably. A couple of them anyway. She couldn't remember what the others were for.

Not important. They needed to find James.

On the far side, on a slightly raised wooden platform, black robes lay discarded atop a portable clothes rail rather than hung from it. Two lightweight folding tables faced each other, back to back vanity mirrors on top, surrounded by what could be crayons. Stage make-up maybe? The Cresswell Macbeth dressing room.

No sign of Massey. Where the hell had he got to?

With her eyes following Dazz's torch beam, Sparks peered up towards a wooden minstrel's gallery, and the new roof above it, a terrifying thought taking root in her mind. If Massey had been spiked, Christ only knew what stupid ideas he—

Heavy wood slammed against stone downstairs.

'Shit! Where's the light?' Keegan's voice. 'Where the hell is everyone?'

'Up here,' Dazz called.

'Up where? Where are the sodding stairs?'

'In the corner, behind the door. Careful, they're—'

'Did you find the bitch?' Sparks yelled

'No. Halliwell said she stayed up here.'

Sparks looked up again towards the roof. If that evil cow had harmed a hair on James' head, she wouldn't survive the night.

Another bang. Sarah's voice, from outside. 'Guy. Up on the roof. There are people on the roof.'

'Shit. Alright Sarah, go back down to the garden. You two, there's got to be a door, or a hatch. Find it. I'll call this in. Crowder is going to love this.'

Sparks couldn't give a shit what the chief thought. God only knew what was happening on that roof.

Dazz concentrated the torch beam on the back wall, below the gallery. It made sense for any stairs to be in the same corner.

'There,' Sparks cried.

A studded door stood ajar. She squeezed past Dazz and pushed it open with her foot.

'Here, let me go first.' Dazz said.

'No chance.' She activated the torch function on her own phone, aimed it in front of her and grabbed hold of the stair rope on her left, Dazz cursing behind her.

CHAPTER 77

'Tell me,' Massey said, blinking away the throbbing aura that had begun refracting each solitary raindrop, as if they fell in slow motion through a kaleidoscope. He bent forward as another stomach pain hit him, trusting the railing to take his weight because the only alternative was to sink to his knees. No way could he show such weakness. Or maybe he should. He might be able to catch her off guard. Either way, he had to listen to her if it could help end this nightmare.

Breathing rapidly, she shoved the keys in her back pocket and grabbed hold of the railing. 'I woke up. With a man on top of me. And I thought… I thought it was *you*… at first.'

Jesus.

'I reacted… as if it *were* you. Do you know what I mean?'

He had no words.

She thrust the knife at his face. '*I said*, do you know what I mean?'

'Yes.'

'I let him do things to me because I was half asleep, and I thought it was… you. But it wasn't, was it? Because you'd pissed off and left me. And you'd left the door unlocked behind you.'

What? Oh God, no! He stared at her rage-filled face. In his head, he was back there, tiptoeing out of her caravan, taking a last lingering look from the doorway at her naked sleeping body, then going back to pull the sheet over her, before sneaking back out, pulling the door closed… But no, he didn't lock it. Without a key himself, she'd have needed to lock it from the inside, and for that he'd have had to wake her up. But, selfishly, he hadn't wanted to hang around to explain how much he was already regretting what they'd done.

'Would you like to know who my *fucking rapist* was? Would you, James? I'll tell you. It was Finn *fucking* Barron.' She pointed a quivering, still blackened finger towards the ghostly shrouded woman tethered to the rail. 'Her *fucking* husband.'

Horrified, his mind took him back, imagining hearing a rustle in the dead of night. Wishing he could go back and do the things he *should* have done, to keep her safe.

'The bastard had hounded me all week,' she screamed, her mouth contorted in disgust. 'But I wouldn't sleep with him. I didn't even like him, let alone fancy him. He was… creepy. But then there was you, at that party. And you know what happened next. Here's something you don't know though. What he said to me, when I realised it wasn't you on top of me and I tried to push him off? He laughed and said he wasn't about to let the losing team have all the spoils. It was his duty, he told me, while he… raped me, to claim back the trophy.' She pounded a fist on her heaving chest. 'That's what he called me, for fuck's sake. A trophy.'

But then suddenly, she calmed down.

'He told me something else. Much more recently. Just last year, in fact. He said he'd followed us back to the van that night and waited until you'd gone. The pervert had been listening to us at the window. And do you know why? I've figured it out now. It was because the pathetic freak wasn't getting enough at home. That's what you blokes are like, isn't it? I mean, what was your excuse, James? Is *your* wife a frigid bitch too?'

He felt a rage rise in him. God yes, at Trinny, for doing all this. And at Finn Barron, who'd taken advantage of her vulnerability eleven years ago. But mostly at himself. If he hadn't left her so unprotected in that caravan, Barron may not have attacked her and Verity would not be here now, wired to a railing at the top of the tower. And if he'd never given in to lust in the first place at that original charity match after-party and betrayed Helen with Trinny, his own marriage might have—

'You can see it now too, can't you James? It's all her fault. Go on, chuck her over now. One way or another, she's going. And so are we. You and I. Together at last. Won't that be fun?'

Jesus wept.

If he'd never been on the team eleven years ago, he and Helen could have been happy together. Their daughter would have survived. He would not now have a son…

Shit. If Finn Barron raped her, immediately after they'd—'

'Have you worked it out yet?'

'Max... He's not...'

Shaking with rage, she slashed with the knife. 'Max is *my* son. He belongs to *no-one* but me.'

'Do you even know which one of us it was?'

'Whose little swimmer won the race, you mean? Yeah, eventually. Not until I came back here though, and got his DNA.'

Massey felt something huge crumple up inside him.

'So that's two competitions you lost that day, James.' She laughed and turned away. Took a couple of steps, then turned back, the wind whipping her hair into sodden ribbons above her head. 'Can you hear me along there, Mrs fucking Barron?' she yelled. 'My son is your husband's *fucking bastard*.'

'None of this is Verity's fault.' he said, clamping a hand on each rail, blocking the walkway with his bulk. 'She's his victim too.'

'Bollocks. She'll have been relieved to be left alone while he shagged his way around all the local women. Ursula. And Betsy – oh yes, smug bitch that she is, even Betsy opened her legs for him. And Elena, of course.' She gave a little deranged giggle. 'I really put the cat among the pigeons there though, didn't I?'

Something stirred in the muggy swamp that was his brain but refused to surface.

'None of that is Verity's fault,' he said. 'You didn't need to bring her up here. Open that door and let her walk through.' Although he had no idea if Verity was capable of walking anywhere.

'I didn't bring her. She sneaked up early. Oh I knew she'd come up here tonight. It's what she does. She likes to play the white lady. But I thought it would be in the middle of the night. Her usual time. I didn't expect her to steal Finn's keys during the performance. But as soon as I saw the door at the bottom of the steps was open when we came back to get changed, I knew she was already up here, way too early. So I had to think quickly. I waited until Betsy and Scarlett went, and then I came up and...'

She waved her hands to include the three of them on the walkway.

'None of this is the way I planned it. This wasn't supposed to happen until later, after everyone had gone. And I'd already had to change things once when I saw *you* here. You see, it was just supposed to be you and me in the middle of the night, walking out into the sea together.'

What? 'How the hell were you going to achieve that?'

'I was going to call you later and...'

How? He'd never given her his number. But then... of course she must have it. That's how she'd got him up here. She'd called him and told him Verity was going to... Shit. Of course. All those mysterious silent calls he'd thought were from Helen... But who the hell had given her his number?

'And what?' he asked.

'I planned to tell you Max was in trouble. You'd have come. I know you would. But then I spotted you in the queue tonight, and... I didn't know you were coming; you see. So I had to change my plan... Then I thought, why not go with the flow for once? So I gave you the bag of crackers I'd made for Betsy and Scarlett, but then... But then I had to change everything all over again, because...'

In a sudden burst of action, she leapt back up onto the ancient platform, braced her knees and filled her lungs, like a Māori All Black about to perform the haka, all her rage focussed on the crumpled figure at the end of the walkway.

'... Because that bitch *ruined my plan!*' she screamed.

And there was that thought stirring in the swamp again, but still refusing to surface.

It felt like only a moment ago since he'd been so desperate to persuade this woman to consider making a new life with him and the boy she'd made him believe was his too.

Jesus. If it wasn't so tragic, it would be funny.

CHAPTER 78

In the cramped stone stairwell, next to an archway leading onto the wooden gallery, a stout metal gate stood half open onto more steep spiral stairs. Sparks continued climbing. On her left, an identical gate looked out onto the roof. Locked. Through the bars and the dark pounding rain, she saw nothing but ramparts on the right and the tower's roof on the left. No Massey or Red.

'James!' she cried. Was this as far as they could go? Where the hell was he?

Craning his head past her, Dazz pointed beyond her right shoulder. A few more steps to another studded door.

Sparks tried the handle. Locked. She hammered on it, then rammed it with her shoulder.

'James!' she yelled, the sound bouncing around the stone walls and almost bursting their eardrums.

'Here,' Dazz said, 'let me.'

She didn't argue this time, but it took some manoeuvering to allow him to get in front of her, the wedge-shaped steps too narrow for more than one foot at a time. He'd be a lot more effective as a battering ram than she would. In theory, at least. In practice, not so much.

The door didn't budge. And then she realised why. The bloody thing opened inwards. Of course it did.

'We need the key.' She pressed the heels of her hands to her forehead and tried to think. Who'd have a sodding key? Tom Kirk, he'd have one, and she had his number in her phone. Her hands shook as she switched off the torch and searched for his number.

'He's not answering.'

'Try again.'

She sat on the top step and redialled, letting it ring. No answer.

'You have to go and find him,' she told Dazz. 'He has to be still around. Get his key and bring it back. I'll stay here.'

'I'll stay. You go. If you keep yelling like that, it might make her worse.'

'I am not leaving him. And we don't have time for this. Go.'

Dazz gave her a long look, but did as she'd said, backing himself out of the narrow space until he was level with the wooden gallery before reactivating his phone's torch function and making his way out of the tower.

Thick darkness enveloped her, but she kept her own torch switched off to conserve the battery. The cold of the stone step seeped through her jeans.

How long had it been since Keegan would have called this in? Only minutes probably. She doubted she'd hear any sirens from here. She couldn't even hear what was happening on the other side of this sodding door. Massey could be lying dead out there. Or, as high as he must be with whatever Red had put in those bloody crackers, he could be balancing one-legged on a bloody parapet and contemplating his navel. And she was stuck in here, useless.

Maybe she *should* have gone for the key. At least she'd have been *doing* something.

She rammed her elbows against the wood and yelled as loud as she could. 'James!'

CHAPTER 79

'Hear that?' Trinny said from her perch. 'Your girlfriend's not one for giving up, is she? Tough. No-one's getting through that door anytime soon.'

Unless they find another key. Massey had noticed that Trinny hadn't risked putting her key in the lock and giving it a half turn to prevent it being opened from the other side. Despite the knife, she'd be worried he'd get past her and get it open before she could stop him.

He wondered how many sets there were. There'd been four for the village hall.

With the rain easing and the wind dropping, he could see the hall now over the battlements. Once a lifeboat station, he'd learnt. Had the keys been handed back to the various holders yet? He'd lost track of that side of things.

He remembered the fuss Finn Barron had made…

The swampy sludge in his head stirred once more. A bubble rose to the surface and burst. Earlier this evening, he'd been wondering why anyone would want to frame Barron for murder. They'd found no-one with even a remotely decent motive to do that.

Until now.

Thank God his synapses had started firing again. And he didn't feel quite so disoriented now. Perhaps being blasted in the face by half the North Sea had done him the world of good.

Not so Verity, whose teeth he could now hear chattering behind him.

Somehow, he had to get them both out of here. But to do that, he had to keep Trinny talking until his strength returned.

Breathing heavily, panting almost, Trinny twirled the knife and glared.

He decided to take a punt. 'Was it you who came up with the whole Macbeth thing?'

Her head jerked towards him. 'You figured that out? Yes, it was me. It was way too good an opportunity to waste.'

'What do you mean?'

'At that barbecue your big gorilla friend asked me about, it occurred to me how alike the character names in Macbeth were to all the people there, and… well…'

Her voice drifted off. *Keep her talking.*

'Why did you even go, after what Finn had done to you?'

'Because he *owed* me. I went to tell him he was Max's biological father. I'd stolen a glass he'd been drinking from at the club. I did a swab and sent it off for DNA testing. I told him if he didn't make regular payments, I'd chase him through the courts and make sure everyone knew what he'd done.'

'How did he take that?'

'He didn't believe me. He said that no-one else would either, especially after so many years. He accused me of falsifying the DNA test. That's when he told me he'd been listening at the caravan window that night. Why should he stump up, he said, when you could just as easily be Max's father. Then he told me how expensive it was to take a case through the courts and dared me to take it further.'

'And did you?'

He understood why she might not have wanted to disclose straight away that she'd been raped. Back then, long before the MeToo movement, she'd have been ripped apart for claiming one man had raped her immediately after she'd had sex voluntarily with another man, who she'd only just met hours before. She might still be today.

But surely she would never have let Barron anywhere near her again after what he'd done, whether or not he had any intention of admitting paternity. And yet they'd been on good enough terms for him to invite her to that barbecue, and for her to go. And again at the party two weeks ago; it had been Finn who'd introduced her. Why would she allow that, after he'd raped her? Why would she have even come back to live in Cresswell? She had no roots here.

Trinny ran her fingers along the knife blade. A folding knife, its Imperial blade too long to be legal in the UK. Like the one described by forensics as one of the murder weapons. Milo's knife, that he claimed to have got rid of.

'How could I?' she said. 'I'd only just set up in business. He knew I wouldn't want any bad publicity. But then…' A huge grin spread across her face. '…the ideal opportunity fell right into my lap.'

'What do you mean?'

She snorted and waved her hand at him. 'I'm disappointed in you, James. I thought you'd figured it out. Dominic Kingsley killed his father. King Duncan was dead. The play had begun.'

A thought struck him. Hadn't Verity said that Trinny put up a special order of poppy seed rolls just for them, which Finn went along to collect? Every Thursday, regular as clockwork. So instead of shunning her rapist, she'd done everything in her power to insinuate herself into his life. But why?

Another bubble popped in the sludge. She'd spiked their rolls, just as she'd laced the Parmesan and poppy seed crackers. Wait. Poppy seeds. He'd seen the jar in her kitchen. And a grinder. Something slithered in his subconscious but refused to surface. But poppy seeds weren't poisonous. Opium poppies grown in hot countries maybe, but not those sold over the counter in the UK. Yet, if Trinny *had* been lacing their bread rolls, it might make sense of the Barrons' declining health. Hadn't Betsy told them Finn wasn't the man now he'd been just a year ago?

Black seeds, grinder, black dust. Bubbles were popping in his swamp brain by the second now. Each one sparking another. Bloody hell, Maureen Duffy. They'd found black dust. The results hadn't come back yet, but—

They both heard the thuds on the door, then Sparks' voice shouting his name.

Trinny giggled and struggled to pull something from her other pocket. Getting it caught in the fabric lining. *Fuck! A syringe.*

Eyes wide with mischief, she cocked her head to one side. 'Are you ready to jump yet, James? Before the cavalry gets here. This will help. You'll be putty in my hands once this is in your veins.'

In the distance, he heard a siren. 'Not a cat in hell's chance,' he muttered.

CHAPTER 80

Unable to bear the feel of the cold stone step on her backside anymore, Sparks stood with her back to the roof door, rhythmically banging her clenched fists on the wood. Dazz had been gone long enough to have had a new key cut, yet there was still no sign of him returning. But she wasn't about to leave her post. Everyone else would already be doing everything they could to bring this mess to an end. So instead, she concentrated her mind on Massey's.

Time and again they'd shocked themselves with their weird psychic connection, although neither had ever actually tried to communicate with the other on that level. But she'd give it a bloody good try now, using the rhythm of her fists to concentrate her mind, attempting to reach out into his; trusting him, if he could hear her banging at all, to go with it and take heart from it.

We are going to get you off that roof.
Dazz is looking for someone with a key.
I told you; that sodding bitch is crazy.
She'd absolutely been right about that. The woman was mental.

CHAPTER 81

Knife still in one hand, Trinny bit the plastic cap off the syringe, exposing the needle. 'Almost time,' she said.

But was he steady enough yet on his feet to stop her from sticking the bloody thing into his neck if she came at him? While his mind might be recovering, he'd been deliberately trying to appear still weak, so hadn't even attempted to test his muscles.

Keep her talking.

'How did you figure out it was Dominic who killed Duncan?' he asked.

She spat the plastic cap out over the battlements and glared at him. Probably weighing up how long she dare leave it before acting. She had to know there'd be at least one more person around tonight with a key to open that door.

He could hear two sirens now, although still distant. There'd be people on the ground below too, but he didn't dare leave go of a rail to look over. He was a big man. Under normal circumstances he could easily overpower and disarm a woman Trinny's size, but in no way was this circumstance normal. What if she leapt onto his shoulders? His height would be a disadvantage then. She could topple them both over.

'Milo's car set off my camera doorbell,' she said, some instinct to boast about her own brilliance winning out. 'It sounded an alert on my phone at the barbecue. I wanted to know who it was. And I'd already upset as many people as I could, so I was bored.

'Why upset other guests, why not just Finn?'

'Because I was so fucking angry with him. He didn't care he had a son. So I was going to ruin his party if it killed me. Then Ursula started spouting off about her and her mates being asked to play witches at Halloween, and it gave me an idea. I suggested they make some prophesies, like real witches.' Trinny threw her head back and laughed. 'Ursula jumped at the idea. Then I whispered to Betsy that I'd seen Finn hassling Scarlett.

Only a little lie. I knew Betsy would be jealous. He'd just thrown her over. And it worked a treat. She warned him off in a prophesy and he was livid. But then those workmen arrived and spoilt it.'

'Who else did you upset?'

She shot him a puzzled look. 'Duncan, of course. I told him about Elena's affair with Finn. It was true. He had a right to know. I wanted him to punch Finn in the face. But he didn't. He spoke to Elena.' Trinny giggled. 'Then stomped off—'

'How did you even know about their affair?'

'That doesn't matter. I just did. I've made it my business to find out about them all. Anyway, Duncan must have seen by the shock on Elena's face that I'd told the truth. When he went off in a huff, I was a bit disappointed, but not for long.'

She pressed the blade of the knife against her lips and frowned.

'Actually, if you think about it, Dominic could be Finn's son too. Finn was shagging Elena when Milo was just a baby. He could be Max's brother.' The thought made her giggle. 'But anyway, I didn't know it was Dom until later. Max has a telescope in his room. It looks out to sea and has a video camera attached. He's into all that stuff. Like trainspotting, only boats. He leaves the camera running sometimes when we're out and then we watch it back later. That day, it picked up Dominic running across the rocks. Actually, no. It picked up a blur crossing the screen, since the camera was focused out to sea. Orange and green, like the vest Dominic wore all the time. I guessed the rest, and they both caved in when I let them believe I already knew.'

'They just admitted it?'

'They didn't deny it, which gave me leverage. I promised to help them, if they helped me. I even volunteered to get rid of the knife, but I thought it might come in handy, so I kept it.' She held up the knife in her hand. 'This is it. Can you believe the idiot didn't dump it in the sea while he could?'

Jesus. That meant... But he couldn't think that now. 'Why Ben?'

Trinny threw back her head and laughed. 'Oh, James…'

It had been a stupid question. He knew why it had to be Ben, and Fleur. She'd already told him the whole Macbeth thing had been her idea.

In the play, Banquo had died next, and Fleance had disappeared from the story. And so it had to be in reality.

Another sludge bubble popped in his brain. Hadn't Sparks told him it had been Trinny who suggested they should stage the play here at Halloween this year?

'But why wait a year?'

'Because of you, of course.'

He had no idea what she meant.

'When Duncan was killed, they cancelled the charity match, which in retrospect turned out to be a blessing. Finn had made sure I knew you'd be playing, you see, and I so wanted you here, although back then I had no idea what I was going to do. But now… One door left unlocked, and look at all the consequences.'

She started to laugh again. A giggle she was losing control of. Gently, she depressed the plunger on the syringe, and watched the wind whip away the little drop of liquid that emerged.

'So you waited until they'd rescheduled the match.'

'That's right. I decided I didn't just want you there for the after-match party, I wanted you investigating my crimes. So I could ruin your life, like you ruined mine.'

CHAPTER 82

Up on the watchtower platform, staring over the side and fiddling with the syringe, Trinny ignored Sparks' rhythmic beating just below her feet. Massey took the opportunity to shift his own feet and loosen his knees, ready to spring if he got the opportunity.

He needed to get Trinny down from her perch. The only way off this roof for all of them was through that door. No way were any of them going over the top.

Soon, a key would be turning in that lock and Sparks would insist on being first through. He knew she would. He could feel her intensity on the other side of that door. And if Trinny was still up there, she would plunge the needle meant for him straight into her neck.

She'd told him it would make him putty in her hands, not an unconscious dead weight she couldn't manoeuvre. But, whatever the hell was in that syringe, a dose calculated to make a man as big as him docile and pliable could kill someone of Sparks' size. And that wasn't happening. So he had to get Trinny down from there.

Gripping both railings, he edged backwards, closer to Verity, an inch at a time. He risked a look back and saw she was conscious.

'Where d'you think you're going?' Trinny yelled.

'It's alright, I'm just checking Verity's okay.'

'Get the fuck away from her!' The fury had returned.

He stayed where he was, pretending to look at Verity again, but all his attention in front of him, on Trinny.

CHAPTER 83

'She's up in that tower thing,' Keegan said, leaning as far back as he could to see what was going on up on the roof.

Tom Kirk shook his head. 'That's not good. It's right above the door. Whatever weapon she's got, whoever's first through, they won't stand a chance.'

'And there's no other access.'

'None that's safe without fall arrest gear.'

Once he'd handed over his keys, Keegan had told Kirk to organise the volunteers to clear the grounds of remaining visitors, although the storm had already done much of their work. Kirk had then returned to offer what help he could, so at least they had light in the tower now – on the ground floor anyway.

When he'd heard sirens, Keegan had contacted control, demanding a silent approach, and now there were two patrol cars, a police mini-bus and an armed response vehicle on the road outside the gates. Road blocks had been established, allowing through two fire appliances and turning inquisitive locals away. A couple of officers on the field below the tower with night vision scopes had reported a tall male figure – presumably Massey since there was no-one else it could be – standing halfway along the battlements and leaning heavily on the railings; a female figure standing in the lookout turret; and something white – a heap or bundle at the southern end of the walkway next to the iron fire basket. They'd noted some movement, but couldn't be sure it wasn't just some material blowing in the wind.

Just as Keegan repeated back the report over the radio he'd acquired from a patrol officer to check his understanding, Finn Barron pushed his way forward, shouting about having lost his keys and his wife. He heard at least some of Keegan's words.

'Something white? Where? Verity is wearing a white coat.'

Shit.

'Would she have taken your keys to get onto the roof?'

'What? Why the hell would she?' Yet still the man almost fell over his feet as he craned his neck upwards. 'Verity!' he yelled. 'Get down here. Now!'

Keegan had no time for the man's bombastic haranguing tonight. He motioned a couple of officers forward. 'Get this idiot out of here, now.'

So it was confirmed. They had three people up on that roof, at least one of whom – Verity Barron – looked to be incapacitated and possibly in need of emergency care. Not to mention that daft sod, Massey, who could well be in need of a stomach pump. But how the hell to get them down.

Beside him, the Fire Service Watch Manager hummed and hawed about a safety assessment. And, to be fair, it wasn't their job to be first in line up a ladder to face a mad woman holding any kind of weapon.

He needed a plan, and he needed it now.

'Dazz,' he shouted. 'Get over here. This is what we're going to do.'

CHAPTER 84

Fists clenched, leaning forward with every muscle straining, Trinny snarled at him. *'I said, get the fuck away from her.'*

'Why? What are you going to do about it?'

She shifted her hold on the syringe, her thumb poised over the plunger. 'I'll stick you with this.'

He sighed. 'You're going to do that anyway, so what's the difference. I just want to check Verity is alright.'

'The *bitch* has never been alright in her *life*,' she screamed, starting to lose it now.

'Not since you started drugging her anyway. And Finn.'

'Ha! You noticed. LSA: same thing I gave you. Long term, it can really mess with a person's mental health. I've enjoyed watching their paranoia, seeing them become more pathetic by the day. I make a special batch of rolls every week especially for them and he comes along to collect them, trying his luck with me every time. As if I'd ever...' Her face twisted in disgust.

Massey concentrated on Sparks' rhythmic banging. When that stopped, he needed to be ready to act. He needed Trinny away from that door by then.

'You haven't told me how you managed to incapacitate Ben and Fleur.'

'Ha, that was easy. Ben and Ursula worked for a wholesale butchery. They brought meat home to sell on the sly. I knew Ursula was staying at Betsy's. I called in and told Ben she'd forgotten to drop off a leg of lamb for me that I'd already paid her for. He took me down to the cellar to pick my own, apologising that it was still frozen. I picked the biggest and as soon as he turned around, I clobbered him with it...'

'What about Fleur,' he prompted.

'I um... I was just about to go and find her when she started coming down the cellar stairs. So I started to run up them, rambling on about needing a joint of meat for family coming to visit. A load of rubbish, by the way, I have no family other than Max.

'Anyway, the stairs were narrow, so she had to back up to let me out first. I kept talking so she wouldn't notice Ben's blood on the leg of lamb. When I reached the top, she started to walk me to the front door, so I told her I'd let myself out. She said okay and turned away from me. I hit her with the lamb, then went back down to the cellar to set the fire. I really thought I'd killed her too. I've been thinking I should maybe have gone to the hospital to turn off that chamber thing she's in. Not that it matters now...'

She lifted the syringe and studied it.

'...We won't be here anyway, will we James?'

CHAPTER 85

Sparks heard a noise. A scuff of stone. Dazz coming back? But she kept on beating the door. She knew Massey would be waiting for it to stop, bracing himself for the moment he'd need to do... *something*.

She heard it again. Footsteps on the spiral stairs. A barely-there sound of metal on stone. Then light as the door below the wooden gallery swung open. Then the top of Dazz's head. That big silly cowlick she'd fallen so in love with.

And still she kept her fists banging.

Having heard nothing from the other side of the door in all the time she'd been up here, she knew they were safe enough to talk, so long as they kept it low.

'She's on some sort of platform directly above and behind that door,' Dazz said. 'There's a planked walkway straight ahead, with railings either side, up to here.' He laid his hand against her ribs. 'Sheer drop on the left over the stone ramparts, an apex roof on the right, with skylights. We have no idea what weapons she has, but we have to assume the worst. Guy is organising a distraction below to try to get her attention, and to hopefully get her down onto the main walkway, but we have no guarantees. Massey is conscious and standing, but no idea how compos mentis he is. Looks like Verity Barron is up there—'

'What? How?'

'No idea. Maybe Red used her to access the roof. She's at the far end, probably incapacitated, right next to a bolted-on fire beacon basket.

CHAPTER 86

'Why kill Maureen?' Massey asked, still doing his best to appear below par, so she wouldn't realise quite how much he'd recovered so far. 'What had she ever done to you?'

'Nothing. But she had to die. She was Lady Macduff.'

'How did you rope in Milo and Dominic?'

She giggled. 'That was so easy. They owed me. I told them I'd kept the knife, to make sure they did whatever I wanted them to do. And they did. Milo got Michael away. Dominic took the dogs and got rid of them—'

'You know he didn't kill them though, like you told him to. Right?'

With a scream of fury, she gripped her weapons tighter, but stayed in the turret. Clearly, she hadn't known that.

'Dominic took them to a boarding kennel and paid for a two weeks stay. He might have murdered his father, but he loves those dogs.'

Full of pent-up aggression, she stepped from one foot to the other, her narrow perch too small to allow any sort of pacing. 'You know you almost caught me on my way home that night, don't you?' she spat.

What?

And then he remembered. Driving out of the village hall car park that night, he'd almost knocked her over. She had blood on her lip. He thought he'd hurt her, but she'd distracted him by telling him how many men she could have slept with on that caravan holiday, and then by allowing him to think *he was* Max's father. Had that been Maureen's blood?

'A bit of a coincidence actually,' she said. 'because I almost got run over on my way back from Ben's house too, just after I set that fire.'

CHAPTER 87

They argued about who should go through the door first. Their first argument, if you could call it that. Sparks was always going to win, and she knew that Dazz knew that too.
He'd have felt the same if it had been his own work partner up there. But also, it made more tactical sense for her to go first. While he would always have the superior strength, she was far more agile. And being a lot smaller in stature, she was much more capable of unhindered movement in the narrow space on the other side of that door.

Continuing the rhythm of her banging, she felt Dazz reach past her and slip the key into the lock. Tom Kirk had assured them it was well-oiled, and it turned soundlessly. Red couldn't have heard unless she had her ear pressed to the door on the other side.

Their big concern had been that she could have left the key she'd used half turned in the lock so they couldn't open the door, but she hadn't.

Checking his watch for the hundredth time, Dazz reversed back down to the wooden gallery to wait for their cue: three narrow beams of light aimed through the tiny window on the north side of the tower next to him. And there they were.

***

Keegan ran up the line, making sure everyone was ready. He checked his watch, signalled the okay for three flashes to be aimed at the window on the front of the tower. After the third flash, he raised his hands and counted off ten seconds.

Then, on a count of two more, like an orchestra conductor, he swept his arms down and a huge cacophony split the air.

***

'On ten' Dazz yelled, and hurried back up the stairs, where Sparks tapped the seconds out with her foot.

'Ten,' she said, and stopped banging her hands on the roof door. She turned in the narrow space and picked up the baton he'd brought for her, while Dazz counted five more.

'Five' he said.

Sparks yanked open the door and rushed through first, her baton aimed above and behind her, barely conscious of the noise from below. Dazz followed, focusing ahead, both of them yelling at the top of their lungs.

'Weapons down. Put your weapons down!'

***

Sparks had stopped banging. Massey braced himself, ready to spring, knowing something was about to happen but not what. Hoping he had enough strength back in his muscles to carry him through.

He counted the seconds.

Two, three.

On the street, sirens split the air, horns blasted. At the base of the tower, whistles blew, people yelled, and an old air raid siren wailed.

Trinny jumped in shock. She dropped the syringe, but held onto the knife.

Four, five.

The door yawned open. Sparks burst through first, baton raised, twisting her body to her right, as sure-footed as a mountain goat. She rapped Trinny's knife hand, disarming her, then pulled her from her perch and forced her to her knees on wooden planks.

Dazz leant over the battlements and waved his hands in the air.

On the ground, Keegan sliced his own arms down. People stopped shouting. Whistles stopped blowing. But it took a few more seconds for the message to be radioed through to the patrol vehicles and fire appliances on the street.

It all happened so quickly, so simply, that Massey didn't have a chance to move. His hands were welded to the railings. His muscles, still tensed, began to tremble. He fell to his knees, all that strength he thought had returned deserting him.

Sparks saw him fall, loosened her grip. *'James!'*

Snarling in fury, Trinny seized her opportunity. She broke free, leapt back up into the turret and threw herself over the top in a swan dive.

CHAPTER 88

NSEC Hospital. Massey lay on his side on a trolley bed, hugging his knees, agonising pains ripping through his guts every other minute.

'You look like shit,' Keegan said.

'I feel… *Nya!* Another spasm hit him. 'I feel like it too.'

'Trinny didn't make it, just in case you're wondering. Cracked her head open on the edge of that mounting block. Nearly flattened yours truly in the process.'

He was glad, but devastated in equal measure. He'd learnt tonight that the ideal of her he'd harboured in a corner of his heart had never truly existed.

How could he not have seen it? For years, he'd held onto some lust-filled fantasy of her. Over these past couple of weeks – now he was single – he'd even romanticised the fantasy to the point of hoping to make a life with her and the ten-year-old boy she'd led him to believe was his.

But she was a monster. A murderer and an arsonist. Possibly the most evil person he'd ever met, since she was prepared to kill perfectly innocent people purely because they fitted into a warped game she'd created in order to wreak revenge on him for something he'd never even been aware he'd caused.

Or perhaps, by abandoning her in such a cowardly way that night, it was he who'd created the monster within her. He suspected that was something that would wake him up in the night now and then in the years to come.

'It was seeds from those Morning Glory plants in the courtyard, by the way,' Sparks said, waving a hand in the direction of his agonised foetal position. 'Ipomoea something or other. The seeds contain a compound called D-lysergic acid amide – LSA – very similar to LSD, except they can play havoc with your belly. Related to sweet potatoes, believe it or not.'

'You don't say.'

'And that black dust? The report came through. It was ground up Morning Glory seeds. We asked the doctor treating Verity to check for it in her blood. Came back positive, so odds on that's what the bitch gave you too.'

Dazz poked his head around the door. 'You've got another visitor, mate.' He cocked his head to Sparks and Keegan. 'Time for us to leave.'

***

He didn't have the energy to deal with Helen right now, but it looked like he didn't have the choice. Still listed as his next of kin, she'd have been contacted automatically as soon as he'd been taken to hospital.

'Don't worry,' she said. 'I'm not staying long. I've got a lift waiting for me in the car park.'

Small mercies.

'Ray Flowers, by any chance?' he asked.

She looked for a moment as if he'd slapped her, but rallied quickly and gave him a tight smile. 'I heard what happened. Sounds like you were lucky.'

She probably didn't know yet that the villain of the piece was the same woman he'd been unfaithful to her with eleven years ago. The reason she'd miscarried their baby girl. He wasn't about to enlighten her now.

'Sorry. No police widows' pension this time,' he said, clenching his fists under the sheet rather than give into the stomach cramps in front of her. 'You'll have to be content with the divorce settlement.'

Her left hand moved to her belly. 'Speaking of which,' she said. 'I'd appreciate it if we can both be adults in all this and get things settled as soon as possible. No need to hang around, is there?'

His heart thudded. 'Why the hurry?'

'If you must know, because I'm pregnant.'

Something high pitched screamed in his ear. Even lying down, he felt the blood drain from his face. All those years they'd tried for another baby without success.

'But I thought—'

'You thought what, James?'

'We tried so hard, and you… we didn't…' He thought his tongue had seized up for a moment. 'Is it mine?'

Her whole face twisted. 'Didn't what, get pregnant? Of course not. I started taking the pill right after you killed our baby. I came off it as soon as I knew I was going to leave you. So no, *this* baby is not yours.'

Suddenly his whole body convulsed as the biggest spasms yet almost tore him apart. He crawled off the trolley bed. Bent double, he headed for the bathroom.

He heard her laugh, but didn't see her leave.

CHAPTER 89

Sunday, 27 October 2024

Sunday lunch service was dwindling by the time they arrived at the Snowy Owl and asked for the quietest table. Just three of them. Himself, Sparks and Keegan. Dazz had dashed away earlier to pick up his daughters and Massey felt envious that his friend had children in his life when he didn't. Sarah had left as soon as everything had quietened down last night. She'd taken Keegan's car home, so that Keegan could drive his to the hospital, while he was ferried off in an ambulance.

They'd given him something to ease the stomach cramps before discharging him a couple of hours ago. And the nausea, of course, which had manifested itself in the wake of Helen's visit and probably had more to do with what she'd told him than with the LSA Trinny had spiked him with. Helen and Trinny: the only two women he'd ever fallen hard for in his entire life, and both of them complete nutters. What did that say about his judgement? And for Christ's sake, how could he not have known his wife had been on the pill for *eleven* years?

How could she have led him to believe for all that time that she was as devastated as he was every time their lovemaking failed to result in a longed for pregnancy? Longed for by him alone he could see now. Christ, she'd even drawn up ovulation charts to work out her most fertile days – allegedly – to help maintain the charade. And to have achieved that level of deception over so long, Helen wasn't merely two-faced, or three-faced; she had to be fifty-faced at least. She must have never ever forgiven him even one iota for that single night of passion with Trinny. But still, how could she possibly have strung their marriage out for so long if she felt such antagonism towards him?

The only reason he could think of was so that she could retain the power to make his life miserable. If they'd divorced earlier, he'd have been free to find someone else, become a father, and to live a happy life.

And what about all the faces Trinny had presented him with, and all that Sparks had told him about Hecate, the witch who was more than just Macbethian, who she herself had played in school and who Ursula had told them Trinny believed herself to be. Not only a witch but an ancient goddess. Associated with the moon, she supposedly had three faces: maiden, mother and crone. Well, he'd certainly seen all of them in Trinity Moon this time around.

Was her name even real, or made up to fit the fantasy?

Just a minute... mother.

'Where's Max?'

'He's still with his schoolfriend,' Keegan said, shaking salt over his skin-on-fries. 'The lad's mother says he can stay there until something's sorted out. Family Liaison are reaching out to his grandmother to see if she—'

'But Trinny said she had no family.'

Sparks snorted. 'And you believed her? She was a lunatic. Every word that came out of her mouth was a lie. We found her mother's contact details at the cottage, along with Red's personal papers. Would you like to guess what her real name was? No? I'm telling you anyway. She was called Judith Moon.'

The name was so incongruously *not* Trinny, that Massey almost laughed out loud.

'Definitely bat-shit crazy,' Keegan said. 'Bloody good buns though.'

Their mouths fell open.

'Jesus,' Sparks said. 'Are you for real?'

'What? Shit, no. I didn't mean... I was talking about her skills as a baker.'

'Yeah, right,' Sparks said, looking around to make sure they were still too far away from other diners for them to hear. 'So she admitted everything, did she James?'

'Just about.' He laid his spoon down after just one taste of his soup – the only thing on the menu he thought he might be able to face. 'She figured out that Dominic had killed Duncan and that Milo knew. She volunteered to get rid of the knife for them, which of course she didn't, in return for some favours when she needed them. She said that the idea to imitate Macbeth had come to her at that barbecue, so both of you were right on that.'

'Why wait for more than a year though before she did anything?' Sparks asked.

Massey sucked in a big breath and blew it out again. He didn't feel comfortable yet with the whole idea that all this murder and mayhem was very likely down to something he'd caused to happen all those years ago when he'd failed to make sure Trinny's caravan door was secured. He probably never would. Yet that's what it came down to.

'It was because the match was cancelled last summer after Duncan's death,' Keegan said. 'Wasn't it? She wanted you there to admire her handiwork.'

'Sort of,' he said. 'She told me she wanted me to have to investigate her crimes. She also said that we almost caught her twice. One evening, I almost ran her over outside the village hall on my way out. I know now she'd just killed Maureen, but she said she was coming to see me before I left for the day. It wasn't until I thought about it later that I realised she'd come from the opposite direction to where she lived. And she had blood on her face. It was dark. I assumed she'd bitten her lip with the impact, but it was probably Maureen's blood. If she kept the clothes she wore that night, they could have more of it on them. She put both hands on the bonnet of my car too. The prints might still be recoverable despite the rain, so...' His felt his mind start to drift.

'What was she wearing?' Keegan asked. 'The search of the woods has thrown up some nylon fibres caught on a branch.'

'Some sort of dark nylon zip-up thing, I think.'

'They're doing comparison tests with some of the clothing she had at home,' Sparks said. 'She might have kept the sneakers we've been looking for too, if we're lucky. And you've just reminded me; someone ran out in front of *my* car on the day of the Stoneyriggs fire. Maybe that was her too. *Bastard!* I should have mown the bitch down there and then and been done with it. We need to be looking for a striped, turquoise top with a hood too. Like a beach cover-up.

'There's something I don't get,' Keegan said. 'Why the hell was Verity up on top of that tower?'

'Apparently she liked taking Finn's keys and going up there at night. But Trinny said something about having had to change her plans on that.

She knew Verity was likely to go back to the tower last night, but had expected it to be much later, when there'd be no-one around to see her. I think Trinny planned to follow her and push her off the top. Like in the play, when Lady Macbeth dies, and it's assumed she committed suicide. Or maybe she planned to leave some sort of evidence that would make us think Finn had killed his wife. I don't suppose we'll ever know.

'She told me she'd intended to call me later and lure me up to Cresswell by telling me that Max had got himself into trouble somehow. She said we were supposed to walk out into the sea together in the middle of the night, just the two of us, and drown.'

'How on earth did she plan to get you to do that?' Sparks said. 'The LSA she'd given you would have started to wear off by then.'

'Those crackers weren't meant for me. She hadn't expected me to be at the play at all. She said she'd made them for Betsy and Scarlett. Just her nasty little practical joke on them, I think. It was the stuff in the syringe that was supposed to be for me.'

'But if she didn't expect you to be there, why did she have that with her?'

'I know the answer to that one,' Keegan said. 'Verity hasn't said much, but she did say she'd seen Trinny run back home for something in between the witches scenes, so she probably decided she had to change her plan as soon as she saw you arrive and needed to have the syringe on her. No idea why she didn't stick you with it as soon as you came through the door onto the roof though.'

'She might have, if she'd been able to get it out of her pocket cleanly,' he asked, rubbing his neck as he imagined the needle piercing his skin. 'Pretty sure that's what she'd planned. Do we know what was in it yet?'

'A stronger concentration of the LSA, apparently. Bloody dangerous stuff. I looked into it. You can buy seeds for Morning Glory in garden centres everywhere, and online, but they're coated with a substance designed to stop people wanting to ingest them. Same principle as that stuff they use to stop people biting their nails. That's why she had to collect uncoated seeds from her own plants. She started grinding them up when she decided to feed them to Finn and Verity. Once Finn was hooked into them, she'd have been able to do pretty much anything she liked with him. It'll have been him who told her about all the affairs he'd had, which allowed her to set up Duncan at that barbeque.'

'But at least,' Sparks said, 'Tom Kirk's fears that someone would be arrested in the middle of the performance weren't realised. Red had the decency to finish her part and wait until the final battle scene was finished before throwing herself off the tower.'

'And she can't put a spoke in your career any more now she's dead.' Keegan said. 'So don't even think about coming clean with Lou. Three murders solved. Three killers off the streets – if you count Milo, who was probably more his brother's victim than a cold-blooded murderer. And three landscapers exonerated – of killing Duncan at least. Everything will be squared away without you throwing yourself on your sword.'

'Three is a hugely powerful number,' Sparks said. 'Colin Chirnside talked about the unholy symbolism associated with the number. 'Did you know that Shakespeare often used people's fear of bad things happening in threes? Especially in Macbeth: three witches, three prophesies, three murders, the three faces of Hecate – or should I say Red. You should have seen the big circular metal thing we found on the wall in her lounge. A bloody great Stropholos of Hecate—'

Keegan spluttered his beer. 'You must have looked that up. You had no idea what the hell it was called when we were there.'

'It rang a bell though. I did say that. Three loop things within a circle. Also known as Hecate's Wheel. She really did see herself as a goddess.

Massey gave his lukewarm soup a stir, not wanting to admit that he *had* actually seen it when he'd paid his ill-advised visit to Trinny's cottage.

'And talking about prophesies,' Sparks continued, 'the moon may not yet have waned, but you've just faced death smack in the face and here you still are. Result all round, from what I can see.'

THE END

MASSEY and SPARKS

Follow the series

Sign up for all the latest news at www.jacquelineauld.com

#masseyandsparks

A FEW WORDS

When I first heard of Cresswell Pele Tower, it captured my imagination and began percolating in my subconscious. Last year, I saw they were hosting a Halloween event at the tower, which sparked the idea of writing about another Halloween event there, which in turn resulted in this book.

Situated in the Northumberland seaside village of Cresswell, at the southern end of the beautiful Druridge Bay, the tower is a Grade II* Listed Building and Scheduled Monument, built in the 14th Century by the local Cresswell family as a defence against the marauding Border Reivers. For generations, the tower was left to fall into ruins and had been placed on Historic England's heritage at risk register. But, following a survey two years earlier to investigate its structural integrity, the Cresswell Pele Tower Project began raising funds in 2016 to rescue the tower and its surroundings as a community resource for future generations. You can find out all about the restoration and the work of the project, now a registered charity, since its completion in 2021 via the website: https://cresswellpeletower.org.uk/. Or you can visit and see for yourself the wonderful work that has been achieved there.

If you do visit you may notice that, to fit the needs of my plot, I've twisted a detail or two of the tower's construction, in particular access to the roof, for which I apologise to any purists out there.

Cresswell Village Hall was originally built as Cresswell's lifeboat station and opened in 1875. Generations of the same families manned the lifeboats there until the station was closed in 1944. Find out more about the building and its history at https://cresswellvillagehall.com/.

However, the village hall's caretaker in my story, Margaret Charlton and her ancestors are fictional, as are all my other characters.

Ben Quinn's house Stoneyriggs, the Barrons' house with its landscaped garden, Elena Kingsley's home with its squeaky gate, Trinny's cottage with its little courtyard and her Blue Moon Bakery, the Duffys' bungalow, and even Ellington & Cresswell RFC are also all complete figments of my imagination. The Drift Café is real though, as is the ice cream shop, Cresswell Ices, and both are well worth a visit.

Although Shakespeare is a required author within the National Curriculum in England now, he wasn't during my own schooldays and my only real experiences of his works before tackling this plot have been of acting the part of Philostrate in *A Midsummer Night's Dream* at school and watching the Royal Shakespeare Company's performances on their first ever season at the Theatre Royal, Newcastle upon Tyne in the mid 1970s, where I worked at the time. But an ancient pele tower at Halloween clearly needs witches, so why not, I decided, go the whole hog and rustle up a little Macbeth?

That decision sparked a huge learning curve for me. And once I'd actually visited the tower, I realised that capacity and logistics could be an issue in staging a full Macbeth production there, so I needed a rethink. My solution, before I discovered that 'immersive theatre' was actually a real thing, was for the audience to be guided around the tower, its grounds and its recently restored 18th century walled garden to watch successive scenes being played out, while also being roped into the performance itself as 'extras' for the banqueting and battle scenes.

I was keen to include Macbethian quotes in Shakespeare's actual words, rather than more modern translations, partly because all of his works are in the public domain, but mostly because I think they add a necessary spookiness to a Halloween-themed story, although I did change the verse form to continuous prose to aid wider understanding. I had no idea at all about what an iambic pentameter or trochaic tetrameter were before I started writing this book.

While it would be wonderful to think that the people who look after the tower might consider staging just such a performance on another Halloween, I have no idea where they'd find someone as accomplished as Colin Chirnside as director and costume designer, and I'd hate to risk bringing down murder and mayhem onto the residents of the real life village through the curse of Macbeth.

ACKNOWLEDGEMENTS

My most profound thanks must go to all those who have chosen this book to read from among all the thousands of crime novels published every year. If you've enjoyed it, it would be wonderful if you could also leave a review on the platform of your choice to help others find it.

Huge thanks also to my early readers for their invaluable feedback: my mother Shirley, my friend Jacqueline, and my brothers Geoff and David, each of whom, once again, have brought a different kind of critical eye to my manuscript.

Special thanks must go to Steve Lowe, Volunteer Coordinator and Engagement Officer at Cresswell Pele Tower for his knowledge and generosity in showing me around and answering all my questions via email and in person during one of their busiest days of the year.

Thanks also to Phil Walton, Age-Grade Safeguarding Officer at Gateshead RFC, an old school friend and brother-in-law of my brother, for keeping me straight on the earliest age at which a young person can play adult rugby and the requirements for under eighteens, who need not only parental permission, but also permission from the Rugby Football Union to play at that level.

On Shakespeare, whilst I did decide to use The Bard's original Elizabethan English language, I nevertheless found the modern translations and scene-by-scene analyses I found online invaluable in helping me understand Macbeth well enough to mirror the plot of the play within my own. So, thank you too to all of them, but in particular the Royal Shakespeare Company and LitCharts, for their helpful online resources.

ABOUT THE AUTHOR

Jacqueline is the author of the Massey and Sparks crime thriller series, set primarily in the North East of England, and winner of the Lindisfarne Prize for Crime Fiction in 2022 for the opening of her debut novel, *The Children of Gaia*.

Writing crime fiction is something Jacqueline took up seriously only relatively recently after retirement from employed work, having spent three decades working in the pub trade and two in the charity sector.

Born and brought up in Low Fell, Gateshead, Jacqueline now lives in the south-east corner of Northumberland with her husband Kevin, the source of many of the off-the-cuff comments she includes in her writing.

Jacqueline draws inspiration from the countless beautiful settings, and grittier locations, around her in the North East of England, and from her years spent observing human nature and the complicated social entanglements of her regulars from her time working behind bars in pubs, hotels and nightclubs, although she has no idea if any of her regulars actually did commit the sort of murders she writes about.

FOR BOOK CLUBS

Is your Book Club looking for its next read?

This Book Club Kit Companion is currently available to all to download from my website:
www.jacquelineauld.com/The-Power-of-Three/

The Companion contains: a welcome letter, an author bio, a collection of ready-to-go discussion points, a Q&A with me - mostly about the book, recipes and info on locations featured in the book.

I love chatting to my readers, so please don't hesitate to contact me via the online form if you'd like to arrange an in-person discussion at your Book Club meeting:

www.ingramcontent.com/pod-product-compliance
Lightning Source LLC
Chambersburg PA
CBHW011549070526
44585CB00023B/2512